Paul Hyland

was born in Dorset a month after India gained independence. An award-winning poet and travel writer, his books on English places, *Purbeck* and *Wight*, are modern classics. His African journey, *The Black Heart*, followed Joseph Conrad, Roger Casement and Dan Crawford up the River Congo.

Paul Hyland is married to Maggie Ware and lives in North Devon where W. Bowden's Indian Balm was made and marketed for eighty years.

INDIAN BALM

TRAVELS IN
THE SOUTHERN
SUBCONTINENT

Paul Hyland

Flamingo
An Imprint of HarperCollins*Publishers*

Flamingo
An Imprint of HarperCollins*Publishers*
77–85 Fulham Palace Road,
Hammersmith, London W6 8JB

Published by Flamingo 1995
9 8 7 6 5 4 3 2 1

First published in Great Britain by
HarperCollins*Publishers* 1994

Author photograph by Maggie Ware

ISBN 0 00 638099 9

Set in Linotron Meridien

Printed in Great Britain by
HarperCollinsManufacturing Glasgow

for Maggie
beloved fellow traveller

CONTENTS

LIST OF ILLUSTRATIONS

Madimsingaya, a Koya toddy-tapper from Kokiragudem.
Sai Baba playing cards.
At the cock-fight.
Sannasamma, a Konda Reddi woman from Cheeduru.
Yuniah and Suvarthamma baptizing a new convert.
The Horn Dance at Pedagudem.
Konda Reddis: the watchman from Geddapalli, the headman of
    Cheymaluru and boy high in the hills.
The first TV ever to visit Sivagiri.

ACKNOWLEDGEMENTS

I am indebted, most of all, to my wife Maggie Ware and my cousin Joy Tilsley. Maggie willingly shared both her own experience of India and my labours during the making of this book. Without Joy's hospitality, introductions and inspiration my journey would have been much more difficult, and parts of it impossible, and I would be the poorer for not having got to know her at last.

Some of those who helped me remain nameless, some names have been changed in the text and many of the following deserve to be more than names in a list; I hope they will appreciate the use I have made of their contributions and understand why I have left so much out. One way or another everyone here assisted me with the journey and the research that became this book:

A. Parvathi, B. Azariah, B. Deenabandhu, B. Samuel and Premaleela, B. Saraswati Pillai, C. R. Prabhakar and Miriam, C. Rathnam, C. V. Ramana, C. Zephaniah and Naveena, D. Ramesh Babu, Joyce Harding, Hetta Hyland, J. R. K. Brahmaji Rao, J. Victor Sundararaj and Daisy, Thomas and Beena Kadavill, K. Michael Stanley and Deepika, K. Obanna and Grace, K. Rathnamma, K. Satyanaryana and Rathnam, K. Shanth Rathnam, Eva Mair, K. T. and B. Mathews, R. T. Meneaud, M. Jagannadha Rao, M. John Victorbob and family, M. Joshi and Santhosham, Colin and Joslyn, Juliane Montgomery, M. Shesha Rathnam, Dorothy Munce, M. Vidya Sagar, N. Surya Rao, Win and Jack Platt, P. Savithri, Colleen Redit, Olive Rogers, R. V. Rama Sastry, Santi Babu, U. Savarna, Jeff Saward, S. Baji, Mahendra Solanki, S. S. M. Gopala Rao and Sita Lakshmi, Christine and David Taylor, John Tilsley, T. K. George, T. Suguna, V. Babu Rao, V. Satyanaryana, Enid Wagland and Y. Ydidiah. S. Yuniah and Suvarthamma have my warmest thanks for their patience and for sharing with me whatever they had.

I am deeply grateful to my agent Bruce Hunter for his advice and acumen, to Mike Fishwick of HarperCollins for his faith and encouragement, and to Richard Wheaton for exceptional editorial warmth and skill.

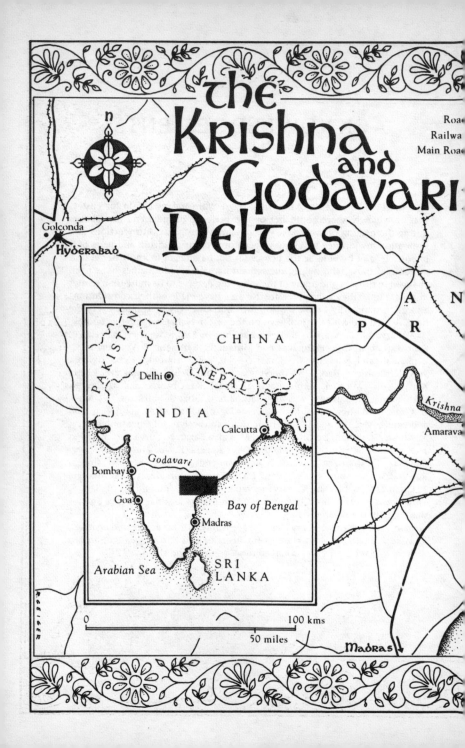

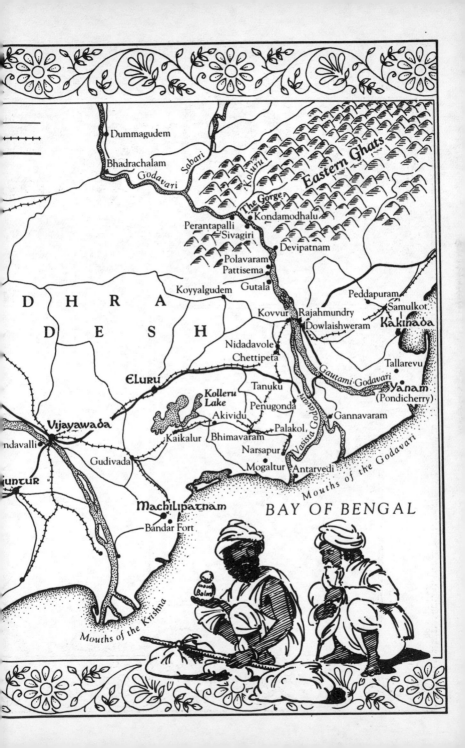

HOLY FOOLS

Devon

AT HER HUNDREDTH birthday party in North Devon my grandmother lay on her bed in my parents' house. Propped against
pillows, she was bolstered up by her own stoic spirit and by the
love of the family who filed through her room. Her sallow skin
was at once wonderfully smooth and deeply lined; it clung ever
more closely to her beautiful bones. Coiled silver hair was a
glorious weight upon her scalp. The room smelt of lavender and
camphor.

The Queen's telegram was one of a great array. It had been
hard to get; the Private Secretary had wanted proof of granny's
birth but my mother persuaded him to make do with the date
on her marriage certificate. Her memory had grown precarious,
and she asked one of my many cousins who she was and where
she was from.

'I'm Joy,' said my cousin, 'from Narsapur.'

Suddenly alight with pleasure, the old lady broke into fluent
chatter in Telugu, a language she'd hardly spoken since she left
India at the age of twenty-two.

She was born Lily Bowden at Kakinada, on the eastern delta
of the River Godavari which flows into the Bay of Bengal, on
21 April 1872. Forty years before, her grandfather William
Bowden had been an apprentice stonemason in Barnstaple,
eight miles from where we celebrated his granddaughter's
centenary.

As I drove down from London for that party I had no idea
that a circle was closing. My parents had been in North Devon
for just a year and I hadn't discovered my roots there. I loved
quarries and stone carving, not knowing that my great-great-

grandfather had started out to be a mason. As it was, he broke off his indentures with two full years still to serve, married his sweetheart in a hurry on 15 February 1836 and, a fortnight later, boarded the *Star* at the Packet Wharf, Bristol, for Milford Haven where they'd embark upon the East Indiaman *Perfect* for Madras.

The *Perfect* was delayed by contrary winds on the run from Greenock on the Clyde. The Bowdens and their party had to wait. Their leader was a dentist from Plymouth, Anthony Norris Groves. He'd originally been invited to India by Captain Arthur Cotton, a Royal Engineer he'd met in Baghdad in 1833, whom we'll meet again on the Godavari river. Groves's wife and baby daughter had died in Baghdad and he found himself free to travel to Bombay, across to Bengal and down the Indian east coast to Ceylon.

Inspired, he returned to England to recruit a missionary party. In 1835 he delivered an impassioned address at Ebenezer Baptist Chapel, Barnstaple. In that congregation, William Bowden and his shoemaker friend George Beer, both about twenty-four, and the women they loved, Elizabeth Folland and Elizabeth Toms, had been fired with Groves's vision of India. The four of them found their vocation. They signed up with Groves's group and got married in quick succession. Their passage to India was to be some honeymoon.

They stayed in a very cold Milford Haven for almost a month. It was an odd party. It included two French Swiss women, one a teacher and the other a farmer's daughter; two German men, a journeyman tailor and a brilliant linguist; the mason and the cobbler and their brides from Barnstaple; the Plymouth dentist and his second wife of a few months; not to mention a pair of frivolous hangers-on, the dentist's fox-hunting cousin and his bibulous brother-in-law. It must have seemed a long March, going nowhere in Milford with that motley crew.

What dream possessed the Bowdens' heads? If God was for them, in a pagan land of dust and idols and lovable souls, who could be against then? In any case, strong measures had been taken against bad Hindu habits like *suttee* and *thuggee*. Human sacrifice had been prohibited. Prohibited but still practised, as William Bowden would discover. As, to my dismay, I would discover. That story will keep. In Milford the party waited with their private hopes and fears. Not until Good Friday, 1 April, did the *Perfect* with its cargo of holy fools weigh anchor and slip away from the snowbound coast of Wales.

The North Devonians were comforted by pens of cows, rams, pigs, goats and geese: a commissariat put aboard in Scotland to sustain their party through the voyage. It smelt like market day. Rough seas at once sent them all to their berths. Then a favourable wind revived their appetites and raised the master's hopes of a fast run. Captain Snell had served under Nelson at Trafalgar and was full of tales of the South Seas. The doldrums hardly delayed him and rather than call at the Cape he resolved to go for the coveted record. They saw no land between the Cape Verde Islands and the mountains of Ceylon.

They marvelled at wandering albatross. Winds deserted them in the Indian Ocean and Snell resigned himself to being robbed of the record. The tedium was relieved by tuition in Telugu from Dr Hermann Gundert, later famous for his monumental dictionary of Malayalam. The young linguist from Tübingen must have terrified the rustics from Barnstaple. They exasperated him by refusing to repeat '*manushyudu*'. They thought he was sending them up. How could the word for simple 'man' have that many syllables? This, thought the Herr Doktor, was not so promising. He went overboard to cool down. An invigorating swim was one better than the makeshift shower they'd rigged up on deck. The lookout's cry of 'Shark' put an end to that exhilaration. The crew caught two. Gundert tested his finger on a tooth and drew blood.

Elizabeth Beer took part in none of this. She was prostrate with seasickness the whole voyage; more than once they feared for her life. She vowed, after reaching the Godavari delta, never to go to sea again. She kept the vow. Indian *terra firma* it was to the end of her days. To her relief the *Perfect* dropped anchor in Madras roads at evening. Did she sleep that night? Did any of them? What did they imagine lay in the dusk beyond the breakers? Were they pleasured by dreams, possessed by nightmares, or filled with the peace which passes understanding?

I don't know. The *Madras Almanack* baldly catalogues the year's arrivals, among them: 'July 7. Perfect. W. Snell. Greenock

3

8th March, & Milford 1st April 1836. Passengers – For Madras
... Messrs Groves, John Groves, Bowden & Beer; Dr
Gundert . . .'

I do know that it wasn't until the next morning, Friday 8 July,
that they disembarked into a lighter, crossed the perilous bar
and landed through pummelling surf. It was exactly fourteen
weeks since they'd weighed anchor. Next day the *Perfect* sailed
on for Calcutta.

My grandmother died six months after her hundredth birthday,
and two years later an elegant shop at the end of Butchers' Row
in Barnstaple stopped selling a celebrated ointment that had been
manufactured in the town for eighty-five years. As a child I loved
the scent of its essential oils when my mother rubbed it on my
bruises. I sucked it on a lump of sugar whenever I had a sore
throat. Its two-tone blue tin claimed that it cured muscular complaints, skin diseases, burns, eczema, piles, cuts, chilblains and
rheumatism. It was called W. Bowden's Indian Balm.

The Balm smelt of heat and distances, of a luxuriant East, of
fakirs and snake-charmers and golden temples: catalyst for a
child's imagination. My great-great-grandfather had concocted
it, I was told, but nobody knew much more. Now I know
the Balm's strange history. Now I appreciate how exceptional
William and Elizabeth Bowden were in the India of the Raj.

Independent India and I are the same age; news of it was a
persistent strand in the talk that threaded together the supper-
times of my childhood. But not until 1991 – when the bomb
that killed Rajiv Gandhi seemed to finish the Nehru dynasty,
when Dravidian separatists tugged once more at the reins of
power and Hindu extremism reared its many heads – did I begin
to think of making my own way from North Devon to the
Godavari delta.

The Godavari cuts India in two. Of the twelve rivers sacred
to Hindus, it is second only to the Ganges in the hierarchy of
holiness, and it springs from the same mythic underground
source. The literal Godavari rises fifty miles from the Arabian

Sea and flows east and south until it breaks through the Eastern Ghats – where a formidable gorge and exquisite lakes between mountains and forested hills compose a tropical landscape as beautiful as any in the subcontinent – before fingering its way to the sea through a delta that is the greatest rice granary in south India: the river flows from Bombay, near as damn it, through Maharashtra and Andhra Pradesh all the way to the Bay of Bengal.

I planned for travel in a region that the guidebooks ignore, in a time of crisis; or in the latest phase of the incorrigible turmoil that is India's life. India is an insupportable idea rolling into the twenty-first century; a juggernaut of symbols, munificent and mundane, dragged teetering across the uncertain ground of incoherent historical clichés. To the outsider it is naked enigma. To the insider it is illusion.

Glimpses of the British in the Delta, 1611–1947, and of the Bowdens and their Balm, are sub-plots in the story of my journey. Their places are markers on my map, but my pilgrimage is now – through today's enigmas and enchantments, strange meetings and conflicts – to the Delta and Narsapur, home of my cousin Joy. I'd met her a handful of times. I didn't know her, but I knew her reputation as a powerful woman, and as a student of Telugu language and culture, more Indian than English in all but blood. She represents the fifth generation to work as missionaries and traders on the Delta since our great-great-grandparents arrived in 1836. She will be the last. Those who call her 'mother' or 'grandmother' are Telugus; her concern is with their future.

I wanted to get to know her, and to meet their India. I had the jabs, began popping the pills and put together a first-aid kit, remembering what a pioneer explorer in Paraguay and Brazil wrote to Bowden's Indian Balm Co., Barnstaple, in 1901:

I was often obliged to load the pack horses with only what was absolutely necessary to existence, and every ounce weight was critically considered. The Indian Balm however always went into the pack as next to food it was the most indispensable article.

I'd got one tin of the stuff left, half full. It went into my pack last. It was both ointment and talisman. I was ready. Once they eventually set sail, the holy fools' voyage to Madras had taken fourteen weeks. My flight took fourteen hours.

2

COROMANDEL LANDFALL

Madras

A PALE-FACED baby girl blinked at sunlight in the low doorway
of a palm-leaf shelter; before she crawled any further a woman's
dark hand flashed out, slapped her hard and withdrew her,
yelling, into the shadows of home.

The shelter straddled the broad potholed pavement of a tree-
lined street just off Nungambakkam High Road. Not far away,
such houses huddled on the stinking mud banks of the Cooum
river that meanders through Madras to the Bay of Bengal; they
queued up beside the railway tracks too, but this shelter was
solitary, in a select district. Beyond a scalloped wall, workmen
clambered like termites in the ruins of an Odeon-style residence
and a pile-driver rising high among trees wheezed and stunned
the earth.

A sign on a pole planted in the pavement read, 'For a bright
career – UPTRON Academy of Computer Learning'. Steel gates,
decorated with a portrait of a slavering dog and set between
marble pillars topped with wrought-iron lamp-stands, suggested
where a bright career might lead: a showy garden, brilliant balustraded verandahs and arches into a shady interior. Engraved
on one gatepost was the name 'Sri Devi' above a painted carving
of Shiva's trident. Outside the gates a swirling pattern had been
drawn on the ground in white chalk to welcome Lakshmi,
goddess of wealth. It seemed hardly necessary. A barefoot
gardener in white turban and *dhoti* paddled in bougainvillea
prunings.

A few doors away a servant was delicately sponging down an
advocate's trim hatchback. Yes, it was Sunday morning and I was
recovering from jet-lag, from my first Madras night's dreams.

7

Yesterday morning I'd peered from cloudless sky at interminable desert, a mutating beach of shimmers and shifts, waves and ripples, building sandhills, riven ridges and dry watercourses like a web of nerves. The emptiness was awesome. Then I saw lonely shapes, tracks going somewhere, small enclosures like runes on parchment, greige fields between dunes, clustered habitations. The thin scum of life on the planet filled me with tenderness.

I'd spent weeks thinking about what I'd find when I landed. It was like staring down from thirty thousand feet: a schematic landscape thickly populated with phantoms, streets where abstract ancestors had walked. Sentimentality thrives on distance. I was excited about walking out of the country of the mind to meet the place and people close up, and apprehensive about whether the past would come into sharp focus and make a shape I recognized.

After the Indus valley, Delhi; after Delhi, a twelve-hundred-mile hop south. Hills of clinker, emerald valleys, bald uplands, quivering lakes and reservoirs, crystalline rivers spanned by rare bridges. More water, more green, and then blue forested mountains at the world's edge . . . I roused as we dropped towards the ocean, lumpy red hills, a wide city beneath a canopy of trees, vivid grass between runways. Inside Madras's Meenambakkam terminal we all converged upon Immigration's computer screens so patiently, so quietly. Was I in India?

The taxi was. A cow with splayed hoofs and a twisted head stopped two lines of traffic dead until it had finished licking its arse. The rest of us were in a hurry: hefty Ambassador taxis, nippy Maruti cars, auto-rickshaws like hornets, thumping motorbikes, whining scooters, jangling cycle-rickshaws, bicycles and primary-coloured lorries, with explosive air brakes and black breath, all flowing, weaving, swirling round temporary obstacles like too many corpuscles pumped down arteries clogged by the accretion of palm-leaf shelters, wickerwork stalls and heaps of rubble and rubbish at the roadside.

Behind the flux, imposing gateways opened on to the Officers Training Academy or the Military Hospital; then I saw the hill called St Thomas Mount, supposed site of the apostle's martyrdom in AD 72, where my relatives found friendship with other ranks in barracks, and where members of a non-conformist church gave them three hundred rupees before they sailed north. Across the Adayar river, Mount Road ran directly to Fort St George where Robert Clive first got to grips with India. And twice tried to kill himself.

Death was a close companion at each intersection. Inimical vehicles, fast and slow, butch and frail, clashed at junctions but meshed miraculously and flew off on predestined paths. From the air it would have looked beautiful. In amongst it, it was ear-splitting. A man pushed an auto-rickshaw's chassis to the side of the road, leaving its battered bodywork grounded in the stream. Only traffic lights stopped us. Immediately, between the straining wheels, women came begging at the windows, slack babies like tools of the trade in their arms. Each mother's appeal was rhythmical, repetitive, barely audible. The lights changed and they were lost, flotsam in our dangerous wake.

Are people compelled, in places such as this, to sign a sterner contract with life? Or is it that travellers from the West are forced, for once, to read the small print? Volleys of rifle-fire plucked me back to the Sunday morning street where the busiest things were browsing goats, house crows and butterflies. Volleys turned into the tattoo of drums carried by a troupe of musicians preceding a litter hung with garlands. Bearers seemed to stagger under the weight of flowers heaped upon a body without gender, wreathed with heavy scents, naked feet first, a propped-up head with eyes sunk out of sight. All the mourners were male. They strolled beside the litter towards the burning *ghat*.

It was a morning to watch things go by, to begin to learn to focus, to ready myself for strange meetings. 'Sir!' A boy's voice and running footsteps destroyed my mood. 'Sir, sir!' I waved him away. He persisted. If he'd been a fly he'd have flown. He stayed at my heels. 'Sir, sir!' I felt my face fall into a shape I grew to recognize and smile at inwardly, a grimace of impatient tolerance. He gazed up beseechingly and patted my back pocket. 'Sir!' I patted it too, to check it, and felt keys dangling from the stitching. I pulled the whole fob through the bust seam and rattled it, grinning and thanking the boy, fumbling in other pockets for change. Phew! I'd be able to get into my room, into my padlocked luggage. He didn't wait for money but laughed and ran off only pausing at the corner to wave.

One day in 1823 Cornelius Traveller walked to the beach for his usual stroll. The breeze that blew up in the afternoons was some relief from the heat and humidity through which everyone swam in slow motion. Traveller was a respectable missionary, but on this particular afternoon he'd dared to flout decorum. He'd left his top hat hanging on the wooden peg behind his door, fitted a straw hat on his scalp instead and flagrantly paraded it against the backdrop of breaking surf. Such a breach of etiquette did not go unremarked and could not go unpunished. Dismissed from Madras, Traveller had to hang up his hat in some other distant vestry.

Now I gazed across these same sands at ships lined along the horizon beyond a kaleidoscopic market. Stalls on bicycle wheels, with fretwork canopies supported by pillars, sold *puris* or *paan* or pineapples; hand-painted panels showed pale, plump faces rapt in contemplation of *samosas* or ice cream; barrows were stacked with lurid bottles or spread with misty green glasses wet from rinsing, ready for refills of milky coffee. A pressing engine throbbed, chewed up sugar cane and dribbled juice into tumblers.

Wiry, wily men offered rides on raw-boned horses. A tiny man walked in the large shadow of balloons that rattled when he punched them. I followed him between stalls that stretched all the way to the sea: glass bangles, plastic novelties, tools and toys set out on the sand. A blind, badly burnt woman plucked at her sari and sang with matter-of-fact feeling into a microphone wired to a loud-hailer; relatives accompanied her on tabla, hand-pumped harmonium and collecting tin. Small coins chimed. The bell of a test-your-strength machine drew a huddle of youths and soldiers. Vendors fired boomerang copters into the breeze; they spun far and high, and back. Women in pristine saris rustled and jostled to get out of the way, girls in Punjabi suits giggled, boys in best shirts and trousers blew raspberries on kazoos.

From a gleaming array I bought the most important item on my shopping list, a steel pot in which to boil water. At a cool stall, like a pulpit moulded from wet sand, people queued to buy water by the steel-cupful. A girl's throat pulsed as she poured it down without touching her lips. She had dramatic features, ivory jasmine blossom plaited into heavily oiled hair, a gold nose stud and bell-like ear-rings, linked by chains to rings in the top of each ear. In her dark sari she was perfectly groomed, and sensuous, though black skin made her unmarriageable to any caste man. She stood in vivid contrast to a passing Muslim girl, fair where skin was visible beneath azure robes, and her escort of older women comprehensively veiled in black *burkhas*.

Men sold fish at the water's edge. The ocean crashed. The undertow dragged and sucked. Boys bathed for fun. Women in wet saris and men with *lungis* hoisted between their legs paddled in the spume to do *puja*, or worship. Shaven-headed devotees tugged at trousers and curled their toes. They should have had knotted hankies on their heads. The air was full of the strong ethereal sound of men blowing conch shells, heavy ones, shiny, white as the moon. The conch breathes the sacred syllable OM, it is the abode of Lord Hari; Lakshmi stays forever within its sound. One who bathes in water from a conch bathes in all the holy waters. One who bathes in water from a conch with a right-handed spiral – rare, expensive and auspicious – is freed from all sins.

The holy fools landed on this beach after fourteen weeks. In the museum at Fort St George – among muzzle-loaders, musty uniforms of sepoys and governors, massive padlocks that secured this first British bastion in India, tarnished patens and chalices from old churches, portraits of notables peering through murky varnish, and fading letters of Robert Clive – I found a modest watercolour in which sailing ships punctuate the horizon while lighters with many oars and pocket-handkerchief sails are beached in the surf; bearers haggle to carry the trunks of over-dressed Europeans who shelter beneath umbrellas and top hats or bonnets; natives in loincloths strain to steady a boat and set a step-ladder at its bow in order that *memsahib* should effect as dignified a landfall as is possible on the Coromandel coast.

Madras was the Queen of the Coromandel. She was born in

the spring of 1639 when an agent of the English East India Company, Francis Day, sailed down the coast to visit the Portuguese fort at San Thome. Then, four miles to the north, he did a deal with the Rajah of Chandragiri for a few acres of surf-wrecked beach between the River Cooum and the sea near a fishing village called Madraspatam. There he and his superior and their Indian brokers built a fortified 'factory' which they christened on St George's Day 1640. As a site for a post, and so near the Portuguese, Fort St George had its pros and cons, but Day conceived and promoted it because he wanted to combine pleasure with business: he had a favourite mistress at San Thome and desired their 'interviews' to be 'more frequent and uninterrupted'.

Many soldiers and merchants, moneylenders and prostitutes switched allegiance from St Thomas to St George. Hundreds of weavers and dyers settled outside the English fort: embryo of Black Town that grew up to satisfy the white town's hunger for 'excellent long cloath better cheape'. A later Black Town became the trading and banking centre of the city. Within its hectic warren, its grid-iron pattern of narrow streets, lives the soul of Madras. At times, between 1865 and 1905, at least four Bowden sons worked as merchants, freight brokers or insurance agents at Second Line Beach, Armenian Street or Erabalu Chetti Street. Frederick Henry Bowden also set up his factory for Henry's Great Indian Remedies in the Black Town, now called George Town.

I was within sniffing distance of Indian Balm. In tree shade outside Fort St George's main gates I bought a cold drink from a stallholder who insisted on one rupee over the odds. I'd have protested more loudly, but here it seemed almost reasonable. A policeman shouted for refreshment too. He had the prosperous belly of most policemen and swallowed his drink fast. No money changed hands. It made sense. When I approached the gates he demanded my passport, but only glanced at its cover and smiled.

The fort's towering ramparts, broad moats and angular bastions were monumentally clumsy, touchingly anachronistic. Within, after the tallest flagpole in India – a mast salvaged from a seventeenth-century wreck – and chill classical façades of government buildings before which endless overheated queues barely shifted, I found St Mary's Church a delight on a human scale. The oldest Protestant church in Asia, its first stones were laid on Easter Monday 1678; constructed as a rectangular box with an arched cannonball-proof roof, it was consecrated in October 1680 and beautified much later.

Did it reform the English in India? A chaplain of 1676 had been advised 'that persons here are a great deal more civilized than formerly they have been. If it be so, there is great cause to admire the patience and long suffering of God, but withal cause to fear that if those things be not reformed, He will not always keep silence.' The graves outside, including stones from the old guava garden beyond the Fort's walls, span the years 1652 to 1755; their bones could tell tales.

But they didn't rest in peace. A petition of 1709 protested how scavengers unharnessed buffalo from their carts at evening and tethered them in the graveyard. Toddy men climbed and tapped the palm trees there, then spent the nights selling the fermented sap to the scavengers, basketmakers and other pariahs who haunted the burial ground, while vagabonds and beggars used the tombs as beds. 'And what unclean uses the neighbours thereabouts doe make of that place we forbear to tell.'

Elihu Yale, who helped found this church and Yale University in the USA, was married here. Here Robert Clive married Margaret Maskelyne. Arthur Wellesley, later Duke of Wellington, was best man at another wedding. Though the Bowdens might have felt more at home with non-conformists of their own class at Black Town or St Thomas Mount, their sixth son, Francis Meno Bowden, married Harriet Mary Mahoney VanSomeren, daughter of Madras's Surgeon-General, here at St Mary's just before Christmas 1872.

A jovial, reckless auto-rickshaw driver rushed me southwards from St Mary and St George, past all the delights of the long Marina beach and promenade, towards the town of St Thomas: the old Portuguese settlement of San Thome at Mylapore. If he'd had a driver like mine, Francis Day's uninterrupted 'interviews' with his favourite *senhora* might have been longer still.

I walked the last bit. Beyond a smart lighthouse, concrete tenement blocks trespassed on the sands. They were gutted, not by fire but by neglect, and still occupied. They'd been built by politicians for fisher caste families. Hating these new inhuman homes, fishermen rented them out, the story went, and stayed on in their old houses of driftwood, woven palmyra and palm-frond thatch. A makeshift town of them stretched down the shore above the tideline. From their shadowy interiors I was studiously watched as I trod the burning sand.

Separated from the squatters by a wall, a big white Costa del Sol villa rose up, a boat-shaped water tank on top with cabin, port-holes and all. Real nets and floats were spread out to dry above the breakers. Pillars of coiled rope cast thick shadows. Garish fishing boats, like the *barcos* of Portugal's Atlantic coast, were beached in surf. Beyond, squatted an oil rig. Beyond that, a hazy tanker crawled up the horizon.

San Thome Basilica, 1890s Gothic, stood a stone's throw from the beach. It is the latest church to be built over the tomb in which the martyred saint, Doubting Thomas, is supposed to have been buried. 'In this domain . . .' says Luis de Camões in *Os Lusiadas*, 'are held those holy and blessed relics of the body of Thomas . . . who put his hand into Jesus Christ's side. He travelled here to the town called Mylapore . . .' where one day a mighty tree-trunk was carried in by the waves. For all his men and elephants, the king of Mylapore couldn't shift it, but Thomas effortlessly hauled it ashore to build his church 'and the more the Brahmins considered the apostle's miracles and his sanctity the more they feared for their own authority. . . .'

King Alfred the Great sent Sighelm and Aethelstan with alms to Rome, says the Anglo-Saxon Chronicle's entry for the year 883, 'also to St Thomas and St Bartholomew in India'. To his immense delight, Vasco de Gama found himself greeted by Thomas Christians on the Malabar coast and here at Mylapore in 1498.

Within the basilica's ornate incense-laden Victorian dusk I found the image of Our Lady of Mylapore before which St Francis Xavier, patron saint of missionaries, wrestled with demons all one night in 1545. At the heart of the church St Thomas's marble crypt was bright. I stepped down into it. Most of the tomb's contents were removed long ago. But I stared at a reliquary said to hold the head of the lance that pierced the saint on St Thomas Mount and a fragment of bone from the hand that reached out to touch the risen Christ. What had

Doubting Thomas said? 'Unless I see . . . and touch . . . I will not believe.'

For all my doubts, I felt alarmingly moved. The holy fools would have disdained both my scepticism and my sentiment. In heat and light I walked inland. On Kutchery Road an elderly widow in a white sari watched traffic and me from her balcony: stained stucco, stout pillars and delicate fretwork above a sign for 'Amaravathi Chits & Investments'. I took a small side road past a tiny workshop where a man was crafting the body of a *sitar*.

Then, as if a magical master had tickled its belly, I saw rather than heard the notes of a *raga*: an ascending scale, the towering *gopuram* gateway of the great Kapaleeswarar temple, a dream mountain populated by intricately lifelike images of gods, goddesses, sages and demons, a pagoda grown out of the *Ramayana* and the *Mahabharata*. I left my sandals outside with a beggar woman, felt paving stones sticky with libations under my feet, wandered among fragrances and flames and powders of saffron and vermilion. Holy men smeared with ashes smiled at me. Women put their children on the backs of stone elephants hoping I'd snap them. Sculpted guardians flanked entrances to Shiva's inner sancta and notices said 'Hindus only'. I hoped that the world I wanted to explore would not always be closed to me.

At dusk, back in the heart of town with a train ticket for Vijayawada in my pocket, I squeezed between stalls on which fruit and vegetables from the Nilgiri Hills were perilously piled. The produce was immaculate, the stallholders wretched. I pushed through a dim entrance down narrow passages heavy with the scent of jasmine, the peppery tang of marigolds. Here in the garland market men threaded thousands of stemless flowers; folk lodged on dark ledges; leaves and filth accumulated underfoot.

Outside the maze I passed two men up bamboo ladders painting a sign, one with red paint, one yellow, just distinguishable in the dark. How could the day's violent colour ever fade? People settled under makeshift shelters and shut their eyes. Little shrines had entrances like strip-clubs, with loitering men and seductive pictures of gods and goddesses. I climbed into an auto-rickshaw and made for my bed. We swerved between lorries and almost brushed scooters away with a honk of our rubber horn. One boy, riding side-saddle on the rack of a bicycle, bared his white teeth at us. It was a cross between a grin and a snarl.

MURDER METROPOLIS

Vijayawada

ALL AT ONCE, six hours north of Madras on the Coromandel Express, something stood taller than palm trees: hills, lumpy ones like bubbles in boiling toffee, some full, some burst, some subsiding back into the plain. The roar of bogeys turned hollow and, through the bridge's girders, I had a stroboscopic vision of the Krishna river: weirs whitening its surface, a narrow stream in a wide bed, bathers in shallows, wind leaning at *dhobis'* washing lines, a fisherman wading, his spun net winking into the water.

High above the muddy bed two men squatted on a rock, base for a pylon carrying power across the river; high above their heads lodged a clump of vegetation brought down in the last floods. Before I could take in the significance of that rotting bundle, the train stopped, precisely on time. Vijayawada, the town at the head of the Krishna delta.

I gathered luggage, said goodbyes and squeezed out of the carriage against the tide of hawkers pressing to climb in with baskets of fruit and trays of snacks and drinks. With their cries – unintelligible but for 'Caffee-caffee-caffee-caffeeuh' – and the station tannoy echoing in my ears I climbed stairs from the platform in search of the retiring rooms. It was only mid-afternoon, plenty of time to book in for the night. A cool corridor, a line of promising grey doors.

'No room at all, sir,' said the attendant, 'all are full.'

'Five minutes!' said the auto-rickshaw driver.

He'd won the fierce competition for my trade in the station

forecourt. I'd picked him for his honest face, refused to pay the absurd fare he'd demanded, insisted on 'Meter' and loaded myself in. I'd learned a thing or two in Madras. He'd chaired a conference of his mates about my destination, to which the vain repetition of 'Swapna Lodge, Durgaiah Street', pronounced every possible way, had been my pathetic contribution. Then he'd tugged at the handle like a handbrake that started rather than stopped his mean two-stroke machine. A yank-start not a kick-start. After barely three yards, a flat. I'd heaved my stuff out into the dust but no one else would take me.

'Five minutes!' said my driver, gazing at the expired tyre. A crowd gathered and, despite their advice, within ten minutes the wheel was changed. Less tread, more air. We swept off around the forecourt and stopped dead. At the exit devotees of the Lord Ayyappa, distinguished by black *lungis*, waited to exact some sort of tribute. I knew it would pay me not to understand this transaction. I didn't.

The Krishna river flows west to east across the subcontinent. It was once the boundary of legendary Narsinga, the Vijayanagar empire which held almost the whole southern Hindu peninsula against invasive Muslim pressure from the north, while growing rich on southern spice and cotton and an ambiguous relationship with the Portuguese on the Malabar coast. This Hindu oligarchy was founded by two Telugu brothers in 1336 and effectively ended by a victorious Muslim alliance in 1565.

It is fashionable, and ideologically imperative for some, to see those centuries as a golden age of Hindu revival. Indians are particularly adept at dreaming the past. Great glories there were, but they belonged to a period of opulent stagnation. Or was it regression? In the first quarter of the sixteenth century the empire's most celebrated king, Krishna Deva, had prisoners ritually sacrificed in order to solve certain technical problems in the construction of a reservoir.

If you want a good water supply, let blood flow. It made sense. Human sacrifice had ceased, banned by the East India Company in 1835, by the time the Bowdens came this way. Believe that if you like. What is certain is that my ancestors saw the Krishna delta transformed by the vision of their friend the hydraulic engineer Captain Arthur Cotton. Later, in welcoming the Governor of Madras to Bezwada, as Vijayawada was then known, the president of the reception committee could say:

> Before the beneficent scheme for irrigating this thirsty land came into operation, Bezwada was only a small village, and partly in ruins, from the people having died in the terrible Nandana famine . . . of . . . 1832. Now it is a town, and increasing year by year with such rapidity as to be a source of wonder to all who knew its former condition. Indeed, it seems likely to become again, as in ancient days it is said to have been, the largest town in these parts . . . No longer struggling for a bare existence, or held in the grasp of *sowcars* – money-lenders ¬ the people rejoice among their smiling crops, and the money-lenders have become almost extinct.

Vijayawada is indeed the largest town in these parts. Sadly, the money-lenders survived, and more; they're a thriving species. What I'd heard of the place had half prepared me for a bustling, anarchic, nightmarish sprawl. Bustling it was, though most of the traffic was bikes and cycle-rickshaws, but I enjoyed the warmth of its people as I unravelled the maze of streets and narrow alleys. It was only later, and far away, on reading in *The Hindu* of some vile atrocity perpetrated here, that I learned Vijayawada's popular nickname, 'the murder metropolis'. I felt hurt on its behalf, as if a friend had been insulted.

There were a couple of flashy new hotels, pronounced 'hottles', but my rickshaw driver had dropped me where I'd asked, at the door of Hotel Swapna Lodge. Smiling boys in blue shirts and shorts had grabbed my bags. The ceiling in reception was propped up by timber scaffolding. It was dirt cheap, as opposed to flashy. Room 303 had a ceiling fan, a fluorescent tube, a bulb above the bed, a squat loo, a washbasin and a window with no netting. It was both dirt cheap and clean, if you accepted that the build-up of ancient and modern bloodstains on the mottled green and blue walls was simply part of the fabric. I'd add to the paintwork's patina before the night was out.

I set out to cross town on foot. Failing a more promising-looking eating house, I thought I'd try dinner in the station's Krishna Restaurant. At a small store next to one of the flashy hotels I bought a packaged milk loaf and a pot of mango jam. I crossed bridges over the canals. The setting sun looked great in them; let's leave it at that. There were palmyra-leaf slums and huge salacious hoardings advertising censored films. 'Night of Love'. 'Five Men, One Woman'. Whips and leather. That sort of thing. There were coloured lights, banners across the streets, and scores of kerb-crawling cycle-rickshaw-wallahs clicking their tongues and clapped-out bells at me in vain.

Afraid I'd lost my way, I decided to ask a policewoman. I'd been surprised to see one in town earlier, in knife-edged khaki trousers and well-fitting brass-buttoned jacket, but this one was especially shapely. She enjoyed her swagger as much as I did. Her hair was swept up from her handsome face and packed into her beret in such a way that I couldn't help imagining it loosed, falling. She would have been wasted on a film poster. The smile was as jaunty as the beret. Her eyes quizzically appraised me. She told me where to go.

Footballers fussed and fouled on TV at the top of the stairs outside the Krishna Restaurant. Wearily I trudged up to them. A steam whistle blew. AC Milan v. Real Madrid. It looked unreal to me. Somewhere someone screamed like a regimental sergeant major. From the walkway beside the TV I watched a train draw out, wheezing. Beyond a tall tiled clocktower and a dozen parked cars, a sign at the far side of the square said 'Mini Stadium' in Telugu, Hindi and English. On the stadium wall a hoarding stood for Four Square cigarettes, and a banner sagged: 'Fitness and Body Building Festival'. Within the walls soldiers with rifles strutted about looking very fit and four-square indeed.

A cashier lurked behind the shabby reception desk. He waved a hand at widely spaced tables. Some choice, for we were quite alone until a delightful waiter made his entrance. He brought me delicious chicken biryani, chapatis and a bottle of cola over-optimistically brand-named Thums Up. A young couple came in and sat at a table in the distance. They massaged hands and gazed engrossed into the muddy pools of one another's eyes.

My bill was less than fifty pence. It was an expensive meal.

Stalls and shops shone in the dusk. Saris, shoes and motor spares. Liquor stores and Marxist book houses galore. Giant cut-out movie stars or politicians, often one and the same thing in India, loomed against the sky. A cement Mahatma Gandhi stood like a battered doll on a plinth. Vladimir Ilich Lenin sternly surveyed Vijayawada's night life. I dodged through jangling traffic and bumped into the policewoman. She was amused.

'Did you find station?' she asked with shoulders aslant, a subtle hint of that sexy swagger.

'Yes, I did, thanks,' I said.

'Well, if you are needing assistance . . .' She disciplined a phalanx of scooters, rickshaws and handcarts with a thrust of her baton and hustled the unfinished sentence off into the dark.

If anything it was darker still in the Ambassador Restaurant and Bar. A waiter switched on a light at my request, but switched it off the moment I'd read the menu. The dive's regulars probably lived under stones. I ordered a beer, a Spencer Sixer, and drank it like cough medicine in the meagre glow of blue lightbulbs and two flickering TVs blaring Hindi soap. Some men – the place was a male preserve – ate solitary meals, but almost all huddled around quarter or half bottles of whisky. One man was paralytic when he staggered in. I escaped before I'd finished.

The boys in blue welcomed me home like the prodigal son. In Room 303 I draped my mosquito net over the window, plugged in my element, boiled water in my steel pot, got into bed with a tooth-glass of tea, screwed ear plugs in and went straight off.

Then I woke up, too suddenly. Felt disembodied. Searing pain reassured me on that point. Pain in my left eye. I might be blinded. Scared, I switched on the light and saw blood on the sheet, saw it with both eyes. In the mirror blood ran down my cheek. It was 4.30 a.m. I bled from a minute puncture beneath the eye. The pain was much bigger than that. I bathed the wound but the bleeding wouldn't stop. Nor the burning. Bowden's Indian Balm was soothing though.

I woke. 6.30 a.m. Number 304 hawked and spat volubly. Yogic

cleansing, I thought sourly. My eye still bled. Whatever insect or dream-borne vampire bat bit me, it must have injected anti-coagulant. 304's hawking was too enthusiastic. He was spewing up as if from his very *chakra*. Had he been a devotee in last night's dive, meditating on Bombay soap and whisky? I sniggered suddenly, remembering a German girl who'd once moaned, 'I vant to womit.' But I had to get away from that convulsive retching and check that at least a little of yesterday's world was left.

The corridor led to a balcony. Bodies lay there swathed from head to toe. They were breathing. I leant on the concrete parapet and inhaled the morning: wood smoke, clatter of cooking pots, a man crying wares, frying spices, tinny film music on some radio, twittering children, croak of grey-necked crows, clacking rickshaw bell, and a car's reiterated toot-toot-toot all down the next street. A man on the balcony above Rama Krishna Diesel Spares cleaned his teeth with a neem twig and spat, spat.

I savoured the idea of breakfast, black tea with bread and mango jam. I wondered how today I'd get to the tempting sites I wanted to see. I started when a hand touched me. It was one of the boys in blue with a white towel thrown over his shoulder.

'Hot water?' he said, and broke into a smile.

None of the shrouded shapes stirred. I dabbed at my weeping wound and nodded. This boy was beautiful. He smiled with big eyes and perfect teeth. His hair was lightly oiled. Beneath downy unblemished skin his bones were very fine.

'Hot water,' I said. 'Yes, good.'

'Photo?' he said, pointing at his heart.

I paused at the door of 304. Merciful silence. I crept into Room 303 to fetch my camera.

4

HEAVENLY CITY

Amaravati

MR ANANTH wanted to be very helpful indeed. He was a managing partner of Samrat Tours & Travels (Recognized by Govt of India) in Museum Road. He switched on a fan above our heads. Faded brochures about Great Britain rustled. But the recital of my needs quickly bored him. A blow-up Singapore Airlines plane hung by a thread from the ceiling; a slow puncture had sent it into a sagging surreal nose dive that must have already taken weeks.

'These are local requirements only,' said Mr Ananth. Round the world in a deflatable was more his line. And soft landings.

'Yes, I'm afraid so,' I said foolishly, dabbing with a tissue at the weeping wound beneath my eye.

He dusted the edge of his desk with an index finger and muttered darkly into the phone. After a few calls he brightened.

'Just wait some time,' he said. 'I will fix you up.'

Some time wasn't even long enough for him to answer my question about the black-garbed devotees I'd seen in town. They were undergoing forty-one days of *mandalapuja* or austere penance, including abstinence from alcohol, tobacco, meat and sex, before setting out with meagre rations on a barefoot twenty-five-mile pilgrimage in the footsteps of thirty million other macho men – and a few pure, that is non-menstruating, women – through once thick tiger forest to the temple of Lord Ayyappa at Sabarimala . . .

He'd only just got going when in walked a tall thin wispy-haired man who made *namaskaram* to Mr Ananth and shook my hand.

'Krishna Satyam at your service, sir.'

He gave me a card and, as they talked unintelligible rupees,
I tried to interpret its elegant Telugu script and engraved gods.
A Hindu tract? I turned it over. The backside said: 'Shiva Durga
Taxi Travels, c/o Nirmala Paints & Ha d Wares, Behind Laxmi
Talkies . . . We Suplyes A/c Cars Also.' I paid in advance.

The Ambassador, built on the lines of an old Morris Oxford
or maybe a tank, was not air conditioned; the windows were
wound down. Syrupy song on cassette, with stuttering tabla and
honking car-horn accompaniment, filled the interior and half
the world. Mr Satyam said something to the driver.

'One moment,' he shouted over his shoulder at me.

We stopped. He vanished into a store across the street. I leapt
out and haggled for oranges off a handcart. The driver and I had
each peeled one before Mr Satyam was back with the week's
shopping in a plastic bag. Behind Laxmi Talkies he disembarked
for good.

'This man, Prakash, I have told him all where you are going.
All is paid for. No extras. I wish you good day.'

My first destination was the Akanna-Madanna temple on a
hill above the river. Prakash drove left, right, left, left, mostly
in the opposite direction, like a minotaur in a maze. We halted
beside a lurid statue of Indira Gandhi and a stationary yellow
cycle-cart with fruits and bottles painted on it. 'Naturally
delicious! Naturally Kissan!' Prakash hooted extra loud and long
until a boy ran from a doorway, jumped into the front seat and
we were off between stalls like a Brahmin bull in a street market.
I wanted to shut my eyes and see everything at the same time.

A steam-roller stopped us. Coolie women heaved baskets from
their heads and cast gravel before it. A big advertisement for
motors was the backdrop for an everyday scene: a thin grey-
headed man in baggy shorts dismounted from his cycle rickshaw
and struggled to push it up the slope; his burden was a plump
Brahmin wearing the regulation thread and a white *lungi*.
Comfortable fat versus straining sinew. For once I thought I
saw something clearly: prosperous high-caste India can never
progress faster than the malnourished India which must drag it
into the future.

*   *   *

Inside the temple gates *sadhus* sat beneath a bo tree. Their brows bore the mark of Shiva and their saffron robes were printed with Sanskrit verses in vermilion. Chinking sounds turned out to be not temple chimes but hammers striking chisels, iron on iron; squatting on a beam that glittered like granite, two masons carved scalloped mouldings down its length. The shadow of my stonemason ancestor followed at my feet. What sharp, clean lines would he have seen here? What hard, exact task did he feel called to do?

High above the Krishna, within temple precincts, a priest blessed a mulberry-coloured Ambassador. Jasmine garlands hung from its mascot, joss sticks burned in the grill, limes adorned the bumper, and on the ground a camphor flame flared in the lee of an artfully placed stone. The priest recited Sanskrit texts. His thumb impressed the owner's forehead with red *kumkum*.

Higher up still there was a shallow cave, rough-hewn and stained with powders of crimson and yellow; it was crowded with pictures of gods and garlanded images that grew out of the ground beside an earthen mound encrusted with all the ochres and pricked with black holes, open mouths of the holy cobra's den. A young priest attended to a family whose small boy offered him a split coconut, a banana and, to be blessed and taken home to the family shrine, a picture of a Naga or sacred snake.

My eyes brimmed with colours, my nose breathed scents, my ears overflowed with strange sounds, my mind crammed itself full of imponderable questions and my heart beat to and fro. When the senses are so intoxicated it is hard to see. Small bells chimed in the temple proper. Devotees with shaven heads filed into the inner sanctum between elephants and four-armed guardians of the gate. Beside a monumental Nandi, the sacred bull that is the vehicle of Shiva, a baby yelled as a priest pierced her lobes with gold ear-rings. I grinned at her; the priest frowned back. The father of an older girl welcomed me to her betrothal party in the wedding hall.

'What is your name? What is your country? What is the purpose of your visit?'

They posed for my camera, smiling and giggling and looking desperately serious, gathered on a dais before an image of Shiva

Nataraja, the lord of the dance; within a halo fringed with fire, which is the cosmos, the dancing god creates and destroys, he moves and is still, his right foot firmly planted on the back of a demon dwarf. The party shared their pleasure with me and sent me on my way with my hands full of sticky sweetmeats which I shared with the one beggar who approached me in the temple, and with driver Prakash and his boy.

If it is possible, we left Shiva, sublime and terrible; we left the snake gods, relics of pre-Aryan cults; we left pilgrims and their *pujas* – acts of worship; we said goodbye to families and their *samskaras* – sacraments and rites of passage. We sped down the hill, through the turmoil of town traffic and out across the road bridge that spans the Krishna. We were on the main highway from Calcutta to Madras.

Sickly music filled the car. Patchy tarmac roughly two vehicles wide ran through shanty suburbs past an occasional modest temple. Then palm trees and fields. Prakash reclined on the bench seat and drove demoniacally, one hand on the wheel. He overtook everything that moved, the way a carpenter's plane overtakes a block of wood. I needed a sedative. In front was a wide lorry in Toytown livery. That'll slow us down, I thought. We overtook it, though it was overtaking a second primary-coloured lorry at the time. We bounced off the jagged edge of the tarmac and hurtled through dust. A third Toytown lorry was coming the other way. At least four horns were blaring. The shearing, squealing, messy, metallic shambles somehow didn't happen. Just.

I saw terror in the eyes of a woman shitting at the side of the road. I think she was shitting before we came into her life. I banged on the back of the front seat with both fists. Prakash and the boy turned round. Prakash the overtaker. I wanted the name of a good undertaker. Frantically I fanned with hands palm-down. He smiled at me in the mirror and slowed. I nodded. Had he not proved what a very fine driver he was? I put fingers in my ears and then pointed at the cassette deck. He turned the music off. I smiled. The rest of the journey was just fine.

To get to the heavenly city, after barely missing the direct and instantaneous route, we had to drive twenty miles south-west from Vijayawada to Guntur, then twenty-two miles north to

Amaravati which lay only twenty miles upriver from Vijaya-wada, but on the south bank, in another dimension.

After more than twenty years in India William Bowden had had his very first furlough in England. He left Elizabeth in Barnstaple for her health's sake. Landing at Madras in November 1858, he returned by road to his beloved delta via Guntur and Vijaya-wada. Somewhere on this road he had an unexpected meeting which deeply moved him. While waiting for fresh bullocks to take him on the next stage, he visited a godown where prisoners in chains had halted. He went to preach to them and found that they were from another world, but one he knew well. They were Koya tribals who hunted the hill jungles flanking those reaches of the Godavari that he had first reconnoitred, in com-pany with Captain F. T. Haig of the whisky family. The Koyas had been sentenced to fourteen years' imprisonment for their part in a local rebellion which had followed the so-called Indian Mutiny. Bowden wrote:

> They listened with great attention, and I was struck with their manly bearing in their chains. A low-countryman in these circumstances would have been all importunity for help, but they asked for none; but after I had left them, one of them obtained leave to follow me a few paces, and asked if I could help them in the way of obtaining leave to be imprisoned in the Guntur jail, rather than the one they were going to nearly 100 miles below Madras, as their wives and children in that case would be able to know of them from time to time. Five of the hill chiefs were hanged on account of the rebellion, and I learnt from these men that I had met and known four out of the five. Mrs Beer went to see one of these chiefs before he was hanged, and he mentioned my name to her.

Prakash drove me through the sprawling, dusty busyness of Guntur comparatively sedately and I was glad to visit neither hospital nor jail. Thick traffic included scooters with whole families aboard, and one with a man carrying tall panes of glass;

they rested on his thighs and leant against his nose like a makeshift windscreen as he bumped across ruts and swerved between lorries and bullock carts.

We were on the road to Amaravati now. It was rough but led through a sumptuous landscape of paddies, cotton and tobacco fields, palms and eucalyptus groves. Now and then there were long stinking chicken houses half-walled with wire mesh. We met two men on bicycles carefully negotiating the pitted road to Guntur with sky-scrapers of egg trays at their backs. I feared for them when we swerved to avoid a lorry lurching along in its own small dust storm. One rider's loss of balance was all it would have taken to make a sixty-dozen-egg omelette.

We overtook carts and wagons stacked with fruit and veg. One ox-cart groaned under a load of slate. We swept through villages in which occasional low houses were built of this thin-bedded rock; most were of mud-and-wattle, and roofed with palmyra fronds; petty stalls sold *paan* and cigarettes; some were festooned with bananas; between humble neighbours, surprisingly ambitious concrete houses reared up where some villager, perhaps a merchant or a lawyer or a money-lender, had made good.

To make good here, in a village in the Guntur district of Andhra Pradesh, you do what you'd do in London or Tokyo or New York. You buy and sell something, preferably money. Or advise those who do. Or go to law on their behalf. You do not grow anything or produce anything or do anybody any good. You play on need and greed and misfortune. They are called market forces and the market is god. Serve god. To make the most, it is best to make nothing. Just profit. Making nothing but money, you make good, even though goodness is the last thing on your mind.

We reached the second destination on my mind, a dusty street between rickety houses, shacks and shops, where a remake of *High Noon* might have felt half at home. So this was Amaravati. Fragments of a pillar edict of the mighty emperor Ashoka, convert to Buddhism in the third century BC, were found here not very long ago. So this was legendary Amaravati, sacred site on the outskirts of the provincial capital of the Satyavahana empire, where in the second century AD the Andhra culture of the

Krishna valley reached its apogee. Here blossomed, in the words of Coomaraswamy, 'the most voluptuous and the most delicate flower of Indian art'. The Buddha's influence spread from here by sea to Burma, Indonesia and beyond. The town's name belongs to the glorious city where the old god Indra, warlord and lord of heaven, has his abode. Amaravati is the heavenly city.

The main drag aimed straight for the gates of the Amareswara temple. Gates is too small a word. They opened at the base of a six-storey *gopuram*, an elaborately moulded tapering tower typical of Dravidian temples. Prakash naturally assumed that I, like the road, was aiming for Hindu monuments not Buddhist ruins. He parked beside the temple. All at once I saw the Krishna river's majestic breadth glittering as far as the blue lumpy hills.

A pair of small girls begged like the professional limpets they were. At the bathing *ghat*, the steps to the water, a woman slapped the dirt out of sodden clothes and a man painted concrete posts deep blue with Telugu lettering in pink and lemon. The *ghat* was sponsored by Suji Graphics. A battered lorry in Toytown livery, with the slogan 'Work More Talk Less' on its cab, had backed into the river. It was being washed down and loaded up at the same time. Men with baskets of sand on their heads waded to it from a sailing boat whose gunwales lifted little by little.

Within the temple precincts boys with coconuts and questions gathered round me beside a diminutive garlanded Nandi. I grew impatient and wanted to find the Buddhist relics. Prakash had disappeared. His boy stuck to my heels. We made signs at one another. Nearby, a low mound surrounded by a paved path is all that remains of Amaravati's great *stupa* or memorial dome. Much of its best carving is in the Government Museum in Madras and the British Museum in London, but I knew that some was still here. At last Prakash popped up again, incredulous that I had done with the temple so quickly, and reluctant to drive on to the museum.

'No photo,' said the man behind the desk.

'Photography Prohibited,' said a sign on the wall.

'I'd like to buy a guidebook.'

29

'No guidebook,' said the man behind the desk.

'No photo,' said the man who followed me around the exhibits with his eye on my camera.

I shrugged, being as slow on the uptake as I possibly could.

'But,' he added softly after a long pause, 'you may take, if you give . . .' And his hand was more eloquent than his tongue.

'No,' I said, much angrier with him than he deserved.

I stared hard at reliefs, medallions and panels from the *stupa*, and at fragments of the stone railing – the biggest, most richly decorated ever carved – that had surrounded it. Here, and palpable, was the collision of Satyavahana high culture with both the Buddhist north and the Mediterranean. Roman traders carried something of Andhra's spirit home; Indian scholars commonly went west, and European craftsmen probably brought skills to the Coromandel coast. There was more than a hint of Greek grace in the *stupa*'s architectural detail; some of its crowded figures had Western faces. One enchanting carving stays in my eye, in soft focus: the face of a *yakshi* or maiden spirit emerging, either unfinished or broken, from raw rock; just rough stone, beads, a braid and a delicate expression of pained surprise.

Prakash drove back towards Vijayawada across country on a rutted mud road often running alongside irrigation channels. It was an intensely fertile, conscientiously worked landscape. Women waved from the fields. Scarecrows gaped. A flock of tan-and-white sheep hurried as if on high heels. A red tractor drove in small circles, perilously packing down layers of rice straw round the central pole of a growing rick.

I repeated the name 'Ondavalli' like a mantra, but sensed from their animated and apparently inconclusive discussions that Prakash and the boy had no idea what I wanted to see. We herded a flock of blue-and-white schoolgirls with oiled plaits and arms full of books. They giggled and pointed. In the village ahead we stopped at a garish temple. I didn't know where I was going but I knew I wasn't there. We pressed on. A mournful pye dog stood in the road with pups hanging in clusters from her teats.

'That's it, there it is,' I shouted, pointing at shadowy apertures in a rocky hillside. It had to be the place.

'OK,' said Prakash tentatively. He and his boy were seeing the cave temple of Ondavalli for the first time.

It stood, four storeys cut into the hill – stepped plinths, stairways and deep pillared halls – supported by massive masonry. A path flanked by trimmed shrubs led up to it. The sun was low. The road was orange. The rock was warm. The darkness inside was profound, perfumed with sandal paste and spices. This monument of the sixth or seventh century was empty, but not abandoned.

I climbed to the second floor and with my finger traced the lotus blossom cut into a capital. I stood by a huge pillar carved as an elephant's head and trunk, and felt the weight of the place. A man in a white *banian* and *dhoti*, with staring eyes and buck teeth, appeared from nowhere. He lit a lamp and rang a bell. Devotees soon approached up path and steps. On the third level gods or sages sat in the lotus posture, and stylized lions with bulbous eyes gazed across the rich alluvial valley and the Krishna river to Vijayawada and the hills.

In the dimness I began to distinguish carvings on the inner pillars: *yakshas* and *yakshis* in relief, dancing as they might on a medieval church. The man with teeth beckoned me. I slipped off my sandals and followed him through a gate he'd unlocked into still deeper darkness. The inner sanctum was close and aromatic. The floor was sticky with libations. He lit a candle. Fitfully a mighty figure manifested itself. So near, my eye could not encompass what seemed larger than the blackness it displaced, and yet lay cramped as if in a procrustean cave. Lord Vishnu it was, vast, dark faced and vivid eyed, asleep upon the coiled serpent Sesha, head and feet pressed at the walls; head sheltered by Sesha's five-hooded head, feet massaged by the goddess Lakshmi; and growing from his navel a lotus on which sat four-headed Brahma, god of creation. The cave was full of him.

I edged out with the devotees. The sky was deep blue, Vishnu's colour, the colour of infinity. I found myself standing on a carved *graffito* that, with a start, I recognized; one which felt cruder and older than these gods and lions and lotuses. It was a labyrinth, mirror image of ones I'd recently seen near Tintagel in Cornwall. Precisely the same maze appears on coins from Knossos, on a tablet from Pylos, *circa* 1200 BC, and scored on a crimson-painted pillar in the House of Lucretius, Pompeii, with the words: *Labyrinthus hic habitat minotaurus.*

I rose from my knees, a millennium or two adrift. I'd come here today, exactly where I wanted to come, thanks to Mr Ananth, Mr Satyam, Prakash and his boy. Now, rising and staring out over the valley, I didn't know where I was.

5

AUSPICIOUS DAYS

Machilipatnam

THAT NIGHT I was caught up in labyrinthine toils. The Minotaur was a Brahmin bull. Kali was Mistress of the Labyrinth. A young woman was rumoured to have emerged from hypnosis beside the Cornish mazes in a state of mortal terror, convinced that men had been sacrificed there. Always the labyrinth's heart was hot with human blood. I woke amazed, in the archaic sense of that word.

By morning the puncture under my eye had sealed itself with a black clot; left undisturbed, it didn't weep. For five rupees a rickshaw-wallah pedalled me along sandy roads to catch my bus; he waded like a man in a mire. I gave him six and trudged through chaotic approaches to the bus station. Beneath the roof it was cool and orderly. An Express ticket to Machilipatnam was sixteen rupees. Forty-three miles. Less than a penny a mile. People stood or sat in clumps while swallows flew between them, skimming the shiny tiled floor. Like shuttles they shot straight through the building at knee or ankle height. I marvelled, unamazed.

Speedily and safely the packed Express bus emerged from shanty suburbs, passed shrines to Ganesh and Hanuman, and rattled along beside the Bandar canal. It might have been a lazy English river, except that palms stood upside down in it, reflections shattered by bathing men and water buffalo. Paddy husk flew from winnowing fans. Ox-carts and lorries heaped with sugar cane queued outside a molasses factory. Beside a masticating ox and an upset cart with one wheel off, blacksmiths with tongs lifted a red-hot tyre from a ring of fire. By the time the iron had contracted, doused and steaming, around the wheel's

33

felloes, we'd dragged our dust cloud another mile down the road.

After five weeks in Madras the holy fools sailed north for the town then known as Masulipatam, just beyond the Krishna delta. The mason, the cobbler and their wives were accompanied by John Vesey Parnell, later Lord Congleton, who had offered to see them settled in. After a couple of days' sailing, they dropped anchor in the shallows, five or six miles offshore; boats ferried them towards a long low beach, bristling palm trees, and glimpses of the flagstaff of Bandar Fort, which they reached a mile and a half up a grubby mud-banked river. Soon afterwards Mrs Thomas, a judge's wife, described the environs in a letter home:

> Masulipatam was an ugly place; a swamp, two miles broad, between the town and the sea; nothing to be seen but wide sandy roads, with prickly-pear hedges, enclosing black-looking Palmyra-trees, and red-tiled houses peeping (no, not *peeping*, they are not coquette enough for that – *staring*) out from among them; altogether, a most *vapid* sort of place.

In mid-August 1836 the holy fools landed there and stayed for eight months. The fort, whose brick ramparts were crumbling, was garrisoned by the 47th Native Infantry Regiment; the last British battalion had been withdrawn, but the fort's population of six thousand or so still included about thirty Europeans. The town of sixty thousand, dominated by twenty temples, was in decline. Parnell introduced the Devon rustics to the white gentlemen; the judge sent him two hundred rupees for them; Dr Morton of the 47th offered medical care whenever they might need it; others rallied to their aid with utensils and sticks of furniture.

In August 1611 the *Globe* had put factors ashore at Masulipatam, the *bandar* or port of the Kingdom of Golconda. Thus it became the East India Company's first station on the Coromandel coast.

Peter Floris and Lucas Antheuniss, probably defectors from the rival Dutch company, had put themselves and £600 into the voyage. They ordered cottons from Masulipatam weavers and dyers, and after eight months sailed on to Java and to mixed fortunes in the Gulf of Siam. Floris returned at the end of 1613, sold Thai and Chinese goods to Golconda merchants, ordered more cottons and repaired a leaky *Globe* in the estuary near Masulipatam. Then he sailed to Bantam, where he traded for pepper, and was back in London by August 1615. Carried ashore, he died three weeks later. The voyage's profit of at least 318 per cent on cottons and pepper and Chinese silk didn't do Floris much good.

But Antheuniss returned from Siam to Masulipatam in 1616 and began to build up the Burma trade. The town's business history was manic: its governors creamed off profits; its chintzes were not always popular in Java; and efforts to oil the wheels of commerce were not necessarily appreciated at home. Hearing that its factors had spent almost £4000 on a mission to the Court of Golconda, now Hyderabad, the London directors of the East India Company wrote in 1636:

> You have to the life expressed your own vanity, folly, and riot unto those people, and wasted so much of our estate in such a lavish manner as if we sent our ships and monies hither for you to make shows and pagents for those people to scorn at.

Two hundred years later, not much vanity, folly or riot was left. The town the English company had held for so long – apart from periods when the Dutch regained it, 1686–90, and the French won it, 1750–59 – was being let go. Still, it was a good place for holy fools to acclimatize and to continue Telugu lessons. Under Dr Morton's eye, Elizabeth Bowden gave birth to her first child in January 1837. He was named William after his father.

It was an auspicious day, the first of several declared by the astrologers, when I arrived at Machilipatnam. The town was full of wedding parties. Nothing could go wrong. An old rickshaw wallah pedalled me up Rabindranath Tagore Road to Hotel Suntosh, which means 'joy'. Deenabandhu, my contact, had booked me in. Reception had no record of that. Still, Deenabandhu said it was the best. The best cockroaches and the thickest dust in town, at three times the price of Swapna Lodge; plus leaky plumbing, mud in the bathroom, butts in the ashtray and vomit on the pillow.

'Clean sheets tomorrow a.m.,' the boy in khaki announced joyfully. That was helpful. I was too hungry to worry.

'Where can I eat?' I asked the man at the desk.

'Westarian?' he seemed to say.

'No, Indian,' I replied, remembering that Deenabandhu had recommended the Western-style restaurant attached to the hotel.

'No, wegtarian, you want?' the man tried again.

The posh restaurant had in any case closed down. The vegetarian café nearby was full of workmen and rickshaw wallahs eating off water-lily leaves or stainless-steel trays.

'Meals?' said the maître d', which meant, as I later learnt, rice with all the etceteras rather than mere tiffin.

I nodded in ignorance. Meals soon clattered on the table: small bowls of curry, okra, spicy rice, beans, dahl, onion raita and curd. A big platter of boiled rice. Poppadoms. Chapatis. Bananas. Poor men glanced at me and mimed discreetly, hand to mouth. It was very helpful. Blissfully I shaped ball after ball of rice and sauce with my right fingers. If I'd chosen it, it couldn't have been tastier or cheaper. I washed under the tap.

In the shade of a palm-leaf umbrella a delicate old man, like a picture-book fakir in a turban and beige and white cloths, hawked melons at one end of the market. At the other, a young Ayyappa devotee sold bananas: shaven and brawny in a black *lungi*, he was a holy skinhead. A fortune-teller squatted beside a silhouette of the human palm and cowrie shells on a mat. A sacrilegious man whacked a sacred cow that scooped peanuts off his handcart with her tongue. The outline of Christ crucified was chalked on the road; only his face was coloured in, but he'd attracted a liberal sprinkling of coins, and pedestrians, cycle-rickshaws, ox-carts, mopeds and motorcycles were careful not to cross him.

Through crowds I thought I caught sight of a grey-haired white man, the first European I'd seen since Madras, but as he strode by I saw that he had the blond eyelashes and sensitive pink skin of an albino. A cut-out film star/politician dwarfed both a Memorial Hall celebrating Machilipatnam Lions Club Golden Jubilee, and palms in the public gardens whose arched gateway bore the town's name in the old style – Masulipatam.

The old style town was not hard to find: wide, sandy streets flanked by open drains and one- or two-storey whitewashed houses with pillared verandahs and red-tiled roofs heavy enough to keep out rains and heat. Doors of vivid green or blue or aquamarine, or of weathered wood, opened into impenetrable interiors. Every threshold was painted yellow and, sometimes, further doors opened into sunlit courtyards beyond. Through one such house I saw sacred basil growing on an altar and glimpsed, in the darkness between the doors, a lithe figure and the gleam of heavy hair combed, tossed back and combed again. Always a voyeur, the voyager. I stared hard, trying to piece things together. Here for the first time I felt that if I looked over my shoulder I might see my ancestors. Tutti-frutti concrete houses and occasional lorries and cars felt like intruders. Down a side-street cows browsed and goats sat with a woman on the mud verandah of her reed-thatched house. There were remains of old brick buildings, a small temple's stained white walls, huge brass pots, a polluted watercourse and a man on an Enfield Bullet who halted beside me in a dust cloud.

'What do you want?' he said. He meant nothing rude by it. He meant what he said, which I had to translate to myself: 'What is your desire and how can I help you?'

I explained what I was doing in his town.

'Very interesting,' he said, 'but sorry I am young.'

Bandsmen in crimson uniforms and turbans with cockades piped me back to the main road. Another orchestra serenaded newly-weds beneath a canopy pitched on a roof-top. At the town centre I met a wedding car discreetly draped with garlands; the windscreen was solid jasmine. It drove at funeral pace behind a gold and biscuit-coloured band playing a trilling, wailing wedding march on drums, trumpets, clarinets, saxophones, a sousaphone and an electric guitar with amplifier and speakers on a handcart. I was welcomed and thrust towards the car to smile my blessings on the groom. It was an auspicious day indeed.

In the inner sanctum of the temple beside the Hotel Suntosh, a priest gave me a banana and a hibiscus flower. Before me stood the god Ramalinghaswara, snake head upon tiers of gold, and a dark goddess with a name I couldn't quite catch. The bell that devotees struck was a ship's bell whose inscription reverberated longer than its chime: 'Iona 1841'.

Old men in white sat in the shade on the raised floor of the *mandapam*, or pillared hall outside the sanctum. One, a retired schoolteacher, explained that the gods were versions of Shiva and Parvati. He was fascinated with my ancestors' story and told me of another Englishman who built nearby St Andrew's Church to keep his wife there, embalmed in a glass coffin. Pyedogs lay in the shadows, languorously licking themselves. Bright blue elephants flanked a stairway to a second hall. Parked on the precinct's clipped grass was a shrine like a carnival float, with pinnacles and a rusty 'tiled' roof, a temple pillar like a tall funnel on its bonnet, and a driver's seat and steering wheel in front of the sanctuary. Its gods were fading and its tyres were flat.

An apprentice priest with a pink plastic basket and the demeanour of an evangelical curate pushed me through a turnstile to the Vishnu temple next door. He was young, but with greying hair and hypnotic marmalade-coloured eyes which implored me to share his zeal. The sanctum was locked fast but I admired cells in which dwelt Hanuman, the monkey god, and Garuda, man-bird and vehicle of Vishnu. The earnest priest pressed on me two bananas and half a coconut, divine food, and begged me to return.

Led by yet another glittering Indo-Jazz band, a long procession of unladen ox-carts and drivers clogged the street in protest against terms and conditions. I watched them and their passion dwindle in the distance. By now I'd checked out of Hotel Joy and into the cheaper, cleaner Revathi Rest House whose proprietor also owned the adjoining cinema and filling station. My room overlooked Nehru roundabout and a traffic island beneath the HP Petrol sign where rag-pickers sorted scraps into saleable bundles and sat until dusk as if at home, laughing and crying, adjusting their saris, unfurling and furling their hair.

The proprietor wasn't much in evidence, but was devout enough to come when *puja* was being performed in reception. While I waited to phone Deenabandhu, a priest offered a split coconut and bananas to the gods in a glass-fronted shrine mounted high on the wall behind the desk; a ghee lamp and joss sticks burned; sandalwood paste and vermilion were applied. The proprietor took it all calmly. The manager, a thin greasy grey-haired man always punctuated by coloured powders, was sweaty and exultant. He took coconut milk in his shaky right palm, sipped from it and passed it over his head. At long last I got through to Deenabandhu. Then the lights went out. Ceiling fans freewheeled to a halt. Darkness grew hotter. No sooner was Deenabandhu in the door than he asked the manager to start the diesel generator. Lights and fans came on. Deenabandhu was a man who got things done.

He was head of the Department of Zoology at Noble College, which took its name from a missionary who started work here five years after the Bowdens landed. He told me of radical schemes to help slum dwellers and the village poor, and about their foes: landlords and money-lenders. Not to mention cyclone and flood, which killed fifty thousand here in the spring of 1977. That was the worst. Just five months ago floods caused great destruction, though radar warning allowed people to evacuate the area and relief schemes ameliorated the damage. When pushed, Deenabandhu confessed that he was centrally involved in several grass-roots aid projects. How many hours were there in his day?

As he led me through town to the Peacock Restaurant I showed him my tin of Bowden's Indian Balm. He sniffed at it and smiled.

'I'm following their scent,' I said. 'I want to see the British fort, the beach, the old Dutch and French quarters, oh, and the place where Kalamkari cloth is made.'

'No problem,' said Deenabandhu, 'except for the fort. There is nothing left of that.'

A flaming wick in a bottle lit crucified Christ; his outline was coloured in now, pink, a white man in a *dhoti*. Red chalk gore oozed from nail-holes and spear wound; he'd collected many coins. A raucous band in scarlet with gold braid and turbans with green cockades accompanied a garlanded wedding rickshaw, all illuminated by vertical fluorescent tubes carried like *Star Wars* swords by relatives and powered by a generator on a handcart pushed by a coolie. It was an auspicious night.

'Four of William and Elizabeth's seven sons were born in this town,' I told Deenabandhu, 'including my great-grandfather.'

So auspicious was it, next morning, it was hard to hire a car. They were all at weddings. Taxi drivers who'd rushed me when I first arrived didn't want to know. Deenabandhu found one, at a price, to drive us to the Kalamkari co-operative in Desaipeta, a village suburb. The workshop was full of low benches and a smell like vomit, but no workers. They'd gone to find coolie work because the government had failed to pay for a big order supplied to their Lepakshi Handicrafts Emporia. I looked at teak printing blocks, at inks, at fruits, flowers, stems and leaves from which dyes were made, at bamboo-and-rag 'pens', and para-phernalia of the fifteen processes – buffalo-dung bleaches, mordants, lost wax and all – through which each cloth takes two months to pass.

Design after intricate design was spread before us, in ochre and madder, pink and indigo, myrobalan yellow and iron black. In 1663 Samuel Pepys bought his wife 'a chint, that is, a painted Indian callico, for to line her new study', and in the same year François Bernier described Emperor Shah Jahan's reception tent, lined with 'cloths painted by a pencil of Masulipitam, purposely wrought and contrived with such vivid colours and flowers . . . that one would have said it was a hanging parterre'.

Kalamkari has been made here for at least a thousand years. The East India Company came for chints, or painted cloths. Of the pinnace *Coaster's* 1834 voyage we know that 'her return lading of Calico is to be one-fourth in paintings'. Deenabandhu bought a tablecloth and I bought one of the 'celebrated *palampores*, or "bed-covers", of Masulipatam which,' wrote Sir George Birdwood, 'in point of art decoration are simply incomparable'. Double-bed size, £3. *Kalam* means 'pen', *kar* means 'work'. But because some corrupt bureaucratic *babu* hadn't been paid enough, a government order hadn't been paid for and no penwork at all was being done.

I watched the first rib being bedded into a keel. The skeletons of new boats, bright ochre timbers shaped by adzes, bristled beside black hulks of decayed barges. Men mended blue nylon fishing nets and women sorted fish. I drank coffee at a stall with one of Deenabandhu's disciples, Vidya Sagar, who had brought me across paddies, swamp and railway line to the *bandar*, or port, where my great-great-grandparents landed. We prowled around the shells of Port Authority warehouses, cracked open by cyclone, and climbed the faulted outside stair of a cyclone warning post, now silenced for good, to survey a derelict cyclone shelter set like a sad helter-skelter in an unfair ground.

Down sandy tracks we found a village of mud homes with rush or palmyra thatches, and, amongst them, small cyclone-resistant concrete buildings put up with government subsidy. An elderly couple, *dhobis*, laid saris out to dry beside a tank in which water buffalo bathed. Between the houses and the tank were the headstones, wooden crosses and anonymous hummocks of an unfenced Christian cemetery beside a monument known as the Tomb of the Dead. I climbed to the balustraded terrace at the base of the massive white pillar which Manuel Fruvall erected 'on the very spot where his relatives perished, *which for years had been their happy home*', and read the lengthy inscription which begins:

THIS MONUMENT
commemorates the melancholy fate of
ANTHONY and MARIA FRUVALL
their sons

JOSEPH MICHAEL PETER MANUEL and DANIEL
and their daughter
MARY ANN HONEY and her children JOSEPH and
GEORGIANA
and about 30,000 souls
who were all unexpectedly swept into eternity by the ocean
wave which desolated this town on the night of the cyclone
of
1st November 1864 . . .

After a few more turnings we came upon a name which gave
me hope: 'Bandar Fort Post Office'. And more than a name,
the fort itself. A ruinous gateway, brick rubble, an imposing
quadrangle, verandahs, fallen roofs, crude but oddly baroque
details which survived winds and waves but couldn't survive
neglect. A shapely tower stood in the old parade ground. A
notice, planted by the Archaeological Survey of India, named the
fort that Vidya had not seen before, that Deenabandhu believed
swept into eternity.

To label is enough here. To acknowledge is to preserve, if only
in the mind, in dreams of history. I clambered in and passed
beneath an arch to weathered footings, evidence of ranges of
buildings that fortifications had not been able to protect. Here
were the barracks, here the messes, here the jail, and here the
hospital where the ghost of Dr Morton trod his rounds. It was
all I could do to set four Bowden births against thirty thousand
deaths. As I climbed a stairway to the wrecked first floor a snake
squirmed under my foot and slithered away beneath leaves
through a gap in the masonry.

6

A NIGHT'S MARCH

via Kaikalur

IN PALTRY electric light the ceiling fan's shadow spins and the chestnut horse framed on the wall plunges forward above the helpful motto, 'Each must find his own road.' I've slept beneath these hooves for several nights but now I'm up at 5.30 a.m., in time to make tea and pack before the morning power-cut. Today the road I'm seeking is the road to Joy.

The manager is already crammed behind his reception desk. Instantly he panics over my bill. He is a man who needs to wipe his forehead, but wonderful self control stops him smudging the pigments, the vermilion 'I' within the white 'V', that mark his devotion to Vishnu. Ego should be centred in god. Atman within Brahman. It isn't. Maybe wiping his brow is all it would take. But piety prevents him and his anxiety is unceasing.

He bids me farewell like an about-to-be-long-lost brother. It's cooler outside. A man of evident refinement squats beside a ditch with his *lungi* drawn up. I watch entranced as a sow, black and glistening from the drain, approaches on tip-toe trotters and thrusts her snout up his arse. He almost tips forward, but only grunts and waves the back of his hand in the beast's face as if to say, 'Hang on a minute.' There's nobility in his nonchalance. The pig retreats and waits, panting. She wants it hot and fresh.

I've my own anxieties. Does the Narsapur bus really leave at 7 a.m.? A conference of officials at the bus station came up with that time yesterday, but the man at the hotel had with great authority plumped for 3 p.m. And despite my efforts to get through by phone, my cousin Joy doesn't know I'm on my way.

*   *   *

Long before the days of phones and buses the Bowdens and Beers made this trip. After an eight-month stay they continued their journey north. They may have embarked on a coaster, but probably hired an ox-cart to transport themselves and their baggage to Narsapur. Committed to living where no other Europeans lived, they left the quartermaster, the judge and the doctor behind them and moved into a territory where nothing was not strange.

Was their faith of the brash kind that allowed them no misgivings? They were young enough for that. Were they anxious despite their sense of destiny? *Dacoitee*, armed robbery, was bad news, and *thuggee* had had a lurid press. Between 1831 and 1836 Captain William Sleeman had succeeded in committing 3,266 *thugs* and in unlocking the dark secrets and language of a *thuggee* lore which both offended and fascinated English sensibilities. Did the holy fools imagine they might be robbed, ritually strangled and buried in the name of Kali before they'd even begun?

In years to come they returned on foot to Machilipatnam if ever they needed to cash a remittance or see a British physician. It became a routine march. They'd change into pyjamas, set out in late afternoon, stride across country and along the coast all through a cool moonlit night, and arrive in time for breakfast.

Elizabeth Bowden made slower progress in October 1845, borne on a palanquin and heavily pregnant. By the time she reached the fort she was suffering from dysentery and an empty purse. To her dismay she found that good Dr Morton, who'd helped three of her four sons into the world, had left with his regiment. The new garrison doctor prescribed arrowroot, port wine and other luxuries for which she had no money. Almost at once a hamper was delivered at the travellers' bungalow, sent by an officer who'd called upon her there before the doctor's visit. It contained precisely the prescription she couldn't afford. On the twenty-sixth, her fifth boy, Edwin Skinner Bowden, my great-grandfather, was born.

The very first journey of his life was the one I'm trying to make today. He was going home, to a strange place. Perhaps I am too.

Last night the manager tried to help me on my way. He had
been haunting the corridor and popping up in reception even
when he was supposed to be off duty. At last he knocked at my
door.

'We have done this and that for you,' he said, 'this *and* that.'
And he put his fingers to his mouth hungrily. He tapered from
a crown of grey hair like a greasy stir-fry to legs like stilts. 'I am
asking you only because I am old and poor.'

'I want to phone Narsapur,' I said.

'Come,' he said, refraining from wiping his sparkling painted
brow. We ignored the reception desk and were halfway up the
street before he explained, 'Hotel telephone not STD.'

Lads on scooters and on foot swirled outside our Rest House.
Fists flew and the crowd staggered. Steel glinted, shouts cut,
scooters revved. Then something diluted the mob and darkness
drained it to the dregs, a drop or two of blood. The manager
plucked at my shirt and drew me across the street. To avoid
a chiming rickshaw I flattened myself against the slipstream
of a lorry as if it were a wall. At the bus station we found
the STD kiosk occupied, a chair padlocked inside it with legs
in the air.

'We must be making call via operator,' the manager decided
in the middle of the street. 'You will book?' I side-stepped as a
swaying bus with faint headlights and a screaming driver swung
round the corner and almost demolished us.

He never fetched me for the booked call to Joy, despite my
ten-rupee tip. I'd have given more if he hadn't nearly killed me,
but still he clasped hands and fawned and called me brother.

This morning at the bus station a man from Hyderabad
speaks some English. I don't know what 'Narsapur' looks
like: Telugu signs are all twirls and flourishes to me. The 7 a.m.
bus will dock at Stand 8. It heaves into view. There's a rush
while it's still rolling to drop scarves, cloths, papers through
the windows to claim seats. It docks at Stand 10. Trying hard
not to be polite, I use my rucksack as a battering-ram and
force myself on board. There's a spare seat above the rear
axle. My rucksack is too fat for the tin luggage rack; until

folk settle down and I can lay it to rest in the aisle, I hug it like an ungainly baby.

I think I'm on today's one bus for Narsapur. We grind away on time, 7 a.m. We'll get there at 11 a.m., I'm told. Forty miles as the crow flies, ten miles an hour. We leave old Frenchpet off to the right and, rather than take the coast road where I imagine the Bowdens striding home, we turn left and inland past the remains of Vondalapalem, Machilipatnam's old Dutch quarter. The faster our driver goes the less I feel numbing jolts transmitted through pancaked springs and thin upholstery. The dirt roads are mostly causeways beside canals and irrigation ditches, or between paddies and fish tanks. I'm so happy that the brakes are good. We halt, toppling at a terrifying angle, to let a lorry pass; we scrape past bullock carts; we nudge a duckherd and his flock down the bank. The bus is old, prematurely aged, with balding tyres, dents in whatever can be dented and a universal coating of ruddy dust. It may be fast but it isn't a crow.

The conductor relieves me of eighteen rupees. With a stout key he whacks at steel uprights or seat backs to tell the driver to stop or start. People press in and out at every village halt to the accompaniment of clattering from above as tin trunks and cloth-wrapped bundles are stowed on the roof or dropped to the ground. Two superior men across the aisle take up all the space they can, almost edging a poor man in a *dhoti* off the end of the seat.

'You should have taken train,' one says, turning to me. 'This is all too dirty.'

A line of carts loaded with bloated sacks is making for a rice factory where grain is spread and raked on paved pitches in the sun, or piled up high like ochre sand. In a village an old-style mud-walled granary decays on wooden stilts. Boys make bedsteads, hammering frames together or turning legs on handspun lathes, one tugging string to and fro, another wielding chisels. In several wayside shrines Krishna slakes his thirst at a sacred cow's udder. At Gullavaller a shop describes itself as 'Krishna & Co. Fancycongans & Booksellers'. If the bus would only stop, I could browse. I might even develop a taste for fancycongans. I know I'm desperate for a pee.

* * *

46

Forty miles as the crow flies. But a bus is not a crow. I did fly out of town in a black Ambassador, a couple of days ago, with Deenabandhu and a driver perhaps as old as fourteen who perched on the edge of his seat and kept me on the edge of mine as he drove like a demon, groping for the pedals with small bare feet.

We took the road to the beach, the Boy Wonder somehow flying over potholes or squeezing between them, just missing children and goats, buffalo and buses. Some seven miles later, after the salt pans, our tyres sighed as they hit the sand. I stood in the warm murky waters of the Bay of Bengal. Small breakers fondled the backs of my knees. Clothed people paddled against a backdrop of endless beach, two petty shops, one tapering black-and-white lighthouse, a horizon of palmyra palms.

A steamroller's wheels were moistened by two small boys who pressed sodden cloths against them as they turned, bedding down tarmac on the outskirts of Kamsalipalem village. Men tended molten pitch and women carried baskets of gravel on their heads. One of Deenabandhu's workers here is called James Watt; he, with Vidya Sagar and a young woman graduate who teaches literacy to village women, showed us the clinic, the sewing school, the concrete houses. Beside a small temple an old woman fell on me and tried to kiss my feet. A farmer gave us hot milk and boiled peanuts on his mud verandah; Deenabandhu prayed over his one surviving son who last year had almost succumbed to meningitis. It was all part of a holistic project involving housing, health, church, education, job skills and business start-up schemes.

'World Vision awarded this one best project in Southeast Asia,' put in Vidya Sagar.

'Deenabandhu didn't mention that,' I said.

'Deenabandhu,' said Vidya Sagar, 'means humble man.'

I was humbled. The place was full of love. At a coffee-stall coolies grinned at me wildly; England led India in cricket on TV; the evening power-cut blacked it out, three overs to go. It was a relief. The night was balmy, palmy, the sunset saffron, the lighthouse pulsing powerfully. Boy Wonder's toes pressed the accelerator flat on the floor. That night he learnt that water buffalo are invisible in deep dusk. Burnt rubber but no blood.

A man in a *lungi* and a sweat-dark blue silk shirt boards the bus with a bulky basket of peanuts. He sells me a rupee's worth in a twist of paper. The fingernails of his left hand are painted half orange above the quick. Outside, reed thatch is giving way to palmyra fronds, and some houses are roofed with multi-layered terracotta tiles. Mud walls are decorated with white stripes, spots and painted plumes. Patches of garden glow with marigold and hibiscus. For miles I concentrate hard on colour and shape to distract myself from my distended bouncing bladder.

Soon after signs for Kolleru Bird Sanctuary, the great lake between the Krishna and Godavari deltas, we stop at Kaikalur. It is 10.30. People stream off the bus. A dwarf woman with stubby feet and hands, chains and ear-rings of gold, and piercing eyes clambers aboard and begs all along the aisle; my rucksack is an obstacle, but twenty-five paise pleases her. The conductor shows me ten minutes on his watch. I'm off too, looking for an end to pain. Away from us men, women stand discreetly with legs apart and slightly lifted saris. We pee against a wall.

I buy oranges and admire the technique of a camp holy man in spotless saffron and pink: with his silver pageboy hairstyle, long staff and mischievous eyes, he doesn't pay for refreshments. But I'm thinking of my map and my watch. Halfway and just half an hour to go? Almost anything is possible.

'Is late,' says one of the superior pair. 'Narsapur, noon.'

Back on the bus, their seats have been taken; they order the grumbling usurpers off. What, apart from an obnoxious attitude, gives them power? Pure caste? Now we are meeting fish lorries, passing fish tanks, leaving Krishna District and approaching Akividu, the first town in West Godavari District, with its Fish Packers, Fish Feed stores, Fish Consultants' offices, and its brick kilns. Unfired bricks laid out to dry on swelling ground create a mosaic of surprisingly liquid contours from which round houses of bricks and air, all blanketed with paddy husk, rise up smoking and fuming.

A hut's yard and verandah are crowded with figures, Ganesh

and Rajiv Gandhi among them, Hanuman and Dr Ambedkar in cement, a sculptor's manufactory of gods and politicians. In Bhimavaram people push between goods stacked on stepped pavements and hung from shop awnings; we skirt still water, holding still clouds and a perfect inverted pagoda, in the tank before Chalukya Bhim's late-ninth-century temple. It is long past noon. I'm impatient.

At about 1.15 we cross the humpy canal bridge into the heart of Palakol. I peer out hopefully and then see it above rooftops: the great *gopuram* I know from old photographs, the pagoda in whose shadow my ancestors lived for years. Recognition like this is unnerving. I'm coming home to somewhere utterly strange. The road follows the canal's left bank, past shrines and barges with patched sails, all the way to Narsapur. Dazed, I disembark, almost three hours late. Ghee lamps and electric candles flicker before gods and holy pictures in the bus station shrine.

'Holland Wharf,' I say to a group of smiling, baffled taxi drivers across the road by the canal. 'Hostel, Holland Wharf?'

I see a telephone in a makeshift box and pay one rupee to the minder who dials the number I show him.

'Hello, Paul,' says Joy. 'You're late.'

'I know the bus was late, but how d'you know I was coming?'

'Oh,' she replies, 'I guessed.'

A woman with a small ragged child pushes her husband towards me on a low trolley. I drop a coin into his steel cup. Joy waves as she drives past. Then she comes back. Beneath her pale-cream Ambassador with white-walled tyres, the road looks pocked and dusty indeed. Beside her elegant white coiffure and stylish sari I feel wind-blown and travel-stained. I wish I'd walked through the night in my pyjamas.

'Great to see you,' I exclaim. 'Wonderful.'

'Get in,' she says. 'We've kept lunch for you.'

7

DANDY FEVER

Narsapur

BEHIND THE darkened lenses of Joy's glasses the eyes were warm.
And the welcome. Her luxuriant white hair, carefully pinned up,
reminded me of our grandmother's, though a steel-grey streak in
front gave me the illusion that I was looking at a negative of
Indira Gandhi. It was a strong face, not to be trifled with.

There was a tantalizing glimpse of river, then a sign over steel
gates: 'Holland Wharf Girls' Hostel'. Joy hooted, hard.

'The taxi-drivers didn't know Holland Wharf,' I said.

'They wouldn't,' said Joy. 'You must ask for Wollander Revu or
Missamma Hahstel. I am Miss Amma. *Amma* means "mother".'

She stopped hooting as the gates swung open, powered by a
handful of her two hundred and seventy children. Preceded by
a hairy black sow and her piglets, we drove up the sandy drive
like royalty. Some of the girls dutifully chased the snorting tres-
passers, but most of them simply waved and stared at the apparition that was me.

Here behind high walls was a garden of coconut palms, ashok,
soap-nut, mango and frangipani trees, poinsettia, bougainvillea,
and croton, a sculpted lotus in a walled fish pond, and girls of
six to eighteen years old, inquisitive ones, orphans, *harijans*,
Hindus, Christians, rich ones, poor ones, all here because years
ago some holy fools dared to pitch up in this obscure place.

An old house, 'The Lodge', was concealed in the wonderful
accretion of new concrete that comprised the hostel buildings.
A fine old timber doorway opened between the sick-bay and
the juniors' dormitory, but girls grabbed my luggage and we
climbed the outside stairs to a sort of first-floor courtyard.
Joy pointed out dormitories to the right, the hostel office and

her own quarters to the left, and the guest room straight ahead.

Two steep steps dropped me into a spacious, well-upholstered bed-sit with the only sloping, old-style tiled roof in the place, the only mosquito-netted windows, and a delicious view of Nagaram Island across the Godavari river. It was glorious. Two more deep steps beyond narrow double doors led down to my own cubical concrete washroom boasting a flush toilet and a padded Ali Baba basket with a bucket of piping hot water nestling inside it.

The rest of the day was a dream. I can't remember what we talked about, or what kind of curry the redoubtable Suguna, Joy's cook, served up. There were many greetings, many confused faces. I lay down and listened to girlish chatter and laughter, to the rhythmic smack of wet washing on concrete, to small outbreaks of singing, to tinkling bells and to sighing brushes that seemed never to finish sweeping the compound's sandy floor.

With many a 'namaskaram' or 'hello' I crossed catwalks that linked buildings and climbed up to the flat roof of three-storey Australia House, so-called because Australian churches paid for it. I stepped between drying clothes. Down below, young women washed heavy swinging hair with lather from soap-nut kernels. Five girls in a row were picking nits out of one another's heads, though the front one was idle and the back one kept her vermin; a shame they couldn't recruit volunteers enough to make a circle.

The luminous Godavari eased past. At a line of posts in mid-stream a man in a country boat checked nets. On the far side oxen ploughed paddies between ranks of coconut palms. I almost put off leaning on the parapet to stare at the house next door. There was no hurry. It would wait a little longer.

'It's still here, you know,' Joy had said at lunch, to my surprise. 'Just over the compound wall.'

Concrete spawned concrete down there too, but at the heart of it I saw the brick gable-end and tiled roof of the old 'Dutch House'. Hard by Holland Wharf, it was once home to agents who handled merchandise for the Dutch East India Company's Palakol factory. But it had been an empty shell for thirty years when in April 1837, two months before Queen Victoria's accession, the Bowdens and Beers moved into the very building I gazed at now.

The English Company had abandoned Narsapur ten years before. Manchester's machine-made cottons killed the trade in hand-woven cloth. The sand bar at the rivermouth was a malignant growth and ships went north to Kakinada. The holy fools met with bleached skeletons in the Dutch House's compound, victims of the great famine of 1833, a scourge that had recurred with the rains' failure in 1836 and continued for three years. The Dutch had sold off the doors and windows, but solid walls and roof provided a good enough shelter. My ancestors' first Indian home was soon engulfed by pilgrims to the Pushkaram festival held on Godavari's banks every twelve years. On famine's heels, festival; on festival's heels, cholera; on cholera's heels, cyclone.

That first night I sat on top of the leprosy hospital at the far side of town being assaulted by clouds of mosquitoes in the light of vertical fluorescent tubes and shivering with cold in front of a roof-full of people watching a long Christmas programme staged by staff and featuring a nativity play which climaxed when angels appeared to shepherds who fell over and did lots of quaking with legs in the air. Everybody laughed and the PA system screamed. I had second thoughts about thin shirts, and about stars and auspicious days and wise men from the east. We all ate curry off water-lily leaves with our fingers. I was glad I'd practised.

The knell tolled. My dead wouldn't be brought out so I woke up. 5.30 a.m. The girl below my window shook her hand-bell like a fist. This is your early morning call. The pump below my window clanked and sucked. Steel plates clattered. Suguna brought me breakfast on a tray at 7 a.m.: tea, toast and marmalade, a kind of porridge, bananas and oranges. Joy was installed in her office.

Down at Holland Wharf a tanker lorry in Rajendra Kumar's livery waited to roll on to the *Vasista Godavari*, the Oil and Natural Gas Commission's ferry. A brilliant white statue of the *rishi* or sage Vasista, put up for the last Pushkaram festival, meditated on a plinth in front of Joy's old hostel, a cream confection of arches, tiled roofs, balconies and lacy balustrades now decaying in the custody of the Faith Missionary Institute.

In his contemplation Vasista heard and therefore composed the hymns of the seventh book of the Rig Veda; a forebear of that Vyasa who sung the *Mahabharata* and codified the Vedas, he gave his name to this westernmost branch of the river. The goddess Godavari *thalli*, or Mother Godavari scantily clad in fairground colours, stood near a pipal tree, *Ficus religiosa*. The tree of enlightenment overshadowed a shrine before which a sacred bull or *nandi* with amber glass eyes stared from the *ghat*'s top step across the sliding breadth of the Vasista Godavari.

A boy in a boat laden with coconuts under a woven bentwood canopy filled a huge basket and eased it on to the head-cloth of a man who waded out and tipped it by the *nandi*. Behind the shrine women changed out of wet saris. Beyond the growing coconut pile a man crapped. The tanker driver drank coffee at a tiny shack with a flimsy awning and a red-paint name, '★★★★★ STAR-HOT EL'.

I wandered up the street amongst browsing pigs and goats and bullocks. India wasn't supposed to be so quiet. Would an alley be busier? On mud verandahs before leaf-roofed houses of almost infinite neatness, women crocheted lace or sifted rice. The hero Rama, *dharma* incarnate, gazed from a cement shrine. A blacksmith bedded tools into timber hafts while his boy blew up the forge fiercely within a flimsy wooden hut. An iron archway led back to the street and, above a sign for the Sunshine School, sparks from a faulty cable cascaded, fizzed and died. Boys, students of fisheries and electronics, invited me up a rickety stair.

'What is your esteemed name?' they asked. 'What is your native country? What is the purpose of your visit?'

From their bow-fronted balcony between dark under-furnished rented rooms – one hundred and fifty rupees a month for each – I had a fresh glimpse of town: mud and palm-leaf, brick and tile, concrete art-deco and, passing beneath us, a crocodile of well-drilled schoolgirls and boys in pale pink, escorted by *peons* with canes. My new friends relished their grasp on the world; they put their arms around me, held my hand and gazed unabashed into my Anglo-Saxon eyes.

'Will you put autograph? Please, here. Just here.'

Afternoon at the five-star hostel was a full Christmas programme presented by girls and boys, the boys being girls with kohl moustaches and hair crammed into turbans: riotous songs and sketches, rumbustious Andhra dances, and a nativity play in which bejewelled Rajah Herod was booed like a pantomime villain and a glittering angel in a white sheet floored the quaking shepherds. Then, a week or so early, young Mother Christmas appeared in red plastic and cotton wool to call Joy to the platform. I couldn't understand the banter but the girls all laughed at her jokes and hung on her every gesture. Good news. Tidings of great Joy.

Joy's 'daughter' Santhosham – whose name, like Hotel Suntosh but with justification, also means 'joy' – and her husband Joshi tried hard to explain things to me. Their children, Colin and Joslyn, tried too. It was tough taking much in. Joshi and I pored over rivers and canals on the map but hot tides in my head disorientated me. On the roof Colin pointed out the swollen moon and the pulsing lighthouse at Antarvedi six miles away at Vasista Godavari's mouth, but the world lay beyond a throbbing membrane. Something scarified my throat and gnawed the marrow of my bones.

I tried to eat supper. Joy talked of how Santhosham had despaired of the boys her parents found for her. She asked Joy to choose someone. Joy thought of Joshi, a leprosy field worker, although he was a Christian *harijan* and Santhosham was a Kamma, one of the higher Shudra castes. I'd get a grip on caste when my head worked. Santhosham was viewed by Joshi's brother and uncle. They all said yes. Joy broke the news to Santhosham's parents. They took it hard at first: the eldest son never accepted it, he won't eat off his sister's plate; his wife told her father-in-law to fetch his own water because he'd sullied caste.

When Santhosham's father died his sons demanded a Hindu funeral although he'd been a Christian for years. They agreed a compromise: a Christian service followed by a Hindu cremation. Joy bought the coffin. I wasn't feeling too hot myself, but I had to listen. Hymns and prayers had hardly begun when the brothers called, 'Time's up,' pulled his body out of the coffin and dragged him off to the priest and the pyre.

I woke to loud temple music at 3 a.m. I tried to sleep. I tried to wake and get going. People converged on the *ghat* for bathing, or holy dip. Drumming drew me down there: a big bass drum, two double-ended drums and three small drums whose players leant back horizontally as their sticks thrashed at the skins and flushed out my head with a torrent of noise. Reedy shawms whined with flared lips. Anklets of bells chinked. On their heads dancers balanced urns holding gods furled in crimson and sheltered by brazen serpents. These were honoured with powders and incense.

I felt right out of it but dancers drew me in. Too ill to refuse, I almost gaffed by forgetting to kick off my sandals. Within the circle of frenetic sound I followed their feet and aped their poise. I had all the rhythm of a blancmange and the equilibrium of a slowing top. When they moved off into town the ferry boss's right-hand man approached me admiringly.

'You are dancing very well,' he said – I know flannel when I'm not washing my face – and smiled. 'I have seen you. One of these days you go on *Vasista Godavari*. For oil trucks only, no civilians. We tow all round India by sea from Goa. I from Goa also. I come by train because I am suffering seasickness.'

I wished that was all I had, promised to take up his offer and made shakily, hazily for the bazaar where I bought Dettol and aspirins. And Officer's Choice Whisky from a boy with a curved orange three-inch left thumbnail in a back-street liquor store.

The Bowdens had to walk to Machilipatnam for anything resembling a home comfort or a chemist. Just forty miles as the crow flies. I fervently wished I'd walked here from Machilipatnam. Before I die, I thought, at least I could have done that. Tom Coryat walked from Odcombe in Somerset, not so far from my home, to India. It was tough getting out of bed. My eyes burned in their sockets and wouldn't swivel. Coryat took three years in all, but only ten months to do the three thousand three hundred miles from Aleppo to Ajmer, 'all which way I traversed afoot, but with divers paire of shooes'. My legs wanted to snap. Coryat reached Agra in 1616 and Surat the next year, 'his journies end; for here he overtook Death . . .'

After three days my pulse slowed and my temperature dropped from 104°F almost to normal. Joy had to go to hospital, Narsapur Christian Hospital that is, for a test and took me too. I lay on a stained examining couch. Nurses took my temperature and blood pressure, Dr Prabhaka asked about joints and bowels, and an orderly led me, faster than I could walk, across the road to the path lab for blood tests. Blood and heat and fever made me fear I'd faint. I waited for results, watched steadily by a sullen lad in a *lungi*, a doe-eyed girl and a baby with club-feet bound in filthy bandages. In Men's Medical, a warm breeze blew through the open ward; bed frames were warped by the taut cotton tapes that held the patients up; a woman wept raucously to see her father for the first time following his stroke.

It seemed a makeshift fortification against all-powerful foes. A sister, whose twisted mouth made her seem sterner than she was, put fever pills and filaria prophylaxis in my hand. Her key-fob said 'Smiling makes you beautiful'. Joy drove home past the portico of the Bowden-Beer Memorial School. Tablets flanking its main door showed that those pioneer men managed to survive for thirty-nine and seventeen years in India before they died.

Afterwards I found out what I'd got. A textbook dose of dengue fever. Also called Breakbone. Dandy fever. Filtrable virus transmitted by mosquito. *Dinga* is Swahili for 'cramp-like seizure'; *dengue* is Cuban Spanish for 'affected, effeminate', and mocks the patient's gait. Was I suffering from Dengue fever? No, I just dance like that. After a few days, says the textbook I read much later, the patient's temperature plummets to normal for about twenty-four hours. But then . . .

8

CAROLS AND
FIRE-CRACKERS

Narsapur

AND THEN I woke exhausted at 3 a.m. to temple music and a
rash on my fingers and hands. My temperature climbed again
and incubated a headache that truly earned the adjective 'split-
ting'. All anyone could do was bring aspirins and ice-packs and
Suguna's home-made lime cordial. Joy came to chat and tried
to lift me out of the depression which is painfully characteristic
of dengue fever. Girls brought steaming buckets to replenish the
Ali Baba basket, and Parvati, one of the staff, exceedingly slender
and smiling, danced in and out on long feet with her reiterated
inquiry:

'How-are-you-to-day?'

Always her giggle grew to a gale which bent her over and
ended as a squeak which needed oil. Every morning the 3 a.m.
music seeped through the mosquito netting. Joy slept soundly
and never heard any of the nocturnal commotions I reported.
If I would insist on listening, she said, I'd have to live with this
one for a month, until Sankranti. The Brahmin priest, accompanied by two drummers drawn from the barber caste, took a
bindi or big brass pot to the canal, carried water back and laun-
dered the god Vishnu to strains from the temple PA that, in
pre-dawn delirium, sounded like Kenneth McKellar singing
along with Charlie Parker.

Why Vishnu had to wash in canal water I couldn't understand.
What was wrong with the sacred river? Though the canal was
used for bathing, for washing clothes and water buffalo, it was
also a drain and the police were talking because an unidentifiable woman with ear-rings torn out of her ears had just floated

57

down from the direction of Palakol. Still, some folk preferred canal water for all their needs. It tasted better that the colourless stuff from tube-wells that gushed out of taps.

The rash crept up my arms and legs. A cleaver rocked in my scalp. Noise, like Joy's dog Giri exploding outside my window, cracked me up. The Alsatian had confusing eyes full of entreaty and malevolence, and an unambiguous mouth full of teeth. She nipped anyone, even her mistress. She kept some of Joy's closest friends at bay, but didn't deter unwelcome visitors to whom a guard-dog was an occupational hazard and wounds were in any case worth a few rupees' compensation. Only Parvati disarmed Giri with fearless cuddles and a laugh. She made me feel better too.

Even so, I could hardly imagine continuing my journey. The extent of my vision over the dipping fronds of the compound's coconut palms was Vasista Godavari's many-textured surface, the ochre and green shoreline broadening and thinning opposite, and a long diaphanous line of trees through which small figures of men or white oxen or black buffalo passed from the visible shore into light and invisibility beyond. It was consoling. Whatever was hidden on the other side was not dark but luminous.

Then, two days before Christmas, after the off-beat Hogmanay saxophonist had finished his shift, the world was white. Mist. Blank. No river, no far bank, no horizon. Even the pump and the girls' raucous chatter were muted. Written Telugu, with all its graceful curves and calligraphic gestures, and a three-thousand-year-old literature inscribed on palm leaves, is the loveliest language to look at in all India; Telugu talk, as well as poetry, is said to be the most agreeable of all. While my fever ran, its music escaped me; it seemed harsh, jagged, brittle. Battles seemed always about to break out. Doesn't the Telugu proverb say, 'A house full of young girls, and a fire of little twigs'?

That day, mist softened all sound and my temperature touched normal for a time. Banter sounded gentler, but incomprehensible. I wondered if I'd even begin to *hear* it. I had tried. Before leaving home I'd obtained a book from Read Well Publications, New Delhi, entitled *Learn Telugu in a Month* (Easy Method of Learning Telugu Through English Without a Teacher) by Govindarajulu BA, DBM. It gave Joy, who is revered as a Telugu pundit, a good laugh. One young missionary wrote home for Christmas 1906: 'How strange it seems to understand nothing that is being said. It is very difficult, but . . . I have learnt all the letters, 429, and a good many words.' I tried to imagine myself next door, more than a century and a half ago, in the Bowdens' and Beers' shoes.

I was pleased to discover an eye-witness account of them written on 18 January 1838. In *Letters from Madras by a Lady*, the writer describes a holiday 'out in the district, travelling about to see the world a little' with her husband, Judge Thomas. They visited Narsapur, 'a large native village about six miles from the sea', not expecting a salubrious resort but because 'we had heard that two Missionaries were established there, and we wanted to see them'. Two, please note, not four; the women didn't count.

In any case they were of quite another class to the usual run of civil service and military wives. In Mrs Thomas's opinion civil wives were languid, speaking in whispers, pleasant and rather dull; military ladies, in contrast, tended to be noisy, affected, showily dressed and furiously flirtatious. The rival groups were 'often downright ill-bred to each other'. An officer who came to dinner accused Mrs Thomas of despising them from the bottom of her heart. 'Whatever people may really be, you class them all as civil and military – civil and military; and you know no other distinction. Is it not so?' She could not resist the riposte, 'No, I sometimes class them as civil and uncivil.'

But these women, these two Elizabeths, were by all the usual rules unclassifiable. They did not fit into white society, with all its foibles and fine distinctions, simply because they chose to live outside it. They belonged to a mystifying, idealistic species; they didn't count of course, but their husbands might, though Mrs Thomas was constitutionally obliged to patronize them.

'They were English shoemakers, Mr Bowden and Mr Beer, dissenters . . . but good, zealous creatures, and in the way to be very useful. They have two pretty, young English wives, as simple as themselves.' Almost buried beneath her condescension there is a grudging admiration. Her thumb-nail sketch of George

Beer reveals a man of 'great natural talent, strong-headed, and clear and sensible in his arguments; if he had been educated, he would probably have turned out a very superior person.'

Of their struggles with the language one of the simple wives said, 'It is pertickly difficult to us, ma'am, on account of our never having learnt any language at all. I don't know what to make of the grammar'; Mrs Thomas advised her not to trouble with grammar but to learn Telugu as a child learns to talk. Judge Thomas was impressed and said that the two men already 'spoke it really much better than the general run of missionaries'.

It was astonishing: 'They are living completely among the natives, teaching and talking to them, and distributing books. They live almost like the natives, without either bread or meat, which in the long run is a great privation to Europeans.' Especially to Europeans with Devonshire-bred stomachs, Elizabeth Bowden thought, but she reassured her guests, 'The Lord has brought down our appetites to what he gives us to feed them on.'

If the Lord could give them no meat, the Thomases had the pick of all the sheep in the village 'as I suppose the natives would kill themselves for the Judge if he would but eat them'. The Judge wouldn't eat them or their mutton, but he had an animal slaughtered and sent to the missionaries, together with bread and some wine to keep by them in case of sickness.

On Christmas Eve a delicious buffet feast was prepared for staff and friends. Colin and Joslyn had decorated the room that opened on to the balcony. A bough of casuerina was planted in a bucket and decked with presents. Joy asked me to be Father Christmas. Make jokes. In Telugu? I was weak and sweaty. My 'ho-ho-ho' didn't much fancy its chances.

Giri barked. A drum beat in the compound. Rattles chinked. Voices began, gathered themselves, and rose and fell in powerful plaintive praise. A tall man in a shawl and a *dhoti*, with the bandaged remains of his feet bound into small round sandals, leant on the shoulder of a short companion and led the songs with mournful gusto. The drummer beat one end of his drum with what fingers he had, the other with a stick gripped in a gnarled hand. A fourth man carried a hurricane lamp on his left shoulder, his right arm looped over his turbanned head to hold it steady. The lamp cast more pinched faces, sightless eyes, stumps of limbs and ragged clothes into soft relief. The carol singers were leprosy sufferers who lived in a canal-bank colony at Palakol. I shook hands and gave a pitiful gift towards their Christmas feast.

I sweated freely and wanted to weep. The unidentified fever had worked on my feelings as well as my bones. As guests arrived I felt pale, white, almost transparent, though they greeted me as if I was real. Rathnamma, the cook, saluted me shyly; like Suguna or Samelu the *peon*, she was a Madiga, one of an outcast 'caste' of leather-workers. Such people are beneath the four classes or complexions (*varna*) and the innumerable castes (*jati*) which comprise humanity. Untouchability has in theory been illegal since 1949. Outcasts or untouchables are officially called 'scheduled castes'; above them 'backward castes' and then 'other castes' are both included in the Shudra or menial class, the metaphorical feet of Brahma; his thighs are represented by the Vaishya class, or Komati caste of merchants and craftsmen; his arms are the Kshatriya class, or Razu (Raja) caste of kings; his head is the Brahmin or priestly class. It makes sense. But Brahmins can be subdivided minutely according to subtleties of status, and castes are not just occupation groups: Brahmins can be farm labourers. Malas, untouchable farm labourers when they are not entrepreneurs, are heartily despised by their fellow outcasts, the Madigas. And, depending on their debts, just about anyone may be a bonded labourer or free. It all makes sense.

By decree, certain percentages of jobs are now reserved for scheduled castes. So some people try to drop down a caste while others riot and paint 'Ban the Reservations' on walls. Christian untouchables, on the other hand, can register their children as Indian Christian which is backward rather than scheduled. Higher status, fewer jobs. It makes sense. Joy's 'daughter' Santhosham was a Kamma, high Shudra caste, married to an Indian Christian. Joshi was a leprosy fieldworker. Joy's other 'daughter' Gracie, who worked in leprosy rehabilitation, was a Madiga married to Obanna, business manager of the leprosy hospital, one of the Settibalgi caste of toddy-tappers; in the old days he'd have polluted a Brahmin if he came within thirty-six paces.

It was a privilege to meet them. Satyanarayana, the hostel's *chowkidah* or night watchman, was of the Marakulu, fisher caste. Satyanarayana, the leprosy hospital's impressive superintendent, was a weaver, Padmasali caste. Parvati the gale of laughter was a weaver too, but one of the Kykabathalu; Joy was having trouble finding her a husband of the same caste to please her parents. Not that the superintendent's wife was a weaver, she was of the Kamsali, or goldsmiths; her father had given all his daughters precious names; hers was Rathnam, meaning 'jewel'. Goldsmiths, a backward caste, are despised for stealing sacred gold, but hold themselves in high esteem and call themselves Visrabrahmins. Of all the girls who helped Suguna my favourite was a *harijan* with nothing to her name; her name was Savarna, Sanskrit for 'gold'.

All these and more came, with their children, and piled parcels round the tree and talked and laughed and played *karam* on the floor and consumed the buffet banquet with great enjoyment. Then I appeared, ringing a bell and sweating like a river inside Father Christmas's clothes and beard. I tried to pronounce the names on the presents while stepping bare-footed between people seated on mats, distributing gifts and trying not to fall down. I fell into bed and listened involuntarily to the girls' TV.

Then there was civil war, execution by firing-squad, or fire-crackers in the street, big ones, thunderflashes. Then sacred Charlie McKellar. Then there was the pump. Then there were chiming bells, rattles, tambourines and sweet girls knocking on the door, singing sweet carols, dancing and screaming 'Harpy Chrismuss!' Can't remember what sweet words I uttered as I stuffed my head under the pillow. 'Silent night' probably.

Joy had heard nothing of course, not even the fire-crackers. The packed Christmas service included several Hindus. Close by me a woman, gaunt and prematurely wrinkled in a tattered muslin sari, kept patting her appealing son's oiled head and adjusting his skimpy scarlet shirt and pants. I left after two-and-a-half hours when the sermon began. The preacher was a short pale-skinned Brahmin in a white *panchi* who sounded very loud and very stern and very long. We all ate a Christmas meal of chicken curry, rice and curd off leaves. The preacher beside me was presented with a special vegetable dish.

'Not because I am Brahmin,' he glanced up from what he was guzzling at an intimidating rate. 'For dietary reasons only.'

I sat, as if in a dream, through the girls' party that afternoon, the songs, the games, the Lucky Dip. I pulled a pencil out of the paddy-husk. Then in the street outside more fire-crackers went off. Colin and I went to look. Devotees of the goddess Durga sprinted past with detonations and drums and skirmishes, flinging crimson and vermilion powders at each other, flaunting the fresh stains like ecstatic wounds.

At the end of the day, with Joy, Santhosham, Joshi and the children, I sat down to a meal of samosas, tinned ham, chicken pieces and potato salad. It was a treat. Just as Joy tried to tune in her tiny radio to the Queen's speech at precisely 8.30, Giri started to bark. Joy shouted, she barked more, the radio crackled. Then Suguna made her entrance bearing on a platter the Christmas pudding my mother had sent out with me; it was hot, but upside down and snug in its cling-film. We were still laughing when Her Majesty wished us all a Merry Christmas. Joy skinned the pudding, righted it and planted something that looked like holly on its summit. It was exquisite with sweet custard.

Later, up on the roof, I thought of those I loved at home. Stars burned high and deep in the heavens. Rockets let off in the town fizzed up to meet them and exploded into brief galaxies. I shivered.

9

FABLED MADAPOLLAM

Madhavayapalem

FIVE MEN took the strain on a coir rope. They braced themselves across a modest street of houses – old thick-pillared ones beside recent 'art deco' ones – such as they, in coolies' turbans and baggy shorts or *lungis*, could never afford. The rope stretched over a wall to a knot below the crown of a coconut palm. Part way down the tree a sixth man squatted in a sling of rope and old tyre that encircled its trunk and his. He wielded an axe. Neat footwork swung him slowly so that his blade bit resoundingly all round the bole. They were taking it down storey by storey.

A goldsmith beckoned me into his dwarf workshop. His boy placed a stool under me. The goldsmith sat cross-legged one inch off the floor on a seat of woven cane. A small iron anvil like a square mushroom grew from a wooden block. A terracotta pot was his forge: coconut charcoal smoked in a bed of paddy-husk and flushed each time the goldsmith took his blow-pipe to it. He plucked out an ingot with tiny tongs and smote it orange to dull gold with a thick hammer. His spectacles slipped up and down his nose. Outside, with a rushing thud, the palm crown landed. The boy entered with a green glass of tea from a nearby stall.

'Is he your apprentice?' I asked between sickly sips.

'He is a *funny* boy!' said the goldsmith. He plunged the ingot into a plastic bucket of water and adjusted his *lungi*. His trousers hung on a hook above a crescent of light switches that framed his head like a potential halo. 'He may be apprentice one day, he is helper and runner, I am doing this work from sixteen years to now, forty.' He smiled and tipped his head. 'Quarter of a century. But he is a funny boy.'

'I am sorry to stop your work,' I said.

'No, I too am happy.' He slid open a drawer in a miniature chest of drawers. He held out his fist and unfolded his fingers to reveal fine filigree that would become ear-stars.

'Ah, yes,' I said, 'it's very beautiful.'

The funny boy took my glass and disappeared, which was not difficult, he was so slight. His master leant back and fetched a cigarette from a packet of ten Gold Flake. How apt, I thought, and pointed at it. He laughed indulgently.

Just around the corner, a toothless white-haired woman sat, legs outstretched over a gutter, a pale new-born baby girl balanced on her shins. Mother, or aunt, sloshed water over the child from a brass *bindi* while grandmother, or great-grandmother, briskly moulded wet pink limbs in her dark hands, hands long and veined as the tall gnarled tamarind trees at the end of the alley.

There, in a broad space of dappled shade, Mahatma Gandhi sat on a plinth with a *charka* or spinning-wheel at his right knee; he too was pale and baby-faced, but what a history of resistance his image represented. Manchester's imperial power-loom versus *khadi* or hand-spun, hand-woven cloth. On verandahs women were spinning now. Beneath trees, vivid colours defied the shadows: warp upon lurid warp stretched between sticks supported by crossed poles and tensed by twisted guy-ropes staked in the earth. For what else but cloth did the English first come to Narsapur?

Rabindranath Tagore, poet, gave Gandhi the title Mahatma, 'great soul'. But Tagore saw the danger of Gandhi's stubborn sentimentality and sounded a note of warning in 1921:

> But if a man is stunted by the big machines, the danger of his being stunted by small machines must not be lost sight of. The *Charka* in its proper place can do no harm, but will rather do good. But where, by reason of failure to acknowledge differences in man's temperament, it is in the wrong

place, then the thread can only be spun at the cost of a great deal of the mind itself. The mind is no less valuable than cotton thread.

In other words, Gandhi enjoyed spinning and Tagore hated it. Here, men and women worked on the warps together. Some carried babies. Several lugged thickened legs from end to end. Filaria, threadworms that infest the lymph and cause elephantiasis, were common here. Folk walked back and forth, checking and smoothing each long warp by hand, shedding it with laths, combing it with four-foot-long brushes, spraying rice-water to size it, twirling the whole thing over like a bright breaking wave and, at last, winding its one or many colours up on the warp-beam and carrying it indoors. It seemed a comradely business. Even spinning, you could watch the world go by. Weaving was the mind-numbing part.

'Come, come,' said a young man and took me into the house of his neighbour. It was low and dark. At the centre, a woman sat in a pit working a clattering wooden loom beneath a short strip light hanging from string. She treadled, left, right, to shed the warp, and tugged a string to send the shuttle flying side to side. The heddle banged the new weft tight.

'One sari a day,' said my new friend. 'Come, come.'

He took me into his own house and sat me down under a fan.

'You will take coffee,' he said. I recognized him, an old not a new friend. I'd bought cloth for shirts at the shop where he worked, Malleswari Cutpieces, in Gandhi Bazaar. He gave me water which I did not drink, thinking of the elephantine legs I'd just seen. His mother sat on her haunches sorting a pile of red and red-and-white bangles before alternating them with the heavy gold ones on her arm, to go with her red-and-white sari. At last his wife, eyes downcast under his mother's gaze, brought coffee. 'There is no goodness in mothers-in-law,' as the proverb says, 'nor sweetness in Margosa trees.' I drank and thought about the price of love, the price of gold, the price of cloth.

*   *   *

An everyday parable in Vijayawada: prosperous high-caste India can never progress faster than the malnourished India which must drag it into the future.

A Big Man peers through the usual tangle of wires above Rabindranath Tagore Road, Machilipatnam.

My great-great-grandparents
anchored in the shallows five miles
offshore and were ferried towards a
long low beach and up the grubby,
mud-banked river to this Bandar or
'port' of Machilipatnam where boats
are still built.

Contemplating a jammed propeller:
the Oil and Natural Gas Commission's
ferry across the river from Narsapur.

Builder's labourer, Narsapur.

Bindis, buckets and baby over a backstreet drain.

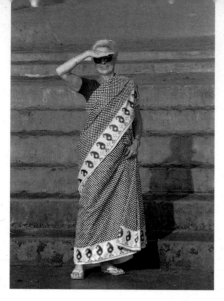

Missamma, my cousin Joy.

Boys preparing to scull an
Ambassador and its passengers
across the Godavari; everything
rocked and one ramp fell, but
the car was safely aboard.

On the canal-boats, Narsapur.

Palakol and the pagoda in whose shadow my
ancestors lived: how long does anything last
here that doesn't last for ever?

Weavers, temple sculptor,
harijan beef butcher and a
couple sorting prawns:
for a moment I yearned
for such simplicity, as
sentimental travellers do;
then I saw their exploitation
their position in society, and
on this mudbank the frailty
of house and livelihood set
against cyclone and flood.

The birth of time: Sita Lakshmi in the hostel garden.

Girls at Holland Wharf Hostel.

'Joy,' I said one day, 'tell me about Madapollam.'

'Madapollam, Madapollam,' she said. 'I don't know the name.'

'It's supposed to be a type of cloth. And to have taken its name from a native town here, before Narsapur itself grew up.'

She went off muttering. If Joy didn't know it, I thought I'd never find out. I thought she'd forgotten all about it.

In 1670 an English factor was despatched from Masulipatam to buy ginghams, longcloth and salempores, or blue calicoes for the African/West-Indian slave trade, from the Madapollam area. He recommended a 'factory' there as there was 'noe cloth in all those countrys better cured'. Two years later the chief agent at Madapollam was ordered 'to cause a good mudd wall to be cast up round about the factory & also to repair the platform' for a defence against Dutch attack, a nasty rumour. The chief was later charged with misuse of funds and, in 1675, there were trade difficulties due to 'strange intemperatures of the weather and great inundation of waters'. Things don't change. Nevertheless, Madapollam was a valued health resort for the Company's factors.

Nathaniel Cholmley, a diamond dealer of Masulipatam, 'the most unwholesomest place I ever lived in', tried in a delirium to kill himself by leaning his breast on a sword. Perhaps he'd had dengue fever. He recuperated in the Madapollam chief's Narsapur house, 'a lodging sufficient for all the Honourable Company's servants; very good & handsome godowns'. The best teak ships on the Coromandel coast were built at Madapollam, so the Company commissioned both the *Arrival* and the *Ganges*, vessels considered infinitely superior to the rotten *Advice* and *Diligence* that had been sent from England. It was natural that sea-going families lived here too. And Mrs Mingham, a widow, whose husband had been cannoneer to the Sultan of Golconda.

'Now about this Madapollam,' Joy said over tea one day. 'I've spoken to Satyanaryana the watchman. It's as I thought. He lives there, a short walk up the riverbank from here. It's called Madhavayapalem. Shanth will show you.'

No sooner had she spoken than Shanth and I were off: to the old quarter that had once been a town with a salubrious downriver suburb called Narsapur. The English simplified 'Madhavayapalem', and the cloth they exported from it, to 'Madapollam'. The cloth was imitated on British looms and 'madapollams' were exported to India in quantities and at prices to make a Gandhi weep.

Shanth, Santhosham's sister, led me past the court and the gaol to a part of town between the bazaar and the high embankment that, most of the time, kept the Godavari out of Narsapur. Our conversation consisted of monosyllabic Telugu and English, lots of pointing and laughter. 'Shanth' means 'peace'. Her husband had habitually beaten her and jumped up and down on her chest before, mercifully, he died. Her son was a continual anxiety; he stole and went missing. Her daughter lived in a hostel sixty miles up the main canal. Shanth was an invaluable worker at Joy's hostel; somehow she brimmed with light.

In Madhavayapalem, children cried at the sight of me. Shanth was warmly greeted. She touched and talked affectionately to everyone we met. We were taken through to the back verandah of a confectioner's concrete house where a big pan of oil fumed on a paddy-husk stove, a man rolled pastry on the floor beside bowls of golden grains, another glazed red ribbed sweets full of syrup, while a third, with fine face and magnificent torso, offered me some of their produce. It was tooth-achingly sticky.

Satyanaryana's wife was making sweets too; she had few teeth left. Some of her neighbours were crocheting white, cream or plum-coloured lace on their mud verandahs. I asked about the empty plots and ruins. Faces filled afresh with terror as they told how, in the cyclone and flood of five years before, water had come up to these eaves, covered that *almirah*, this cupboard, washed those neighbours to their deaths. Beside the embankment a woman, with her sari wrenched up between her legs, vehemently trod mud and slapped it up against the wattle wall of her house.

'See all the trouble we have to build a house,' she said in Telugu. 'Why don't you build us one? And if you think it's so nice, when I've finished you can have it for rent.'

A Christian bus conductor's wife fed us sweets and coffee in her mud and palm-leaf house; under a ceiling of newspapers there was a fan, a TV, a water-filter and a double bed. She didn't know about 'madapollams'; nor did her husband when he returned from his shift. He wanted to know about England, and to show me the two-year-old Hindu boy next door, 'a very honest person' who burst into loud tears on seeing my white face. Shanth got very excited talking to an old carpenter who said there'd been stones and sticks where we stood, for weaving cotton six-foot broad he'd been told. She wrote a word she didn't know on her palm in Telugu script. Back at the hostel Joy read it: 'French'.

Nobody knew about French or Dutch or English godowns. From the embankment, above palmyra-leaf roofs, I watched a black kite gliding over a few *navas* in the pool at the bend of the river. I imagined coolies loading Company vessels, shipwrights hammering at new boats, and poor Mr Fleetwood, chief here until 1676, supervising the accumulation of his debts. In 1678 his widow renounced all claim to his estate and made over her Narsapur cottage to the Company. Moveables were sold, including two slave girls and one boy bought by a Dr Heathfield whom Mrs Fleetwood wasted no time in marrying. In 1681 the *Bengal Merchant* landed agents here from Madras: John Davis as new chief and James Wheeler as his number four. All too soon the pair were accused of oppressing the agents. John Davis was demoted at once, and James Wheeler, who went on to be chief elsewhere, was eventually suspended pending an enquiry and dismissed at his own request.

Later, I visited a small graveyard at the other end of town where my aunt, Joy's mother, was buried in 1969. Nearby I found some old stones. One was inscribed, 'Here lyeth the Body of Katherine Davis the daughter of John Davis Cheif of Madapollam who departed this life the 24th August Anno 1681 Aged 17 months.' Another read, 'Here lyeth the body of Mrs Tryphena Wheeler wife of Mr James Wheeler Merch. of Maddapollam who departed this life the 13th May 1682. Also. . . .' But the rest was indecipherable.

Later still, I read Major Arthur Cotton's remarks in his report of 1844: 'In the lower part of the southern Godavery, a bend has been allowed to form, which has cut away the greater part of the town of Moddapollem, and if neglected, will destroy both the remainder of it and the adjoining town of Narsipoor.' Successive encroachments had by then carried away the sites of the godowns. Of the East India Company factory of Madapollam which closed down a decade before my ancestors arrived there was simply nothing left for me to find.

10

ANCESTOR WORSHIP

Bowdenpeta

A MAN'S HEAD beamed up at me from the canal. He was enjoying an afternoon bath with his water buffalo, scrubbing at them with his bare hands and caressing their submerged slate-blue hides. They wore their customary supercilious expressions, as if every nuance of the massage was no more than their due. A change of element changed the nature of the world. Out of the water, the man would drive the long-suffering beasts down dusty tracks with curses, sticks and stones. In it, he and they were wallowing lovers.

Across the road from the canal, a temple rose like piles of primary-coloured bricks, beautiful and terrible dolls balanced on every last perch. There was new concrete too, sprouting rusty reinforcing steel, waiting for paint and applied theology. Penugonda, famous throughout the delta for its buckets and tin boxes, was not a town to miss out on the Hindu renaissance. I settled back into the Ambassador after stretching my legs. Joy had eased her stiff back and was ready to drive on.

She was taking me, and Savarna the 'golden' girl, sixty miles due north from Narsapur to her childhood home. First of all, we were aiming for Nidadavole and Hebron Hostel where Shanth's daughter stayed. Joy was to open a new church building. I hoped to find William Bowden's grave of 1876, and the place by the headworks of the delta's canal system where the family lived in the 1840s. For Savarna it was a great adventure, and probably the most comfortable journey of her life.

Potholed gravel and patchy tarmac was occasionally cushioned by paddy husk or sugarcane pith. Embanked fields and brickyards were interspersed with palmyra and coconut palms, and increasing numbers of tamarind and mango trees. Now and then there was a banyan, that vast evergreen, with aerial roots that hang like ropes, crutches, new trunks. A seed from one of its small red figs germinates on, say, a palm tree, strangles the host with its sheath of roots and grows on to become a grove. Described in 1791 as 'the most stupendous effort of vegetable nature', its name, 'banian', is said to have been first given by Europeans to one particular tree, at Hormuz on the Persian Gulf, under which *banians* or Hindu merchants built a temple.

We drove beside the Narsapur canal for miles, then lost it and hit the broad main canal where a shuddering bridge crossed over into Nidadavole, a town grown up at the railway junction. We queued above the water in a crush of Public Carriers and ox carts. At the far side a long train slid across the road. There was no time now to call at the hostel so we drove through the sprawling, congested town and out again into the country on dirt tracks. At Singavaram, Joy hooted her way up the narrow village street towards a crowd. We shrouded the Ambassador in its cotton cover and joined raucous hymn-singing Christians outside a brand-new building decked in bunting. Years ago Joy's father, my uncle Crawford, had opened the first church here. After prayers, Joy cut the ribbon and everyone poured into its successor.

I strolled on. The hymns faded. The village petered out into paddies. Boys ran behind a ponderous ox cart and snatched switches of sugar cane from the base of its high load while the driver swore at them impotently. On a raised floor beneath a palm-leaf roof a woman tended her milch cow. Silvery langurs, with clinging young, clambered over a terracotta roof plucking at tiles. A woman flew from her house to scream at them. The monkeys tumbled into line on a mud-brick wall, flaunting extra long tails like fashion accessories and gazing at me out of black faces. The woman stared too, adjusting her sari. Dogs barked. Boys giggled. People were shy here, wary of the white man. It was pleasant to be left alone, uninstructed and in peace.

With harsh croaks paddy birds flung themselves into the air; earthy brown at rest, they flashed white wings, tail and rump in a revelation of grace which, along with strong wing beats and furled neck, quite earned them their nobler name of pond heron. Brahminy kites soared and banked, squealing hoarsely over-head. A roller, or blue jay, chuckled on a wire. A pied kingfisher the size of a pigeon hovered high above a palm-fringed pond; a small blue one, which is really turquoise and white with underparts of glorious rust, sped across the surface.

'This, not river,' said a turbanned boy, helpfully pointing at the pond's shattered surface into which, with many a whoop and whack, he'd just driven half a dozen water buffalo.

'This, not arsehole,' I said quietly, pointing at my eye.

Back at the church, goats played king-of-the-castle on piles of rubble as folk flooded out. Joy introduced me to my mother's old friend, Joyce Harding, director of Hebron Hostel. Savarna made new friends. We all sat down in a dim mud house beside the church and ate a sumptuous meal of chicken and rice off leaves. Men came round with buckets offering more. Beside me, two tiny girls each consumed at least twice what I could pack away.

Two pale Ambassadors, Joy's and Joyce's, waited with the throng at Nidadavole's unlevel crossing. Pedestrians ducked, and riders laid their scooters over, to get under the barriers.

'My father always prayed that this crossing would be open,' Joy said. 'Then he praised God for granting us patience.'

A mournful steam whistle presaged a wheezing passenger train *en route* for Rajahmundry and Vishakhapatnam. There was more ducking and diving at the gates. A diesel loco's brash horn did a leisurely Doppler shift as an interminable goods train trundled through the dusk towards Vijayawada and Madras. We crossed the tracks but not the canal. A mile or so downstream we turned off. Joy's parents' house stood in darkness on the corner. Joyce's hostel – lights and girls and staff and dogs – welcomed us.

'Now, have you got all you need?' said Joyce. 'Oh dear, I don't know what we should do about food tonight.'

'Joyce, Joyce, Joyce,' said Joy, 'we've just had a feast.'

'Oh, I know that, but I so want you to feel at home.'

She needn't have worried. Like a prodigal daughter, Joy teased and encouraged the older woman. Savarna found a soul-mate in the kitchen. Girls tried to teach me the name of the brindled bitch that was suckling young when she wasn't nipping my hand. 'Puji' it was, or 'Pooji', some Indian name like that.

'Oh, that's Podgy,' said Joyce. 'She was so fat as a pup.'

Later we sat down to a snack supper off fluted, faded floral plates that once belonged to Martha Bowden, my great-grandmother who started the hostel, and then to Hetta, my great-aunt.

Joy and a friend called Zefanya stood in dappled shade at the edge of a coconut grove. At their feet were the crumbling cement grave-slabs of Martha, 1927, and Hetta, 1960. Both died in the two-storey bungalow Edwin Bowden had built here at Chettipeta in the hot season of 1886. The building, founded on treacherous black cotton soil, had begun to crack up long before Hetta's death. In my mind, with the help of Joy and Zefanya's recollections, I uprooted all the coconut palms, replanted the garden and rebuilt the house to look like the family photograph I knew, with Martha and her daughters Hetta and Lily, my grandmother, and Lily's son and his wife, Joy's parents, in the foreground.

Joy was reconstructing her own picture. The small riverbed beside us had shifted some yards, she thought, away from the graves on the bank and the old garden where she used to play. Now it flowed through a small hydroelectric station and on into the canal. The Chettipeta school hadn't changed much, though: back rooms where Joyce had first lived on joining the mission in 1949; the school room with faded blackboard, teacher's desk, high beams from which fans hung beneath a heavy tiled roof, and rows of benches crammed with boys and girls. Lily ran the school for its first four years, until she left for England and married life in 1894; Hetta succeeded her for the next half century.

We threaded a route between rice paddies of a greenness that was the visual equivalent of the tamarind's sweet astringency; it puckered my eyeballs. We were aiming for a suburb of Chettipeta established on land bought by Edwin Bowden and given to outcast Christians of the Madiga or leather-working class. Most of their descendants' paddies, Zefanya said, were rented out or share-cropped. Women up to their ankles in muddy water bent to thrust bunches of shoots, the short-duration winter crop, into every last one of the hillocks raised like a rash across the paddy.

'Good wages may be earned in brief harvesting season also,' said Zefanya. 'Then coolies, carpenters and all go harvesting for forty rupees, sometimes so much as seventy rupees, per day. My grandfather the gardener, his wages were five rupees per month.'

Bowdenpeta was one long street. We walked to the far end between tiled houses, old and new, with white walls, fancy carved doors, and verandahs draped with white and puce bougainvillea or flanked by flaming marigolds. Some plots were vacant, overgrown, abandoned by families who'd long ago migrated to Vishakhapatnam or Hyderabad. The furthest house was the simplest of all: a mud plinth, wattle walls waiting for daub, and a palmyra-leaf roof. An apoplectic dog strained after us, but we skirted the arc of its chain and went inside. The interior partitions were screens of sticks. The widow who lived there was thrilled to see us.

'My house was quite destroyed in the last flood,' she said in Telugu. 'I am still waiting to plaster the walls.'

I glanced at Zefanya, raised my eyebrows. Six years? He shook his head. I thought of Martha and Edwin's brand-new house occupied by eighteen Madiga families when the Godavari rose to new heights in 1886, with cholera to follow. 1986 now holds the record. As we made our slow, almost royal progress back through Bowdenpeta, many people showed us marks on walls where the waters reached. One old woman, with both her glistening skin and stone floors speckled white, was vigorously limewashing her house.

Subharsanam, a burnt-out leprosy case, lay on his charpoy as he'd done for nine years, legs quivering, eyes newly opaque with cataracts, seeing me with his hands and ears. Next door, grown children had returned home for their mother's burial; some worked in Hyderabad, one with the Oil and Natural Gas Commission, six of them altogether, called Vincent, Victor, Roosevelt . . . A small boy sat on the ground cracking soap-nuts on a stone with a lump hammer. Across the street, Zefanya's mother gave us tea and snacks as the family crowded round.

Simply being here was heart-warming and humbling. I was handled and hugged like family.

In the house of Yeshya, Joy's parents' cook, we sat in a circle on Joy's parents' chairs around samosas and mixture set down by his white-haired wife Chandraleela, a woman about half my height. Her son Othnie, a slight but handsome man with greying hair, opened bottles of Limca.

'No,' said Chandraleela to Joy, 'we have not yet found a wife for this boy.'

Othnie grinned, twisted his watch round his wrist under the cuff of his lumberjack shirt, and took me off to meet Wilson, his friend. Wilson was a fine broad man, dressed all in white and standing in the shade on his stone-paved verandah. He was the great-nephew of Venkama, one of the legendary figures of my childhood mythology. She'd been Hetta Bowden's companion. I could see her in my mind, in sepia, leaning from the cabin of the Bowdens' canal-boat *Water-Lily*. Here in her old house, perched upon switches for lights and fan, was a tiny photograph. It was not of Venkama, but of Lily, my grandmother, beside her husband Tom. My grandfather never came to India.

'We lose photos and many more things in flood,' Wilson said. 'Three evils are here: floods, monkeys and termites.'

Samuel, lace-trader, builder and church elder, hearing that a new member of the family was in Bowdenpeta, hurriedly arranged an impromptu ceremony beside the mud-brick meeting house. A simple kitchen and restroom at the rear were nearing completion. He pressed scissors into my hands. I cut the ribbon.

He and his wife gave us coconut water in their living room. Samuel was proud of his two-storey house with its white rendering and lilac woodwork. He took me into the garden and upstairs to the kind of penthouse I've always wanted as a study.

'I have twelve-room apartment house in Rajahmundry also,' he said, 'for rents.'

We had come quite a way from the skeletal house with the hungry dog, from the burnt-out case quaking on his charpoy bed. But I still had to visit next door. Next door was brand-new with a balustraded verandah and balcony, and 'Grace Villa' in stylish script above the entrance. Here Samuel's daughter Vinolia Deena lived with her husband, or without him for ten months at a time. They were childless, that curse, endless anguish, empty future. He worked on offshore communications in the Gulf. He was plump beneath his *khurta*, his face was shiny, his oiled hair was thick.

'It must be hard, being away for so long,' I said.

'But it is worth it,' he replied.

And it was. There was a fridge, a TV, a radio, Michael Jackson cassettes, bottles of Vat 69, everything an untouchable could get his hands on, which is every *thing* anyone can get.

Zefanya's wife Naveena served us a good prawn curry. They had heard of W. Bowden's Indian Balm and seen its label, but knew nothing else about it. There were healers near Madras, he said, who used special leaves for breaks and fractures. They descended from thieves who once stole a kid, jointed it and wrapped it in leaves. On unwrapping it they found the bones were knitting. The secret is passed down from father to eldest son.

We barely squeezed past an ox cart as we drove down a perilous embankment towards Chettipeta's older Christian quarter. *Dhobis* worked at the edge of a tank, and saris were spread along its banks. A tatty Mahatma Gandhi stood on a plinth near a bright bust of Dr B. R. Ambedkar, *harijan* hero and father of the constitution, whose birth centenary was celebrated in 1991. There was an upstanding Lutheran church with a proud congregation of Malas, outcast farm-labourers, bitter rivals of the Madigas. Some joker nicknamed the two communities 'lawyers' and 'doctors', MLs and MDs.

Across an irrigation ditch we came to the 'doctors' of old Christianpeta. Sampson gave us tea and biscuits in his concrete house, though he kept his wife out of sight. He was an exporter of crochet lace hand-made in Narsapur and Palakol. His son had an office in Bombay, while he traded out of Calcutta, proud of the new market he'd created in Japan for exotic black lace.

In the humble village behind his house, pigs wallowed in drains and chickens scratched in the dust before low mud houses. A poor man in a *lungi* stopped me.

'I was born in 1914 Great War,' he said in an impeccable accent, 'and served in Second War in Rangoon.'

Did he tell me this because I was English, or because the start and what might have been the end of his life were, for him, its highlights? And what of the lifetime since Independence?

A young woman, called Devadanam, 'gift of God', was resting in a rich neighbour's reception room. Her father had fetched her from Hyderabad for fear that she might die there in a coma. Her face was like wet clay. I sat and watched her anguish. Joy, whose father was a diabetic, gave advice and prayed with her.

In the shadow of a smart Odeon cinema-style house I met Sundriah, Joy's parents' gardener, and Durgamma his wife. They seemed very old indeed. Their daughter and son-in-law lived in the Odeon, but they preferred to stay in their small mud and palm-leaf house next door. They had a charpoy and a chair, baskets and blackened cooking pots, as well as the big brass *bindi* or water pot that was given as part of the dowry. They stood barefoot in the dust near the hearth under spiky palmyra eaves. She stood straight in her cheap sari. He wore a pullover on top of his *khurta* and a scarf wrapped over his bald head and under his chin. He leant forward on a stick whose crook he clutched at his heart. His sightless eyes glinted. His white moustache was neatly trimmed. His smile and his handshake, like hers, were very warm.

Halfway between Chettipeta and Hebron Hostel, on the road beside the canal, we stopped at the Engineer's bungalow. In its grounds a black cow grazed and a curvaceous metal canopy sheltered the bust of one regarded here as a great *rishi* or sage. Under the visionary marble eyes, broken nose, high collar and frock-coat lapels, was the inscription: 'General Sir Arthur Cotton R.E., K.C.S.I. Designer and Architect of the Godavari Anicuts. Erected by the grateful public.' Cotton it was who inspired Groves, and Groves who inspired Bowden and Beer, with the idea of India.

Forty years later, aboard his boat *Echo* in October 1875, William Bowden used Cotton's canals to visit the Chettipeta district. On that occasion he marked out the foundations of two meeting houses. In December he returned and was cheered by what he saw in the villages. Somewhere not far from where the bust of his friend Cotton now stands, as he stepped into *Echo* from the bank, his foot slipped and he toppled into the boat head first. He cut his scalp and right cheek, and bruised his right hip. He felt little pain and continued his canal journey for another ten days before returning home. He died before January was out.

I watched a canal boat laden with sand, gunwales barely clearing the water, making downstream; one boy sat on the tiller, one bailed amidships, and two men let long punt poles drop, then pushed at them as they walked from stem to stern. A small boy drove water buffalo past me; his technique was attempted buggery with a stout stick. He chased them into the water and rode out a short way upstream mounted on one of the glistening beasts.

The water flowed by. I thought of empty lives, full lives, of pushing and shouting and goading, of what most of us leave in our wake for all our fuss and fury. Whatever else the Bowdens' legacy was, I knew that here because of them I'd met with love.

11

LUMINOUS FORCE

Dowlaishweram

THE SWEET SMELL caught in the back of my throat. Under a lonely tiled shelter set among fields and palms beside the canal, a diesel engine coughed and chuntered; its flapping belt drove the cogs and rollers of a crusher into which boys thrust sugar cane from the hip. It was as if the iron-toothed goddess tested their manhood. A man crouched in the shadows to monitor the flow of juice. The morning was dull and cool. An older man with a towel round his shoulders loomed through steam that billowed from huge pans. Broad and shallow, each was set above a charcoal fire in a pit. The foaming liquor would boil down to syrup, and further evaporate to jaggery, that coarse brown sugar made from cane juice or palm sap and sold in every bazaar. The man wiped his eyes and, when he could see, scooped scum off the surface with a giant tin ladle at the end of an eight-foot pole.

Mr Topping, an eighteenth-century engineer, had seen the delta's potential, given a Godavari dam and good irrigation. The British had done nothing. In 1843 Sir Henry Montgomery was sent to enquire into the district's decline. The Great Famine of the 'thirties, cyclones and floods, cholera epidemics and droughts, had devastated it. But the two main causes of its impoverishment were, he declared, firstly 'the abolition of the Government mercantile establishments and the subsequent annihilation of the cloth trade' and, secondly, 'the neglect of existing works of irrigation and the absence of improvement'. I imagine Sir Henry adding, 'And by the by, there's a fellow's done sterling work in Tanjore. Learnt a lot from ancient native methods. Tapped the Cauvery and Coleroon rivers. Royal Engineer. Name of Cotton.'

Captain Arthur Cotton reported, in May 1844, on the prospects for the Godavari delta. He wrote, 'it must inevitably continue to decline, if some substitute for the cloth trade is not discovered. Happily sugar cultivation is calculated not only to fill this void, but to offer the fairest prospect of much more than compensation for the former trade.' Later that year he concluded that, 'after deducting sandy tracts, and sites of villages, besides channels of rivers, there remain one million acres of land fit for the cultivation of paddy, or sugar'. Of the district, he wrote privately to his brother that he 'could not help seeing what it wanted, which was simply everything. So magnificent a country in such a state of ruin was the greatest disgrace to a civilised Government ... With scarcely strength to ride ten miles, I started on this expedition to turn the Godavari out of its bed and make it do something for its livelihood, a river only seven times the breadth of the Mississippi at the spot where I am now pitched!'

Joy and I were making for that spot, on the far side of the Godavari. But first, she had business to attend to up the sandy track to Vijjeswaram, a village near the sharp end of a wedge of land between the main canal and the river. Amongst mud and palm-leaf houses we came upon a crowd of women and one man in a tiled meeting house which, I soon realized, Joy had come to open. How had the event been organized? Then I recognized two women from Nidadavole in white widows' saris. They greeted Joy as a beloved sister, and held her and rubbed her back. They were called bible women, because they carried big bibles and could read them. Only three in the crowd, including one little girl, could do that.

As soon as the brief joyful ceremony was over, the man and his wife took us to their home. He was an egg dealer who had christened himself John. The neighbours, who were of the same Kapu farming caste as he, had white *muggulu* at their thresholds. John and his wife had a cut-out cross in the verandah wall, and a beautifully kept prayer room set apart under the palmyra roof. We ate tiffin there and listened to the women in white.

Ramayamma was one of the Bhagamvaru, or dancing caste. A devout reader of the Vedas and Puranas, she'd been enraged when a neighbour had offered her Christian books. She read them anyway and was convinced. Her angry husband threw all her books out and beat her and beat her again. But when he grew sick she cared for him as best she could. He became bed-ridden, at death's door.

'I asked him "Where are you going?"' she said, looking at me with a smile. '"To heaven," he whispered. "How," I said, "how are you going to heaven?" He could speak no more, that strong man, but he looked up and put his hands, so, in prayer.'

Her dear friend Venkayamma was of the Tsali caste, a weaver, once a young wife plunged into darkness. Most of her children had died. Her husband died. She left her one remaining child, Satyanarayana, with her Christian sister-in-law because, in utter despair, she could bear to live no longer. She went out into the garden to throw herself down the well. But something compelled her sister-in-law to follow her outside.

'She saved me,' Venkayamma said, 'but still I wept and cried out, "Is there a god to help me?" So much weeping, so much tears, my face covered with wetness only, when out of this a hand appeared. It touched me, and wiped away the tears.'

We drove out of the village, out of the palm groves, steeply up a rickety road and on to the anicut. This Anglo-Indian word from the Tamil *anai-kattu*, 'dam-building', is defined as: 'in the Madras Presidency, the dam constructed across a river to fill, and regulate the supply of, the channels drawn off from it.' To the east the anicut stretched nearly four miles, spanning the breadth of the Godavari and the three islands that Cotton found so conveniently situated at just the elevation needed for his dam to feed the network of canals he planned for the delta.

At this end, white water roared through the Western Delta Head Sluice. Immediately to the west, men punted laden boats down a peaceful canal between palm trees and palm-leaf huts, but from my vantage point high above the sluice gates I could see the slumped masonry of the old headworks that gave way on 15 August 1986 when the river's record flood was let loose into the delta at a rate estimated at 3,600,000 cubic feet per second. This massive ruin was the source of so many of the terrible tales I'd heard. But Cotton's anicut was barely completed when Vijjeswaram Head Lock was first destroyed in the floods of 1852, followed the next year by the adjoining Head Sluice.

I was standing on its successor. Men punted steadily down past Vijjeswaram gas-fired power station, recently linked to the grid amidst much fanfare. A week ago, it 'tripped' yet again. Plant officials blamed dust in the gas. Oil and Natural Gas Commission officials denied it. The next morning, at a village on the pipeline between the collecting station at Narsapur and the power station here, there was a blast and billowing flames.

'If some consumers switch off supply at once,' said an ONGC man, 'pressure builds in pipeline and, at times, leads to burst.'

Civil engineering never was straightforward. A big notice announced 'Sir Arthur Cotton Barrage, Vizzeswaram Arm', and the busts of two *rishis* flanked the road: Cotton and Vasista. Joy drove for four miles along the concrete dam, stopping to look down at the island called in Telugu 'the isle of sparrows', where I glimpsed only cockatoos and acres of tobacco. Behind the Dowlaishweram arm I was amazed to see a fine stretch of old-style anicut topped with *chunam*, lime and sand cement, the downstream slope faced with rough masonry like crazy paving: a method of construction on sand that Cotton learnt from the thousand-and-eighty-foot Grand Anicut he had rehabilitated. That was built to span the Cauvery river at some time between AD 100 and 1100. Cotton expected his own much grander anicut here to last only a century.

But his ambition was breathtaking. The task was herculean. The politics were painful. Bureaucracy played its usual tricks on the visionary. Skilled subalterns were refused him because they'd not passed an exam in Hindustani, which has never been spoken here. Cotton replied, 'Let me have men that are deaf, let me have men that are dumb, but let me have somebody.'

Close by the Dowlaishweram 'Headlock Office' there was a colonial red-brick house, all gables and white barge-boards, full of rucked carpets and battered models, faded plans and fly-blown photographs. This had opened as the Cotton Museum in 1988 but seemed already old and tired. It was fascinating, though, when I could find the light switches. Most interesting of all was the shrine to the man known as *sanyasi* in his lifetime, and *rishi* since his death. Cotton's bust stood between candle-sticks in front of bead hangings and glass baubles framing a portrait in which the engineer, white-robed, held out his hands to an Indian multitude above an inscription which concluded, '. . . he is the wisdom incarnate on a glorious throne. He is beauty, he is the seer, his nectar flowed in healing streams on indigent life.'

Joy and I ate a picnic in the museum gardens, where Krishna played the flute to a moist-eyed sacred cow and Sir Arthur Cotton rode a startled but stiff white horse; where a buxom goddess rose from a dry pond and a bronze Cotton stood on a vast black marble plinth with a tiny hat on his head and Charlie Chaplin's stick in his hand; and where the watchman came to reprove us.

'Eating not permitted,' he said sternly.

'But we'll leave no litter,' smiled Joy, offering him fruit.

'OK, you will stay,' he conceded, taking two bananas which he sat down and ate before throwing the skins over his shoulder. They landed near the old shutter-raising machine, manufactured by Ransomes and Rapier Ltd, Ipswich, England, which used to chug along on rails to lift sluice gates and let water run free.

The Dowlaishweram scene was hard to credit in 1847. Boats were built beside the river. Workshops, *chunam* sheds and stores were erected, together with a hospital and huts for five hundred craftsmen and four thousand coolies. Lime kilns went up, embankments bisected the islands, bricks were fired and the quarry face was extended in the hill of good stone that Cotton had rejoiced to find on site. By autumn there were cranes at work, wagons that ran down to the river under their own weight on railroads, and plans for a wharf from which stone could be tipped straight into the boats.

Cotton's problem was keeping people to their work, 'it being almost impossible to find a *peon* who is not more idle than the men he is superintending'. One day he saw a tall, tanned white man in shabby clothes walking among the coolies and talking with them in colloquial Telugu. Cotton was captivated, for he longed for a missionary to work amongst his labourers. The man was William Bowden. With joy they discovered their Groves connection via Baghdad and Barnstaple. The aristocratic engineer invited the powerfully built stonemason to stay on.

William and Elizabeth and their five sons moved upriver into
a palmyra hut in the grove of trees on the river bank where the
Cotton family lived until they moved uphill. Major Cotton, as
he now was, had great respect for the holy fools. He and others
established a fund for what had been the Narsapur Baptist
Mission but now became the Godavari Delta Mission. Cotton
personally undertook to pay for the Bowdens' boys' education.
Of Bowden and Beer he wrote to their friend Groves, 'What
a blessing for India if such men could be found everywhere!'

Joy and I crossed the road from Dowlaishweram Head Lock
to an arena of waste ground, fringed by mango trees. A small
shanty town of palm-leaf houses and stalls had sprung up on it.
Pigs and squealing piglets rooted in the dust. A little apart stood
a sturdy brick church; its bellcote lacked a bell, but a young
man up a bamboo ladder was repainting 'Church of the Good
Shepherd' on the porch. He didn't know how old it was. I found
a plaque which said, 'rebuilt in 1892'. A caretaker materialized,
proud of new paintwork and polish. He pointed out the bell on
the nave floor, and the tambourines and drums in the dim chan-
cel. The old Anglican church now belonged to the Godavari
Delta Mission.

Was this the site of the *tope*, or grove of mangoes where my
great-great-grandparents had lived and laboured amongst all the
clamour of the anicut works? Nobody knew. It was near enough.
Such dramas were played out here. Cotton and his men suffered
such traumas when, more than once, the great river threatened
to wash all their work downstream. The cost of replumbing the
delta swelled from an estimated sixteen *lakhs* of rupees to one
hundred and thirty *lakhs*. From beginning to end Cotton's
response to his critics was the same: 'If it be asked how is this
great sum of money to be obtained, the answer is, Simply by
converting the water of the Godavari into money instead of
letting it run into the sea.'

Two thousand miles of irrigation channels quintupled the
acreage cultivated 'with almost absolute certainty'; five hundred
miles of navigable canals and an equal length of new roads
transformed the district's communications. In twenty years
government revenue grew fourfold, imports tenfold, and exports
twentyfold. By the 1890s the tonnage conveyed on the canals

was twenty times what Cotton anticipated in 1852, and canal navigation was continuous – via the Godavari and Krishna systems and the Buckingham Canal – for four hundred and fifty miles from Kakinada to some way south of Madras. But most significantly the terrible see-saw of extremes, flood and drought, death by drowning or cholera or famine, was arrested.

The statistics floated vaguely in my head. Fragments of the museum's eulogies were safe in my notebook. One ran:

An ancient tale of woe can move us still
We keep the ache of breasts that breathe no more
The river poured down of bliss and luminous force
Could so rain from the all powerful misery above.

I stared through grey afternoon air at locks and sluices, at the Kakinada canal and at miles of concrete striding across the Godavari. Cotton had always threatened to work himself to death. In 1860, at the age of fifty-seven, he retired from India, his health broken and his spirit jaded. He received a knighthood from Queen Victoria and a prescription for a year's rest from his physician. General Sir Arthur Cotton retreated to a delightful rented house his wife had found near Barnstaple, North Devon. Had they talked with the Bowdens about their home town? I turned back from the river to the church of the Good Shepherd.

'This church', a man was saying, 'was the only building here to withstand floods of 1986.'

I tried to inhabit the minds of those men as they stood somewhere here in 1847. Most of us cannot begin to imagine such scope, such sacrifice, such sense of purpose. Cotton believed in his liquid gold, the Godavari's potential, but more than that he believed in living water. He thought stone and cement, rice and sugar cane, but he was convinced that Bowden's work for God would endure long after his grand anicut had been washed away.

12

LOOKING FOR THE DEAD

Rajahmundry

SIR ARTHUR COTTON lived to be ninety-six. Lady Cotton looked back on those Dowlaishweram days with mixed feelings: 'a happy home, full of large, wide interests', periodical attacks of jungle fever, as malaria was then known, and the birth of a second daughter in their rough house. 'It pleased God to take her from us after about twelve months, and we buried her at Rajahmundry in a little graveyard looking down upon the river.'

In June 1848 Cotton, who prided himself on working all day beside his men, suffered sunstroke 'till I found myself quite floored, with a total inability to take food . . . every symptom of a complete break up . . . This is the very height of our oper-ations, with the works in a most critical state, the freshes close at hand, and the monsoon already set in unusually early.'

He'd been lying in that state for some days and nights when the freshes came. They were used to seeing trees, houses and corpses – one year a big black bear – borne down on the swollen river. This time Mrs Cotton feared that it, and the anxiety it brought, would carry her husband off. Rather than let him hear news of the flood from other lips, she broke it to him herself.

'What would you do if you had no God to look to?' she asked.

'I should destroy myself,' he said.

The river rose. Not a vestige of the anicut works could be seen. Before the water subsided a steamer took the Cottons away: Madras, Bangalore, Australia. The Bowdens stayed, William working among the quarriers, masons and coolies six days a week, preaching on Sunday when all work stopped, and travel-ling downriver one weekend a month to keep in touch with the mission's work there. Elizabeth needed all her humour, caring for five sons, running a school for labourers' children and treating the families when sickness, especially cholera, threatened.

That December duty took William south as usual, despite the fact that eight-year-old Robert lay very ill. When he got back, their third son was dead. Two days before Christmas their sixth, Francis Meno, was born. In May 1849 Captain Orr, in charge of the anicut works in Cotton's absence, noted with alarm that the river had risen eighteen inches in an hour. A river four miles wide swelling at that rate is an ineluctable force.

It filled the Bowdens' house. Fortunately, the family had just moved back downriver, though furniture still awaiting collection was crushed when their palm-trunk dwelling collapsed. The Cottons' house too was swept away with all its contents, including the Major's cocked hat in its tin box and *Madam Guyon's Autobiography* which was picked up by boat. Those flood-stained pages were long treasured, as were Elizabeth Bowden's clock and little Fred's Bible, all that a friend could rescue from the Bowdens' Dowlaishweram home before the flood took it.

The Head Lock with its fine masonry, its office, its bridge, its gates and its cast-iron Victorian streetlamps would have looked entirely English on this grey afternoon if, at the steps beside it, a woman in a sari had not been washing her daughter's bottom. The girl waved at us. Joy and I drove off up the high road, past a gigantic image of Hanuman and yet another bronze statue of Cotton. Just beyond a Vishnu temple we pulled in beside a cycle-rickshaw parked by an open drain. The wiry rickshaw-wallah slept upside down on his passenger seat, head on the footrest, legs slung over meagre upholstery. It was the sleep of the dead.

In Betty-Anne's tiny house we took tea. Her daughter showed us the family album while her son ran off to fetch Joseph, his father, who put-putted home on his scooter and installed himself in the Ambassador. After four or five miles, and the Lutheran Hospital where Joy's brother was born, Joseph began to give Joy abrupt orders as late as possible. We overshot junctions, reversed, rocketed down side roads. My impression of Rajah-mundry — once a Mogul fortress at the head of the delta, now a market and manufacturing town dealing in timber, paper, graphite crucibles and tobacco – was staccato, jumbled, slightly insane.

In amongst petty shops on pavements, houses and bustees, big stores in the new pedestrian plaza, godowns and schools, we were looking for the dead. We stopped in a wasteland over-shadowed by monumental concrete piers of what would become a bridge of fifty-eight arched spans across the Godavari. In the background, where the road dived under an old masonry bridge, families had homes of poles, sacks and old saris pitched on heaps of soil and rubbish beneath a hoarding on which a film hero and heroine exchanged an antiseptic kiss. A scavenger's pushcart – a box on small wheels – stood at the tarmac's edge. Chickens and children pecked and played amongst cooking pots beside the traffic.

A pier's iron skeleton reared up on the bank. A spindly crane swayed above piles of stone and sand. Rails led from a mighty concrete mixer to the water's edge. Rusty barges rode the river. The frail indented shore was punctuated by rocks propped in the shallows. *Dhobi*-wallahs slapped clothes on them. Every spare inch of the construction site was spread with laundry. Zig-zag lines of it flickered like vivid bunting. Perched above all this the *pukka* white-painted Chitangri Palace, Officers' Guest House, seemed to hover in another dimension.

Between the high palace and the bridge works, Joseph pointed down into a strange dell. In a dream it might have been a neg-lected maze, all mantled with greenery and pink flowers, but in the grey light of day it was an overgrown British cemetery. Joseph said that it had been cleared for the visit of Sir Arthur Cotton's great-great-grandson in 1987. This was the 'little grave-yard looking down upon the river' where the Cottons' baby daughter was buried, and probably young Robert Bowden too. But was this where his father William had been laid to rest?

Not one grave was visible. We hadn't brought machetes. Joy was wary of snakes. Joseph thought William's bones lay in a later cemetery at the heart of town. We drove off and, after a serpentine journey, halted beside a petty shop where men paused to buy *paan* and cigarettes, or simply to light their tobacco-leaf roll-ups from the lamp kept burning for that purpose. There were tea-stalls with steaming cauldrons and three sets of chained and padlocked gates. One set opened on a Muslim cemetery; one led into a walled lane, graves crammed down one side like single beds with crosses on their headboards, a cow ambling up the other to heavy breathe at me through the wrought iron. Joseph's favourite was a big walled area full of scrub and headstones.

I'd just decided to clamber over the wall when an ancient watchman in *banian* and *lungi* came with the key. In sandals, Joy and I tiptoed between graves and thorns, watching for snakes, but mostly for amber and ginger cones of excrement. The place was a latrine. A man squatted by a headstone. I remembered old complaints about Fort St George's cemetery: 'And what unclean uses the neighbours thereabouts doe make of that place we forbear to tell.' But it didn't seem like desecration. Unpurified by fire, corpses are the last waste product, and I could imagine this old man shinning over the wall each day and systematically shitting on every soldier, collector and missionary in the place. How many months, I mused, would such a political gesture take? Boys gambled on one grave-slab. There was the ruin of a robing-room. Down a deep wide-mouthed well which once watered funerary flowers, palm-fronds and torn playing-cards floated.

Unexpectedly, I felt sick. Not of crap, but of looking for the dead. There were plenty of tombs of the period, but the thrill of the chase had evaporated. Back in England I'd longed to locate my great-great-grandfather's grave. Here, I understood why Joy had never bothered with such sentimental gestures. The living and the dying were more important than the dead. But to humour me she and Joseph searched on, intent on finding William's bones. The card-players watched us all three acting out a bad joke, going through the motions.

On Sunday 6 January 1876, about a fortnight after he fell headfirst into his canal boat near Chettipeta, William preached at Narsapur for the last time. At teatime he looked ill and con-fessed to pains in his cheek and hip. On the eighth, his fourth son Fred, and daughter-in-law Mary, brought him to Rajahmundry for medical treatment. The doctor diagnosed the rising on his cheek as a carbuncle, and lanced it. When the news reached

Narsapur, Thomas Heelis, mariner turned missionary, sailed upriver in his boat *Harbinger* with Elizabeth Bowden and John Beer aboard. Heelis wrote:

> We arrived there on the 13th, at two o'clock in the morning, and hastened to the house where he was. On opening the door of the sick chamber we were almost overwhelmed by what we saw. There was our dear brother and teacher lying on his back on the bed, a perfect wreck; and his dear daughter-in-law was lovingly dressing the carbuncle on his cheek by the light of a lantern held by a servant. From that time he rapidly grew worse . . . when his spirit departed, on the morning of the 26th, just as the sun was shining upon him through the venetians, his eyes were bright, and his face assumed a calm and happy expression as though a vision were before him, which filled him with joy and surprise.

We found no Bowden in that grim graveyard. The watchman suggested we try St Giles. I was weary, but Joy's enthusiasm on my behalf carried me along. We drove to the Western Railway Colony and, after enquiries in a bazaar beside the tracks, found our way down a cul-de-sac to a Victorian village church sitting in a boneyard full of flowers. A plaque inside said it was built by railway people for railway people. A man came in to tell us that only twenty families supported the church now, mostly Anglo-Indian, very few to do with the railway.

'It is time of theological dispute,' he said. 'My wife and I – we are teachers – look after the church in interregnum.'

He took us to the vicarage. One of their small boys handed round tea while the other went to fetch the church secretary and his graveyard plan. He came remarkably quickly.

'This is most excellent tea,' he said to our hostess before turning to me. 'For this tea I visit, if possible, three times a day. I am the Honorary Secretary. My name is Meneaud.'

He was tall and long-boned for a South Indian, a widower of great charm, more English than the English. Than me, anyway.

'My great-great-grandfather was not a missionary,' he winked at Joy, 'he was Renard, "fox", a French pirate wanted for murder who changed his name and found refuge and a wife in India.'

'Our guests wish to see grave plan,' said our hostess.

'The utter transformation of the garden here is entirely due to this lady,' he told us, flattening the creased, foxed paper with his fine hands. There wasn't a Bowden on it.

When at last we dropped Joseph near home it would have been ungrateful to explain how little failure mattered. We stopped for diesel, and for plant pots at a street stall. The pots and the girls who sold them were from Gujarat. They carried them across four lanes of mayhem. Joy suddenly had as little Telugu as they, and could not understand their cries for extra money.

We drove into darkness over Rajahmundry's one-and-three-quarter-mile road and rail bridge across the Godavari. There was a hold up at the centre and for a few minutes I gazed southwards at the lights on the much longer barrage and felt the rumble of a train passing immediately below us. Until his death Arthur Cotton had challenged Indian railway mania and championed canals as the most appropriate technology for the subcontinent. He fought and lost. As men do, who live before their time.

Sugar-cane pith showed white in the headlights. We queued for an age on the bouncy canal bridge into Nidadavole. Traffic built up around us. Men swung down off public carriers and carts and lit up, their faces briefly bright with match flame.

'Dad's prayer will be answered again,' said Joy, 'but let's pray that Joyce will be granted patience.'

Joy knew better than I how worried Joyce would be about the evening's programme. Girls planned to entertain us with songs and dances. Meanwhile, a long dimly lit train thrust southwards through the night. The ox cart beside us lurched sideways; its axle and linchpin ploughed a deep furrow down half the length of Joy's pale Ambassador. She showed exemplary forbearance.

'That's life,' she said.

And life was what I was looking for.

13

WAITING FOR TRAINS

Nidadavole

To go back almost to the beginning: in mid-November 1838 the judge's wife, Mrs Thomas, wrote home from Rajahmundry: 'The Narsapoor Missionaries go on zealously and sensibly, and I hope do the *beginning* of a little good. Bowden and his wife are here just now, that she may be under the Doctor's care during her confinement.' On the twenty-fifth the Bowdens' second son, George, was born. Would he have chosen zealots for parents, even allowing they were sensible zealots? Did he grow to share Mrs Thomas's tentative optimism about the little good they did? Whatever Mrs Thomas's head told her, her heart warmed to the holy fools and she began to describe them as '*Our* Narsapoor Missionaries'.

One hot bright day I thought these thoughts as I sat on a hard slatted seat aboard the Circar Express, waiting to pull out of Rajahmundry for Nidadavole. A woman climbed in, stowed a bundle under the seat across the corridor and settled herself down. Or rather, set to plucking at her sari blouse, leaning and peering, muttering at me. I concentrated on the snack-sellers' cacophony, each tray of drinks, plate of sweetmeats, basket of fruit brandished with harsh, hoarse, rising cries of which the most intelligible was 'Caffee-caffee-caffee-caffee-caffeeah!'

I drank sweet coffee and watched a small community of near-naked children playing with nothing beside low patchwork tents between the tracks. Malnourished men and women heaved baskets of coal off rail-trucks and tipped them into lorries. As we drew out an iron gateway boasted, 'Rajahmundry Loco Shed': bogeys, wagons, black-and-rust steam monsters in various stages of decay or repair, hard to tell which. A locomotive pounded past, all steam and smoke, gleam of brass, glint of fire, a scene from childhood. The driver hanging out of the cab was a white man.

My train ran through a cutting, embankments topped with shanty towns, streams of effluent dribbling on to the tracks. At Godavari station the platform stepped down to the train like a *ghat*. Near the overgrown graveyard, we teetered out over the river on the old bridge, single track, nothing to be seen but the river below; then piers of the newest bridge at intervals, some sprouting cantilevered arches but none joined up. I could see the road/rail bridge I'd crossed with Joy, and Cotton's barrage through haze to the south. In the hot carriage the mere thought of the efforts we make to harness and cross rivers made me tired.

The world was waiting for us at Nidadavole Junction. Queues of it through town and across the canal. That's how Nidadavole was. Comings and goings, and long waits. Since Joy drove away on New Year's Day, I'd been doing all those things.

Slapping and scratching too. Hebron Hostel's mosquitoes were bigger than Holland Wharf's. But I could sit on my narrow balcony and enjoy the trees in the compound: sapota or sapodilla plum, mango, date palm, palmyra, pomelo, peach lime, tamarind, pawpaw, eucalyptus, gourd, casuerina and sacred sandalwood. A gold mohur's feathery crown hid buds that prepared to detonate scarlet. Drumstick or horseradish trees, with corky bark and honey-scented flowers, brandished long stick-like pods that I enjoyed in curry; young roots made horseradish relish; crushed seeds released a watchmakers' lubricant, *ben* oil, also employed by perfumers because it absorbed and retained fugitive odours.

Sunrise on 1 January was a smoky, burning orange behind the coconut palms. Emerald rice sprung from golden paddies. Beyond, diesel and steam trains came and went on parallel tracks, hooting and whistling, or waited fuming until points changed. Across fields, the cement pipe factory's siren screamed for every shift.

I focused eyes and ears on birds and songs in the trees: black-headed and red-whiskered bulbuls, bank mynahs and bee-eaters, grey shrikes and golden orioles, kingfishers and coucals, storks and sunbirds, swallows and palm-swifts, Indian robins and rose-ringed parakeets, pond herons and paradise flycatchers.

Sedentary natural history, with Joyce's reference books at my side, was a delight. The sky went black. White egrets lifted against it. The rain came down. Marvellous smells rose up. I wanted a few drops of *ben* oil on the brain, to absorb and retain the fleeting scents, to find words for them.

Six brothers had been murdered, the *Indian Express* said, in the staff quarters of a mental hospital in Hyderabad. They were alleged to have killed one Vijay Kumar in the hospital campus. Thirty of his friends hacked the six to death with swords, axes, knives and sickles before carrying away drops of their victims' blood to smear on Vijay Kumar's portrait.

Andhra state's unit of the BJP had undertaken to contribute ten thousand volunteers to the 'saffron brigade' that would march to Srinagar, in disputed Kashmir, to hoist the national flag on Republic Day, a Hindu gesture against Islam.

A terrorist of the People's War Group, strong in Andhra, was killed by police as his task force set fire to a bus and a telephone exchange. In the next district, PWG Naxalites, named after Naxal in West Bengal where the left-wing peasant movement began, bombed a police house. Further away, the Border Security Force shot a bomb-throwing Naxalite leader known as Swamy.

Russians, the biggest buyers of Indian tea, withdrew from the auction houses; the ex-Soviet Union's chaos cast a pall of gloom over Cochin, Calcutta and Coimbatore. Andhra journalists protested at the death of a colleague killed by police. Two men had their throats cut in Vijayawada. The Indian prime minister announced the fencing of the whole of the border with Pakistan.

None of this was happening in Nidadavole. The biggest thing was a refuse collectors' strike which left roads full of rubbish and open drains blocked. Fruit stalls surrounded Indira Gandhi's dusty statue; black goats, clambering on her plinth, masticated vegetable waste and did their bit for recycling.

In every street someone invited me in for coffee. In a timber yard on the canal bank, where *dhobis* worked by a Muslim cemetery, old men staggered with great stumps hung from a pole between them and lads ran a mighty silk-cotton tree trunk through a naked whining bandsaw. I asked for the potters' quarter.

Pots were stacked up to the palm-frond eaves: round black ones and terracotta tubs. Through one low doorway cooking pots and vegetables lay on the floor beside a two-ring primus on which the potter's daughter boiled tea. Behind me was a charpoy bed, a low dressing table, a few books and a shrine to Ganesh. One of the split palm trunk pillars had a panel of switches, for lights and fan, nailed to it. My hostess poured tea from pot to cup and back again in long arcs, like a conjuror springing cards.

I raised my steel cup to her wizened mother and thought unsentimentally what a civilized life was possible in this mud house. A second daughter lived in Liverpool. I crouched to get out into the back yard. I picked out a big pot to buy for Joyce.

'How much?' I asked in Telugu.

'No, no, no,' said the daughter in English, 'you, friend.'

Next to one palmyra house men and women were labouring on a brick and concrete mansion. A scarecrow of straw-stuffed cloth, with a crudely drawn demon's face, stood on the roof to repel the evil eye. A coolie grinned at me, scampered up flimsy wooden scaffolding, whistled to ensure I was watching, delved between the demon's legs and, with a flourish, pulled out its penis.

Joyce's neighbours, a Kapu caste farming family, were living in their cattle shed. Their brick and tile house had seen three family deaths in quick succession. On the priest's advice they'd moved out for six months. On Joyce's boundary a termite mound was venerated as a cobra shrine. People offered rice, eggs, flour, saffron and vermilion powders there on holy days, but Joyce was building a new wall, to enclose the hostel, the gardens and the playground called Bowden Park, that would demolish it.

On Sunday morning the whole Godavari Delta Mission church congregation processed through town to the bathing *ghat* by a line of temples. Travellers peered from the wobbly iron bridge. Coolies at work on a new concrete one watched as one Christian after another descended into the canal to die. Each rose again in the pastor's arms and was wrapped in dry cloths by friends in full view of goddess Durga astride her snarling tiger.

There was nothing mundane about the comings and goings here. The long waits were pregnant. I looked forward all one day to a performance of the *burra katha*, 'big story', given in the Andhra tradition by three song-and-dance-and-cross-talk artistes in silks and jewels. Their musicianship and comic timing was given extra piquancy by the fact that when we got to town that night we found it clean but deserted. The strike had ended, a curfew had begun. Unknown to us a politician had been beheaded with knives, there'd been beatings, a youth had died. There was almost nothing, of course, that could not happen in Nidadavole.

Savarna the golden girl, Shanth's daughter Lily Pushpum, and I crossed the footbridge over the tracks. We ran the gauntlet of coolies lined up for hire at the 'Signals Supervisor's Bungalow' with its neat garden of flowers and croton in the best Anglo-Indian railway tradition. In the cool dark station building carcass-like bundles lay shrouded on the floor near the ticket office. A ribby dog lifted its jaws from its sleeping mistress's thigh and snarled at me.

At the 'Refreshments' booth a Shiva devotee drank coffee. A woman in a gold and red sari scratched at rubbish and stones between the rails with a handle-less rake. Much hawking and spitting, tooth cleaning and washing was in progress at taps beside a building labelled 'Cool Drinking Water'. It was chilly enough already. An old man strode up and down – past 'Ticket Collector's Office', 'Station Superintendent', 'Assistant Station Master', 'Chief Booking Supervisor', 'Parcel Office', 'General Waiting Room', 'Ladies Waiting Room' and the station garden of temple trees, bougainvillea and bananas – with water pot and tiffin tin in his hand, a scarf wrapped around scalp and chin, and a lady's stained camel coat over *khurta* and *lungi*.

A man in white, with a red cross embroidered on his patch pocket and a big picture of Jesus hung on string round his neck, kept shaking his tin of *paise* in front of my nose. I gave a coin to a beggar whose naked torso was veneered and varnished with severe burns. Savarna did too, and a man down the platform gave him a note which he took and gratefully touched to both cheeks. A mean-looking guy perched on the concrete base of an iron pillar close by. He had a faded jazzy shirt, a tiger-tooth pendant and piercing evil eyes. He just stared at Savarna, Lily P and me.

Porters in shorts and red shirts squatted on the platform's edge. An official struck an iron bar with panache. It announced something with all the authority of a temple bell. Nothing came. 'Complaint book is available with on duty ASM.' A bare-foot woman with permed grey hair lifted her sapphire sari, climbed down on to the track and up on to platform one just as the Kakinada–Vijayawada steam train drew in, fizzing, fussing and spewing the stink of smoke, soot and steam, fugitive odours that now I'll always associate with Nidadavole. The girls wanted to get on.

Our train was overdue. 'Trains running late are likely to make up or lose time.' It made sense. A bulgy-eyed blind man led by a healthy boy begged all along both platforms, followed by a fit-looking widow in a white tucked-up sari with wrinkly skin and small exposed breasts. Then the train came. Joyce had stressed that we must board the rear portion because the train split at Bhimavaram. The girls wanted to get in the front.

We sat opposite a very dark woman and her daughter, both with vivid eyes, wonderful mouths and teeth. They chatted to Savarna and to a ragged guy in a turban, with fly-away hair and teeth. Even solemn Lily P laughed at two elders who realized they'd boarded the wrong half. They leapt off at Viravasvarum and sprinted breathlessly to the front of the train. The vivid daughter invited me to visit Bhimavaram.

For now we were happy to be going to Narsapur: Savarna to see Suguna and her friends again, Lily P to be with her mother, and me to experience the joys of Pongal. A pale-skinned cloth merchant roused himself on the top bunk and whistled imperiously at my dark neighbour to move over so that he could step to the seat and the floor. Once down, he stood on one arched foot, so that as little sole as possible touched the dirt, and with the other prospected impatiently under my seat for his sandals.

14

FIRE WARRIORS

Narsapur

IT WAS THE EVE of the Pongal festival. Downstairs the generator throbbed and stuttered through the regulation evening power-cut. Joy and I sat and talked in wavering yellow light. What breeze wafted in at the windows was diesel-tainted. Mosquitoes basked beside the dim fluorescent tube; geckoes, like staccato cartoon creatures, stalked them vertically on adhesive toes and picked them off with long tongues. A fresh rhythm outbid the generator: distant drumming, deep and frantic, getting closer. I'd been weary and relaxed, but the nearer the drums came the more restless I grew. Joy knew that my mind was in the streets.

'Better go and see what's happening,' she said.

We slipped down the stairs and padded across the shadowy compound. Satyanarayana unlocked the gates and let us into outer darkness. Stars shivered as if to the drums' erratic pulse. As we turned the corner of Holland Wharf a bright moon burned above the water: the globe of a hefty primus lamp screwed to a board balanced on the head of a woman poised on the top step of the *ghat*. She stood still, with her hot hissing burden. In this light the troupe of drums beat high and low as if compelled by their tattoo to keep the planets in their tracks.

Over and above this boom and clatter two men blew *booralu*, reedy shawms like long oboes with flared mouths, and wound tangled threads of melody in the quaking air. To this music dancers danced with gods in brass urns on their turbanned heads, each pot swathed with crimson silk and hooded by a many-headed brazen cobra. Joss sticks burned. Bare feet beat the earth, anklets jangled, silken arms flung gestures, but the gods passed through the scented night with perfect equilibrium.

The gods had bathed in Godavari's waters. Next, a man said, they would pass across the fire. Where? Near the cinema. When? At 8.30. My watch already said 8.45. It made sense. Back at the hostel half an hour later, Joy called some senior girls to help push-start the Ambassador; she let in the clutch and we all jumped in. Satyanarayana flung the gates wide and a big black pig flitted in through the headlights' beam to laughter and hisses from the girls. The town was dark and quiet, but for a few women drawing elaborate *muggulu* by lamplight on the street in front of their houses. Then a few lights went on as the power-cut ended.

We parked not far from the Neapolitan cinema and made for a small crowd gathered round a fire. A shallow pit, four by twenty feet, had been dug in the sandy street; along its length burning stakes leant together like the rafters of an incandescent roof. There was no sign of gods or dancers, no sound of drums. A man in white stepped down from the verandah of his long low-browed house and invited us in. Stocky pillars supported a heavy tiled roof. Inside it was brightly lit.

'Please sit,' he said and we sat in the reception room where we could keep an eye on the fire.

'This', said Joy, by way of a compliment, 'is a very big house.'

'Oh yes,' said our gratified host emphatically, 'indeed it is a gigantic house.'

Then he disappeared for five minutes. He returned with a plate of *kamalalu* or loosejackets, tangerines with skins one size too large.

'This house, it is one hundred and thirty-five years old,' he said with unusual precision. 'It is British house. You are welcome, please come.'

We followed him through a dim central court, open to the sky, with well-proportioned rooms at each side, in one of which flickered a colour television. We paused to greet his wife before passing straight through the rear portion of the house and stepping down into a paved garden where a few trees, shrubs and the sacred *tulsi* or basil grew.

'I am agriculturalist,' explained our host. 'Please come.'

Back in the house he sat us on one of two orange vinyl sofas in the back room where his wife joined us to watch the television news in English on a black-and-white set. She and Joy chatted in Telugu.

'I am agriculturalist, yes,' her husband repeated to me, 'but all my brothers – we are ten brothers – all nine are lawyers.'

Pronounced, as usual, 'liars'. I peeled and ate my loosejacket being careful to convey each segment to my mouth with my right hand. It was fragrant.

'One of my sons is a liar also.'

Above my head a few loose timbers lay across the joists; between them the view was of rafters and tons of blackened terracotta tiles. Dirty white clothes hung on hooks behind my host's chair. Black-and-white police dragged mutilated bodies from a train attacked by terrorists somewhere in the north.

'I have much interest in nature reserves. Are you visiting our nature reserves?'

Given the average man's attitude to wildlife here, I was pleased to find someone who had other, more benign ideas.

'I hope to go to the Coringa and Papikonda sanctuaries,' I said.

'We can pay money and have some very fine shooting.'

It made sense. A susurrus of activity seeped through the house from the street. Joy and I rose to our feet.

'There will be much time yet, but you may go and see.'

We rejoined the girls on the verandah. Our host was quite right, there were no gods. He introduced his two sons instead, and sent one off on a mission into the night.

'For how long has firewalking taken place just here?' I said, pointing at the blazing pit.

'Last year and last year,' the agriculturist said, 'and last year and . . .' He gestured backwards in the general direction of infinity.

'From times immemorial,' smiled the lawyer son.

His brother returned with bottles of Limca from a street stall and all three men insisted that we refresh ourselves again.

'Well, thank you,' I said and dutifully began to inflate myself with gas.

'No mention,' said the lawyer.

'Tomorrow,' said his brother abruptly, 'if you wish to go there, it is not at all far, I will take you to the cockfight.'

Before I could reply to his invitation, we all heard the throb of drums. It was 10.30. At once the crowd thickened and we were plucked from the verandah of the gigantic house and pushed through the crush to the front. What wood still stood was knocked down amid the spume of sparks. A strong man like a bouncer in a *dhoti*, with a sweaty turban and wild eyes, whipped at our legs with a palmyra frond, driving us back to give the walkers room and the fire air. Then he stifled a few small flames and fanned the embers from red to orange heat. The crowd swayed drunkenly and staggered forward and back. Round and round the strong man thrashed at us violently, grimaced and grinned, fanned the fire zealously.

Drum troupe, *booralu* players and dancers closed on us with a crescendo of sound and frenzy. The professional dancers wore anklets of many bells, black trousers hooped with silver, tight turquoise tunics, pleated and flared below the waist, with epaulettes and ranks of sparkling metal like golden fish scales; they took the god-pots from their heads and rested them on a temporary shrine beyond the fire.

The other dancers, whose celebration and worship this was, wore simple *banians* and *lungis*; all were of the fisher caste – Marakulu – though many of them, Joy said, were in practice masons, builders and tailors. Since nightfall they had been dancing through the town. They were high on it, but sober; entranced, but not by drink or drugs. They breathed deeply, gazed at fire or darkness. Two of them looked nervous.

Now the fire was yellow. The crowd surged as the musicians pounded and whined. There was the scent of sweat, and the stench of *arrack* on hot breath. The light-bearer stood her ground beside me; the primus lamp on her head fizzed in my ear. The dancers balanced god-pots on their turbans and queued at the pit's end with the fishermen. The fire was three paces from my feet; its heat tightened the skin on my face. My bones, like my senses, felt naked.

One by one the men walked the length of the pit. One put his feet down gingerly; the others took steady deliberate steps. The crowd shouted and celebrated the miracle. The fire was fanned. Our feet and legs were lashed. The men returned the way they had come, across the ardent embers. There was no wincing, no smell of burnt flesh. The strong man fanned the fire once more and for the third time gods and men passed over it unscathed.

Dirt quickly quenched the fire. People rushed to pick up cinders – some to kiss them – before the pit was filled. Within seconds it was just another bit of dusty street to walk upon as usual. A place to dance. Within an arena formed by musicians the dancers strutted, pranced and pirouetted with ecstatic dignity. A young woman, in identical tunic and trousers, joined them. The rhythm grew crazier. And a clown – *vashalu* with white face, crimson lips, curling black-paint moustache and tiny white-framed spectacles on the end of his nose – amplified and subverted everything.

He mimicked the dance with camp grotesquery. He stuck his tongue out, ogled the crowd, leered at me and banged on his big bass drum, whirling himself and it around until it seemed that he must fall. He didn't, but when he bowed his head I saw the lion mask he wore like a hat; its tail stuck out behind, two-rupee notes pinned to it. So clown was also *narasimha*, sacred man-lion. If, here, there was a line between the sacred and profane, I'd yet to see it. I tripped over it, as usual.

It was the fisher caste's *puja* or worship, and their party. They, the Marakulu, are officially classified as one of the backward castes in the bottom half of the fourth division, the Shudra class of farmers and peasants. But self-esteem lifts them to the second division, Kshatriya or warrior, the kingly caste second only to the Brahmins. They presume to award themselves the title of Agnikshatriyas. It makes sense. Agni is the god of fire. On the eve of the Pongal festival fishermen are fire-warriors.

15

BOGI MEN

Narsapur

THAT NIGHT Bogi bonfires burned in the streets. A shimmering sky received the fire and transformed it into starlight. Smoke became dawn. Bogi is the first day of festival; garlands of cow dung, dried during the preceding fifteen days of Gobimma, had been cast upon the fires. In the morning they lay like pale neck-laces, ghostly and unstrung, on each blackened hulk of palm trunk that smouldered amongst the ashes; ashes of any old timber or ruthlessly scavenged furniture that had fuelled the blaze. The past is not waste; it is illumination, possibility.

Down by the canal, beneath a post-box like a dull red tin can hanging from a tree, a holy man squatted on the *muggulu* outside the shrine of Durga the dark goddess. A makeshift hold-all slumped at his feet. His skin was the colour of night, his eye-brows and beard were white as the whitest ash, his turban and *lungi* were saffron and his long *khurta* was crimson, the colours of flame. He was *sanyasi*, refining himself, shedding the dross of worldly ties and hoping for salvation, release from the cycle of death and birth. Around his neck, like a garland, he wore a rosary of beads which he counted as he repeated his mantra.

The beads were seeds of the Rudraksha tree which grows in the Himalayas. 'Rudra' is Sanskrit for Shiva, and 'Aksha' is eye. The eye of Shiva is the third eye of spiritual insight. Once, by their occult powers, three demon brothers extorted boons from Shiva and dominated both this world and the subtle worlds from their flying citadels of gold, silver and iron. At last Shiva appeared to them with a benign smile and a look as terrible as truth. Citadels and demons were consumed and, in the same instant, a tear fell to earth from Lord Shiva's eye. That tear was the seed from which the first Rudraksha tree sprang. Worn as beads the seeds are said to control blood pressure, to cure jaundice and cancer. As I approached him, the holy man stood and looked at me with rheumy eyes. His gaze was solemn and soft. He asked for nothing. I gave him a rupee.

At lunch we talked about charity. Joy introduced me to her guests: David, a plump and kindly looking Indian with a wary eye, and two Australians, Ray and Bob, whose church back home sponsored David's boys' hostel at Rajahmundry. David had wisely borrowed an Ambassador and driven his benefactors across the river and down to Narsapur to see what a hostel could be. Ray and Bob were knocked out. The enthusiasm and horror with which they faced all things Indian made me feel like an old hand. To David, their enthusiasm and horror were good currency.

'Here is purpose built,' he said, 'with full facilities. We can do so very much more for children with full facilities.'

Joy thought her own thoughts while she dished out Suguna's best fish curry, drumstick curry and rice.

'David's doing a great job,' said Ray, 'but up there in Rajahmundry those kids of his have got no sickroom, no craftwork rooms, no nothing compared. No room to breathe. We got to go back to that committee and tell them how it is. Folks can go on sponsoring David kid by kid, but what he wants is real capital.'

Joy kept her counsel as she handed round *gongora*, *charu* and curd. She knew too much about Christians and Christian charities to jump to quick conclusions either way. Bob read her reticence and decided to lighten the tone.

'Y'know what?' he asked. 'Caught a beauty of a panther in the headlights up country the other night. What a place, eh?'

Joy painted them a vivid, and puzzling, picture of last night's firewalkers.

'Must've been drunk or drugged,' said Ray.

'I don't think so,' she said.

'Whatever it is, one thing's for sure,' said Bob, 'it's the work of the devil.'

'Oh yes,' said David sagely, 'work of the devil indeed.'

'What a place, eh?' said Bob.

'Why it's off the tourist map I don't know,' I put in. 'Except for a few people like yourselves, I haven't seen a white traveller since Madras.'

'We thought same's you,' said Ray, 'till yesterday we come down to breakfast in our hotel and the dining room's wall to wall English steam-train buffs.'

I needed a siesta. They needed tough talk. 'The only white man I saw in Rajahmundry was *driving* a steam train,' I said.

Outside my door their discussion faded. I woke in time for a cup of tea. Then the hubbub of drums and *booralu* approaching Holland Wharf drew me and my camera outside. Four men bore a palanquin on Y-shaped poles and set it down on these stilts near the *ghat*. The *rishi* Vasista and Godavari *thalli* – mother Godavari – on their respective plinths gazed upon the goddess in the palanquin, upon Brahmin priests wearing white *lungis* and white threads who made offerings to her, and upon female devotees in saris of yellow and mauve who bent their faces to the ground before the goddess and circled her palanquin kissing its four corners. I composed a picture.

A reproving hand swam up at the lens. I took my eye from the viewfinder as its owner spoke softly.

'No permission. Unsocial,' he said. 'Ask this man.'

He looked towards a fine-looking man standing a little apart and apparently aloof. Here, everybody else had welcomed me to take photographs of their rites, but this was clearly a Brahmin ceremony of a very superior sort. I had gaffed. The fine man looked through me.

'This is very sacred rite and place.'

'I did not mean to give offence,' I said.

On leaves upon the ground three priests kneaded some kind of dough, their muscles barely rippling beneath golden skins and noble layers of fat.

'You may take photos,' he said with an inkling of a smile at the goddess, not me. 'But from a distance, not obvious, unseen. If we do not see you, all is well.'

I thought that he – they – could have chosen not to see me in the first place, as they choose not to see so much else, but I kept quiet. I couldn't compete with Brahminical casuistry.

'I'd like to know what this ceremony is,' I said after a pause.

He brought me into focus and I felt that by his act of will I had been retrieved from invisibility.

'This idol is incarnation of goddess Lakshmi; here and now she prepares herself to marry Vishnu,' he explained graciously. 'That is, we are preparing her. All is part of the God, and the *puja* done here glorifies the God.'

The priests had moulded dough into three boat-shaped lamps. Deftly they inserted wicks. Now they offered oil to Lakshmi and filled the boats. Then they lit them and bent to launch them, on slivers of wood, off the *ghat*'s bottom step. The frail vessels tossed in Godavari's slight swell. Flames guttered momentarily, smoked blackly, then flared once more. Women followed them in for a holy dip and climbed out with saris clinging to breasts, bellies and thighs. The flames winked on the water.

The Bhagavata Purana tells us that the gods and demons churned the ocean of milk to obtain Amruth, nectar. One of the many treasures that surfaced from the great churning was Lakshmi, goddess of wealth, necessary consort of Lord Vishnu by whom all things are maintained. She sits on a lotus flower and carries a lotus in her hand. Her emergence stands for the evolution of values – ethical and aesthetic – in the heart of one whose pure mind is churned by its contemplation of the higher self.

Coolies carried the goddess away. The crackle of drums and plaint of shawms faded. I chatted to the lads from Goa who were responsible for the Oil and Natural Gas Commission's ferry, *Vasista Godavari*.

'I didn't want to upset anybody,' I said.

'Do not worry,' said the boy in speckled jeans, 'they are very proud.'

The river had washed the dough boats back to the *ghat*'s lower step and a hairy black pig climbed down and sniffed at one. Oil and dough smelt good. The pig snatched it up. She snorted as flame singed her bristles. Nostrils flared as she pranced up steps gobbling at her prize. She spat fire and swallowed hard. In her agony she learnt a lesson. She stood off and looked regretfully at two flames lifting and settling back on the step with each small wave.

This rare food made her salivate. In her ecstasy she unlearned the lesson. She made tentative approaches to the second boat; she grasped it in her teeth, lifted her head and skipped from the water's edge. Burning oil coated her snout. She squealed and breathed fire, gulping and retreating further from the source of her pain. Discretion and valour warred in the porcine breast. Did she slink away? No. She made wary passes at the third flame, rushed it, guzzled it and ran from the scene of sacrilege, basting herself as she went. I loved her: oh my dragon-pig, oh fire-warrior, my bit of crackling.

At supper I described these incendiary scenes to guests from Madras, Daisy and J. Victor Sundararaj. Both spoke excellent English and, of course, Tamil. Daisy also had fluent Telugu. Victor laughed at my naive mischievousness and spread his palms:

'There is refined Hinduism, and there is vulgar Hinduism. Here's all the snobbery and inverted snobbery you can think of.'

'But despite the extremes,' I said, 'hasn't Hinduism always been voraciously inclusive?'

'Oh yes, apparently,' he said. 'In the Gospel Jesus says, "No man cometh unto the Father but by me", while Krishna in the Bhagavad Gita says, "Whatever god a man worships, it is I who answer the prayer". No answer to that.'

'But exclusivity is essential to the Hindu hierarchy,' I said. 'At least in theory Christianity allows all men to be equal in the sight of God.'

'Hindus do not want to be equal,' Daisy said, 'they want status. Like everyone else.'

'Is *karma* really caste then?' I asked.

'Loosely,' Victor smiled, 'but you are being provocative. Each caste has its *dharma* and Hindus do not have to achieve everything in one life.'

Victor and Daisy have to, though, by the grace of God.

'Tell me how you see the current Hindu revival,' I said, 'and the rise of the BJP.'

The Bharatiya Janata Party's *ekta yatra*, or so-called 'unity pilgrimage', had raised a flag in Srinigar, Kashmir, on New Year's Day and aimed to replace Ayodhya's mosque with a temple.

'Everybody talks about the *ekta yatra* as if it was merely a gesture against Islam and Pakistan,' he said. 'I wish it was so simple. But it's against a secular state that permits, for example, Christianity to run wild among the tribals. *That* threatens the power structure. BJP wants a Hindu state.'

'The secular state is in any case an illusion,' said Daisy, 'like democracy.'

'See how the cult of the Lord Ayyappa has grown in the last decade,' said Victor. 'His devotees claim to undermine caste, and perhaps they do, but they reinforce prejudice against other faiths and against women.'

'Ah, the men in black,' I said, 'the muscular Hindus.'

Daisy laughed. She was a muscular Christian. Her events were the one hundred metres, two hundred metres and triple jump. She scandalized the orthodox by training in a tracksuit.

'She competes all round the world,' said Victor.

'When I can afford it and the Lord allows.'

'She has won many medals.'

'Veteran's medals these days.'

In her sixties, she was still a winner. And Victor was Victor. Both were running the race and would, I felt sure, finish the course.

Down by the canal the Lutheran church towered darkly and merged with the night. Shrines and temples were lit with fairy lights and fluorescent tubes. Near the fairground, adolescent boys rolled together in the straw beneath a cloth. Swathed people slept soundly by their sideshows or beside stocks of pots and novelties and idols. They slept, though the air could not comfortably contain distorted loudspeaker music, brittle chatter, and the throb of drums that seemed always to be moving through darkness a few streets away. People queued to enter shrines beneath great figures of the god Lakshminarasimhaswami and the goddess Durga. Between them stretched a sheet, screen for the open-air film show the kids were waiting for.

Dazed people pressed at booths selling beads, ear-rings and bangles; stared at stalls packed with plastic goods – gods, guns, rattles, conch shells and dark glasses – a cross between a Catholic shrine's souvenir shop and a game show's prize conveyor belt. You could buy Shiva's black *lingam* shielded by a yellow five-headed cobra, a life-like Sai Baba in crimson robes, the lurid god Ganesh with the head of an elephant, pale blue Lord Krishna, shocking pink Parvati, or a purple and red money-box fish with a slit in front of its dorsal fin. Almost anything here could have popped out of an oversized Christmas cracker.

A pale, delicately marked gecko with a big cockroach in its mouth caught my eye on a stall of plaster animals. I bought it and carried it carefully home. Outside their houses women were drawing elaborate *muggulu* on dampened dust. Some, with pattern-books in hand, joined the dots with a deft trickle of white chalk. Some embellished designs with colours and petals. Telugu script writhed. And surprisingly, in a town where so few spoke English, a handful were boldly inscribed 'Happy Sankranti'. And at one lamplit threshold, a kitsch cartoon mouse – vehicle of Ganapati – flourished a paintbrush and a wish: 'Happy Pongal'.

'And you, Walt,' I said. 'And you.'

16

SIGN OF THE CROCODILE

Narsapur

TRYING TO look cool and unconcerned I sat down on the narrow plank seat in the lowest basket of the Big Wheel. Rathnam sat opposite me and smiled shyly. She was the quietest of the nine hostel girls I'd brought to the fair. I was relieved to escape their chatter. The basket slewed sideways and up, then went into reverse and stopped. A smartly dressed boy of three or four was lifted on to the plank next to Rathnam. He looked serious. I smiled. He searched for his mother or big brother in the crowd as we rose jerkily, segment by segment, on an ascending arc. Rathnam put her arm round him.

Ever since we'd left the hostel gates the girls had been very helpful. Pointing things out. Like 'Boy' or 'Bicycle' or 'Bus', in English. It helped a lot.

'Cow!' they said.

'Bull,' I said quietly. It wasn't easy to tell, for this white Brahman bull was draped with rugs and brocades; its hump was upholstered in five colours of cloth; its forelegs, haunches and chaps were hung with bells; its upward-curving horns were wrapped in cloth and topped with plumes like pom-poms; its face was adorned with macramé and its muzzle was disguised by gaudy silk. Ears, eyes, tail and testicles gave the game away.

A boy led it by a cord knotted untidily in the middle. The knot consorted oddly with the luxury and precision of the beast's caparison. The boy whined a tune on his *boora* and collected alms at each street door.

'Cow!' said the girls again, and 'Pig!'

'*Pandi*,' I said, to the girls' glee. It is the Telugu word for pig, and I thought of the proverb: 'If he says it's a Nandi, it's a Nandi; if he says it's a *pandi*, it's a *pandi*.' Nandi is the sacred bull, vehicle of Lord Shiva. One of its horns stands for *tamas* or non-apprehension of reality, the other for *rajas* or misapprehension; it is the symbol of egocentric man. Riding him, Shiva is Brahman, and Nandi is the fully realized soul.

A few yards up the road a small pig, with trotters splayed, stood firm for a dog that had mounted her. He seemed to be enjoying himself. She looked philosophical about it. I said nothing. Another pig lumbered out of a drain.

'Nandi!' I said, pointing. 'I say it's a Nandi.'

'No, no, *pandi*,' the girls chorused, 'not Nandi but *pandi!*'

Clearly labouring under a misapprehension, I lacked the authority to abolish the distinction between sacred and profane.

'Ah, pig!' I said as the truth dawned.

The girls laughed, uncertain which of us was the joke.

'Nandi,' I said, looking through a temple gateway to where a carved bull sat in ecstatic contemplation before the sanctum sanctorum, not moving its gaze even for a split second from Lord Shiva within. 'I say that's a Nandi.'

'Yes, yes,' giggled the girls, 'that is correct.'

'Good,' I said. 'Now tell me what these people are doing.'

A man in white *khurta* and *lungi*, with the white V and vermilion stripe of a devotee of Vishnu on his brow, was standing in the road beside a green statue of Hanuman the monkey. Other men carried palm fronds and instruments: a drum, a pipe and a *sruti*-box, or hand-held harmonium. Women stood in the shade of two palmyra-leaf umbrellas.

'It is marriage,' one of the most talkative girls said with utter conviction. We all smiled at the party.

'But wait, I ask,' said blabbermouth. She came back looking solemn. 'This man's mother dead. Ashes thrown on river since fifteen days. Now are waiting for *Acharya*.'

We recomposed our faces as the *Acharya*, revered teacher, emerged to lead the family in a rite that would oil the wheel of *samsara*, death and reincarnation. Ashes are not confetti.

*   *   *

Now I was at the top of the Big Wheel with Rathnam and the smart little boy who, despite Rathnam's arm around his shoulders, had a hopeless, faraway look in his eyes. I had a bird's eye view of the makeshift fairground, with shrines and queues of worshippers at one side and the street full of stalls and customers at the other. Below, like a twirling multicoloured umbrella, a roundabout with a canvas roof spun children on painted animals outwards by centrifugal force. A gypsy family sat on the ground with all their stuff – bedding, clothes, steel and brass utensils – at their backs and balloons above their heads, selling peanuts. A Little Wheel of frail struts and stressed wires, a miniature of ours, with kids crammed into tiny baskets, whirled frantically in front of the end wall of a house plastered with sado-masochistic cinema posters. Without warning we dropped, and accelerated. It was our turn to spin, to be one with the universe.

At each Sankranti the sun passes from one sign of the zodiac to the next. At Makarasankranti – that's what we were celebrating – the sun leaves the sign, or *rasi*, of Dhanus and enters Makara *rasi*, the sign of the Crocodile. The exact moment cannot be distinguished by eyes of flesh. The thirtieth part of the time taken by the throb of the eye of a man sitting happily at ease is called a *truti*; one hundredth part of a *truti* is the time the sun takes to pass from one *rasi* to the next. As it's not possible to perform the Sankranti rites during so short a time, they may be performed in the twelve hours before and after the imperceptible instant. It makes sense.

Sankranti is a god too, of course, identified with Durga the 'difficult of approach', the black and terrible giantess of many names, with blood-red tongue and fierce tusks, weapons in her many hands and a garland of human heads about her neck. She bears and consumes each moment, hour, day, month, season and year. Her stomach is a void which can never be filled and her womb forever gives birth to all things. She rewards the meritorious and punishes the sinful, and on this day both merits and penalties are many times multiplied.

Each devotee should offer three vessels of food and a cow to a good Brahmin householder, and recite four verses including the prayer, 'May Sankara (Shiva) who pervades the universe always bestow welfare upon me.' A rich devotee should also donate some ornaments, a bedstead and a pair of golden jars. Hence the proverb, 'There is no meekness in cows, nor poverty in Brahmins.' Gifts offered on Makarasankranti gain a *crore* (ten million) times as much merit as the same gifts given on an ordinary day. A bath in the Godavari at Sankranti is worth six months of bathing there on other days, and anyone who won't bathe on the holy day will be diseased and poor for seven lives.

I needed nine lives. I looked at the Big Wheel's axle turning in bearings set into timbers that had obviously split long ago and been bound up many times. Two men wound us up to an alarming speed. They faced each other, swaying and rising and falling with the handle between them that drove the flapping belt that spun the groaning wheel. Rathnam wouldn't meet my eye. The smart little boy grinned. I felt as green as Hanuman.

'You *like* the Big Wheel,' I told myself emphatically.

'Not this one!' came the response from where my throat had been before it became stomach.

One man stood back. His mate alone maintained the momentum. Above her shrine Durga swelled and receded and swelled again. Tamarind trees grew, shrank, grew. Rathnam's friends laughed like little demons. Their voices came and went.

At last we slowed, waited to alight. It was a letdown. The smart little boy was plucked from his seat.

'*Terra firma*,' I sighed gratefully.

'Please, why this terror?' said Rathnam as she bought me a glass of sweet tea and an onion *bhaji* at a stall. The girls' chatter and ineluctable helpfulness engulfed me once more.

'Now, back to hahstel,' I said firmly.

'Not this way,' they protested.

'Yes,' I said, 'through the bazaar.'

I wanted to buy guavas, but they were adamant that they must return by the route we came. How could I convince them that it was possible to do something different? I almost dragged them to market. Once there, I couldn't tear them away from the stalls. One who limped I packed off in a cycle-rickshaw, for two rupees, with two friends who came over tired when the wheels appeared. The remaining half dozen girls gloated over trophies from both fair and bazaar as we walked slowly, so slowly, home. Indians, I decided, have a great love of novelty and a hatred of change.

Was I really seeing this? Two wooden pecking birds with black heads, silver toppers and turquoise feathers stood in front of an enamelled brass peacock, the vehicle of Saraswati, goddess of learning. Close by, Shiva Nataraja, the Lord of the Dance, moved in eternal stillness between a Spanish flamenco dancer with just two arms and Venus de Milo with none at all. Russian dolls in order of ascent led the eye to elephant-headed Ganapathi, and the Buddha meditated complacently beside fluffy yellow ducks with hats and handbags.

These figures formed part of the multitudinous three-tiered display, lit by fairy lights and sanctified by incense burners, that filled one wall of Gopala Rao's reception room. Mr Rao, a devout and prosperous Brahmin, is the chartered accountant who audits the hostel's books. His family have passed down, from one generation to the next, a secret herbal remedy for jaundice. Joy sends for it whenever a hostel girl comes down with the disease. It's infallible, she says. Mr Rao makes no charge.

His daughter Sita Lakshmi showed me round the house. It was strangely tatty and untidy for an opulent household, and on a holy day too. But Sita was nineteen or twenty, well-spoken, self-confident, and beautiful in her silk sari, brand-new for Sankranti. She led me upstairs to a room furnished with a second TV, a sitar in a glass case and a household shrine: lamps before a lurid holy picture and a second statuette of Nataraja.

'We worship him especially for the dance,' said Sita. 'Next week I will dance at NCC camp. You will come?'

'What is NCC?' I said. The words were hardly out of my mouth when, with scrabbling claws and blood-curdling barks, an Alsatian dog launched itself into the room from the balcony. Its chain strangled it before it got to me. Bark became yelp, but only for a moment. Sita explained who I was. It made sense. The dog stopped barking. It quivered and growled.

'I am at college here,' said Sita, 'studying commerce. But I also belong to NCC – it is National Cadet Corps . . .'

As she climbed more stairs ahead of me, I tried vainly to imagine the liquefaction of her silky limbs translated into uniform.

'. . . we do many things, like camping, jogging, parascending. I play in orchestra and I dance. For me, to dance is worship.'

Up on the roof of the concrete house, away from the dog's incensed growling, we looked down at a cow and her calf in a shed beside the house. Sita waved her hand at the shrine, triangular in plan and full of worshippers today, that stood in the street outside the front gate.

'My father built that, for Sai Baba,' she said. 'This house was built by my grandfather.'

Then she pointed to the single-storey tiled house below.

'That was my family's house before. It is one hundred years old. Now it is rented by a very affectionate woman.'

I liked the phrase.

Sita was needed downstairs to give an affectionate welcome to women who arrived one after another. Every foot that crossed the threshold was a sickly yellow, anointed with turmeric to invoke Lakshmi and prosperity. Sita Lakshmi lit the oil lamps and wafted smoke and prayers over her proud display of gods, toys, holy pictures and plastic fruit. Perhaps her mantras fertilized the model farm laid out upon the sandy floor with, as backdrop, a poster of the ocean. Her prayers seemed not to discriminate between Durga's dark visage or Grenadier's bearskin, woolly rabbit or sacred elephant, 'twenties flapper doll or plastic Christus Rex.

Sita applied vermilion *bottu* to each proffered forehead and sandalwood paste to each extended neck. Everyone chattered and asked what I was doing in this female company. I exchanged many greetings and, like the women guests, was given Bombay mixture, seeds and a banana. I got Thums Up too.

'All is done now for Makarasankranti,' said Sita. '*Muggulu*, worship in temple, this with the dolls and all. Tomorrow is Kanuma when cattle must be washed and decorated and worshipped, and first fruits of the paddy harvest celebrated.'

'Thank you for showing me,' I said.

'Now you will come to uncle's house,' she said.

I went to uncle's house. With Sita and her father. Uncle was big, all in white. The doors were magnificently carved. The display was even more eccentric: Krishna with a teddy bear, Mickey Mouse in a car, a doctor and nurse's outfit, two white toy poodles, a village set out on multicoloured gravel. Uncle's threshold was painted bright yellow for Lakshmi and beautifully decorated with red and white and black designs. Above, in a net, hung a coconut with a grotesque face painted on it.

'It absorbs all curses, protects house from evil spirits,' said uncle's son as he gave me another bottle of Thums Up.

Must be an echo of human sacrifice, I thought, but I didn't put the thought into words.

'Come now,' said Mr Rao, 'please come.'

Out in the dark a donkey ran between houses and knocked a man off his bike. The front wheel was so bent it wouldn't turn. The man smiled and smiled. Was he philosophical? Or drunk? Or not cursing and throwing bricks after the beast because it was Sankranti? His smile would be multiplied ten million times.

In the face of so much novelty my smile had become fixed, until the donkey made me laugh. But when Gopala Rao and Sita Lakshmi whisked me over yet another saffron threshold I had to fix it again. In a big way. My Brahmin friends introduced me to a woman who manufactured novelties out of rubbish. Why, I wanted to ask, do you think this is so good? A whole cardboard pitch of cricketers made from the caps of toothpaste tubes. A suite of furniture made of matchboxes. Pictures made out of seeds, or of wire wound round nails. Mr Rao and Sita seemed to think all this was fine. Was it a parable of *samsara*? I wanted release from the cycle. But this tall mannish figure in a sari who took the despised rubbish of this world and reconstituted it as, well, rubbish, she wouldn't let me go. After three boxes of exhibits she produced an album full of photographs of all the things I'd just seen. She'd won State and National awards, you know.

Satyanarayana shot me an old-fashioned look and said something about 'police' when he let me out of the hostel compound.

I wanted to be in amongst it again, the frantic sounds and smells of festival. There was nothing in town. Just silence and stars. Until dogs barked at me, and one began to howl. It was spooky. Then I realized what the watchman had been saying. There was a curfew. The quietest night ever. One shooting star was the closest I came to excitement.

Makarasankranti is the feast of the winter solstice when the sun moves to its northern home. Astronomers put the solstice at 21 December, but priests who thumb almanacs based upon ancient data believe the sun's march north starts in mid January. So it seemed that the precession of the equinoxes, at a rate of 50.27 seconds of arc per year, meant that I drank Thums Up with Brahmins and had my bellyful of novelties three weeks or so too late, twenty-four days after the correct Makarasankranti. We were out of sync. Someone had crashed the cosmic gears.

In Britain and North America, back in 1752, we deliberately mislaid eleven September days in order to catch up with the Gregorian calendar of 1582 once and for all. Why couldn't Hindus do something similar? Silly question. They have a great love of novelty, sure enough, but an indelible hatred of change.

That night news came from the bazaar that a child had been kidnapped at the fair. A boy. Well-dressed. Three-and-a-half. Could he be the very boy who'd ridden the big wheel with Rathnam and me at the moment when the sun was supposed to have moved into the sign of the Crocodile? A kidnapper's plan. Or whim. A spin of the wheel. A child's fate. Found, one ransom note. Its demand: ten thousand rupees and a hundred coconut trees.

17

HELPING THE POLICE

Narsapur

PERHAPS the tale of three men on a plinth should embrace and give shape to the episodes and observations which follow. The very first time I walked from the hostel to the bazaar I'd noticed a trio dressed in white, life-like but glossier, standing on plinths beside one of Narsapur's more prestigious temples. Holy or not, they were a trinity. One I recognized, Rajiv Gandhi, ex-ex-prime minister, maybe the last of his dynasty.

One day I undid a parcel I'd brought from the bazaar and felt sick. Glossy pages used as wrapping paper unfolded a series of unexpected and explicit shots of the aftermath of Rajiv's assassination at Sriperumbudur near Madras, on 21 May 1991 at 10.20 p.m., including the blurred picture of the explosion itself which killed Haribabu the photographer, Rajiv, the suicide bomber and twenty-five others. Rajiv had been one of the most closely guarded men in the world. In a desperate bid to regain power, to recapture his rapport with the people, he let security slip.

'I have been on the road twenty-three and a half hours a day since the first of May,' he said. 'At the end I am swollen and bleeding . . .'

Out of the crowd came Dhanu, a young agent of the Liberation Tigers of Tamil Eelam, most fanatical of the Sri Lankan Tamil separatist factions. A police woman attempted to stop her. 'Let everyone get a chance,' Rajiv snapped.

Dhanu placed a garland over his head, bent to touch his feet and triggered the bomb concealed beneath her *khurta*. Yes, Rajiv on a plinth I recognized.

'Who are the other two?' I asked some people nearby.

'Beside lamented Rajiv Gandhi is big man here, and beside him is good man, public benefactor recently died.'

'But who was the big man?' I persisted. It was hard to get an answer. Someone drew me aside and, discreetly, over a cup of coffee, explained a few things.

'The third man, he is a Rowdy,' she said, 'big in Narsapur.'

For Rowdy read wide-boy, petty politician, gangster and murderer. So, this tale, 'Three Men on a Plinth', might well be subtitled 'Rajiv, the Rowdy and the Philanthropist'.

The Philanthropist made a lot of money, gave some away and died in his bed. The Rowdy sold security. He set up an office and dispatched letters to the gold dealers and money-lenders, who were mostly Jains from Rajahstan, invoicing them for services not rendered. It was a simple protection racket. And when anything did occur, naturally he helped the police.

He grew rich and powerful. He had at least two men killed who stood in his way. He employed faithful *goondas* or heavies to protect him, but one day someone who'd had enough stabbed him to death in the temple. The town was in uproar. People pressed in to view him in his blood. His body was paraded around while trembling traders sat locked in their shops for fear of looting. Transport came to a standstill. Buses were overturned and burnt. Narsapur might have rejoiced. It mourned violently.

One of the Jain gold dealers had once been heard to wish the Rowdy dead. It made sense, this wish, and should have been safe among friends. But it had reached the Rowdy's ears. It was costly, and the debt never written off. The Jain was blamed for the murder although he was away in Rajahsthan at the time. His relatives in Narsapur knew he was innocent, but they sent him instructions not to return in a letter he didn't receive. In desperation they intercepted his train at Vijayawada and turned him around. After some time he did come back to Narsapur, but he was soon visited by a deputation.

'Your arms are all right now,' they told him. 'Your legs are all right now, your heart is good.' He left for Rajahstan.

*   *   *

There are Philanthropists as well as Rowdies, but all too often charity begins at home. The Jesus Children's Home, for instance. Its funds have built its administrators a fine house which is filled with children paid to come in off the street and answer to the register only on days when sponsors and grant-givers visit.

An unidentified 'field-worker' recently wrote abroad to raise money for sinking boreholes in a drought-stricken Narsapur. Why should donors know that in the real town, set between river and canal, tube-wells supply taps on every other street?

Joy's correspondents around the world sometimes receive heart-rending letters from plausible proprietors of meretricious causes. The addresses, copied from Joy's outgoing mail, are probably bought or stolen from the post office. How many pious 'pastors' need a good living. How many 'flood victims' need houses. How many 'orphans' need homes and education. I was tempted to think these good scams if they came off, until I saw that out here the needy can't even afford the stamps.

The smart small boy who had been abducted from the round-about at the Sankranti fair was found a week later, far away in Hyderabad, the State capital, in the custody of a needy man. A crazy man, they said. The kidnapper never realized his ransom demand of rupees and trees. What the police made out of it, and what price the boy paid for his adventure, I don't know. He was lucky.

Shanth's son Prakash disappeared again just before I left Narsapur. He made a habit of it, and of petty crime. He'd been sleeping rough and working for a man who'd killed his last boy. Santhosham and Joshi offered him a home. Joy and I took him there. He was in a catatonic state. When he came to, they got him a job as a mechanic's apprentice. It seemed like a last chance he might just take. He took their money and ran away.

Rathnamma, the hostel cook, brought up her niece as her own. One day she vanished from her job in Kakinada. Rathnamma was frantic and combed the big towns. She was poor, so her case was of no interest to the police. After two years the girl turned up at the hostel with a boyfriend. Rathnamma insisted on a wedding, though Joy said it would be a waste of time. It was. The boy quickly stopped caring for his wife or his child.

Satyanarayana, the hostel's night watchman, lost his son. The boy vanished when he was nine. His parents spent what money they had looking for him in Rajahmundry, Kakinada, Hyderabad, all the places they could think of. After a year, Satyanarayana went on business to Vijayawada. He knew a tailor from Narsapur who'd settled there, and called on him to ask if he'd seen the boy. The tailor said no, but next minute Satyanarayana's son walked into the shop. His lie was justified, the tailor said, because the boy had chosen to live with him and learn his trade. When I met him he was back at home, a tailor, looking for a wife.

Some never come back. The day I ordered a shirt at Narayana tailor's, beside the big red hoarding with the slogan 'Taste the Thunder', a bloody woman floated down the canal from Palakol, gold ripped out of her ears and picked out of her teeth. Joy and Suguna once took in a woman who was pulled from the river at Holland Wharf and pumped out; she'd jumped from a boat; relatives said she'd tried it before for no good reason. A man who tied stone mortars to his arms couldn't fail; for months Joy feared every watery sound, thinking it might be someone she must save. A body came ashore at the *ghat* with an acid-eaten face; it became an attraction, but Joy disliked its gaze and asked the police to remove it. Perhaps she was not co-operative enough, for the police said that nothing could be done. No one had been reported missing. It made sense, and the body floated away before long.

'Please accompany me to the police station,' Joy said.

'All right,' I said, 'so long as you don't press charges.'

She'd been called in, with all her papers, to prove she was of good character and worthy of a new five-year residence permit. Missamma: born in Andhra, beloved founder and administrator of a respected hostel, trustee of hospitals and schools. No problem, I'd have thought. But the good make powerful enemies, and the powerful buy good lawyers. Pronounced 'liars', remember.

Two officers stood on the verandah gazing past the flimsy iron arch and Police Station sign at the entrance. As I parked on sand at the side of the canal road their eyes lit up. Police were either aloof, it seemed, or hungry. These, I felt, had a healthy appetite. They waved us through the door. It was dim in there, crowded and dirty. There was a rough table in the middle with a chair at one side and a bench on the other. Joy and I sat on the bench. Men squatted, backs to the wall, in handcuffs. More lay, behind bars labelled 'men' in Telugu. A blackboard screened the lower half of the matching barred door labelled 'women', but faces rose up to stare over it at us, until lethargy or despair got the better of curiosity and they sank back.

We were punctual, but the officer Joy had to see was at lunch. Those who weren't at lunch were wary. Eight members of Madhava Friends Union had just been remanded to Rajahmundry Central Jail for attempting to murder a sub-inspector and two constables here. A rusty two-way radio, that might have been under water for months, fizzed and gurgled with submarine voices. It hung, unattended, on the wall I faced. The walls needed a good scrub. I felt like a patient who had intended to go to the hospital, but found himself in an abattoir.

A detective sat across the table and casually interrogated me, all the while examining my passport and visa with intense lack of interest.

'But what are you doing here?' he said.

'How long have you been stationed at Narsapur?' Joy asked.

'Four years, Missamma,' he replied at once.

Officiousness evaporated. All at once he was a schoolboy, anxious to please. He whisked us through a door that faced the cells. On the stained wall beside it, a motto was painted in big red letters. 'Duty Before Self'. His superior looked up wearily from his desk. A ceiling fan rotated slowly. This officer had red flashes on his uniform, but his walls needed scrubbing too.

'Very sorry,' he groaned. 'Return tomorrow, same time.'

Satyanarayana's brother was remanded to Rajahmundry Central Jail. A small-time prawn dealer, he'd come to Narsapur on business and drunk coffee at the wrong street stall at the wrong time. Police had been beaten up in the cinema, part of a feud between the Rowdy's mob and the Rowdy's murderer's mob, and as soon as the assailants repaired to the street for refreshment, so the story went, the police took everyone in sight.

Satyanarayana's brother had not stabbed the Rowdy in the temple. He hadn't picked a fight with his friends, or enemies. He dealt in prawns not gold, and drank coffee. Satyanarayana was worried. He couldn't afford to pay for quick answers. When he did find out where his brother was, all he could do was take the 3.30 a.m. train to Rajahmundry and try to bail him out.

He couldn't. He told us that of the two dozen men arrested perhaps four had been involved in the alleged crime. Travelling to and fro cost Satyanarayana time, and forty-five rupees each way. At last bail was fixed at one thousand five hundred rupees. It was a non-refundable donation, innocent or guilty. I gave him money towards it, which he acknowledged with a nod and a ghost of a smile. His brother looked worn but well when I saw him. It had been an expensive business; and still would be, with days spent travelling to court only to have the case adjourned: bus and train fares, loss of earnings, 'bail', the odd bribe and his lawyer's fee of one thousand rupees. Innocence probably cost him four thousand rupees. If he was lucky, that meant five or six months' work, before allowing anything for living or for money-lenders. And he was a lucky innocent because he was the only one who'd been granted bail. He just wanted to get back to work, for he lived hand to mouth. The police had beaten him, but they'd only broken one of his fingers. A doctor set it for him for three hundred and fifty rupees. It had been an expensive cup of coffee.

Whenever I heard such tales, or talked to the victims of routine injustices, I thought about the afternoon Shanth took me to the police quarters near Hanuman's temple, just off the bazaar. The monkey-god's image reared up behind bars, but his mighty war-club protruded through them and its business-end rested on the floor where worshippers could touch it. Uniform rows of tiny two-roomed cottages lay on three sides of a spacious compound. We were warmly welcomed. A Muslim officer's delightful wife gave us tea in a spotless room crammed with a bed and a tall *almirah*. She was not veiled. She seemed irrepressible, and showed us the family album with great pride. Her brother was a doctor in England. Her husband spoke good English. She invited us to stay for a meal. Meanwhile, we agreed to visit a Hindu friend across the compound for a minute, or half an hour. It was the same little house, but chaotic. We perused another album, listened to indeterminate music at varying speeds on a dodgy cassette machine and drank an exotic mixture of tea and Horlicks. I thanked them for the nice coffee. Delightful folk, the police.

Joy returned to the police station to sort out her permit. A man in the cells waved wildly and cried out. She couldn't place him at first. Then she recognized him as a Christian evangelist she'd helped in the past, whose daughter had lived in her hostel.

'I must bring up his incarceration in staff prayers,' she said. 'They'll all remember him. Once he was loath to let the girl come back here. He wanted her at home when she "matured", as he put it. We all prayed she'd have her first period in the holidays. Our prayer was answered. He'd given so much money to other families towards their daughters' maturing that he was desperate to recoup his investment. His daughter obliged, the friends threw water over her for ritual cleansing, but when I saw him next he said he didn't make much money after all.'

'Why is he in gaol?' I asked.

'Oh, he says his wife has put a case against him.'

She recalled a teacher she knew who'd gone home to find his house in a mess and immediately put his sons into police custody. He'd once brought his family to stay, uninvited, at the hostel and then drugged them to prevent them going out in the sun. But most people do things for money, like the nurse at the state hospital who gave a sick woman water to drink and then left her screaming for a bed-pan because she had no money to pay for it. Or the senior police officer, a fine fat figure of a man, who came to look the hostel over. It was a shame, he muttered, that Joy had not been co-operating with the police. They needed fans, new chairs, office equipment. Joy explained that the hostel was a charity that was accountable for its money. It was a shame, she said, that the police did not co-operate with the hostel. The police made no donations, but Joy got her permit.

Someone from the tailor's gave me hot news of a 'Christian' politician's new shirt. It had a lion embroidered on the right breast and his name and all the letters after it on the left. It was all of a piece with his wild black mane, his gold-topped cane and the real lion that he'd borrowed from the circus to help his election campaign. The town buzzed with gossip about him and the mistress he'd just married. There was some argument about money. Two *goondas* had called while he was out, thrown pepper in her face, robbed and raped her. The question was, who'd paid them? Naturally, the politician was happy to help the police.

The next morning there was a fusillade of firecrackers. It was an auspicious day. Gandhiji and Mrs Gandhi were freshly garlanded. So too, beside the temple, was the trinity. I walked towards a *pandiri*, or colourful canopy, spanning a side street, with garlanded dignitaries beneath it making speeches through a raucous PA system and nodding sagely on the platform.

'Excuse me,' I said to a smart policeman as tall as myself. 'What's going on here?'

He turned on me with immense suspicion. I don't know why. It was not good for me to be there.

'What do you want?' he demanded.

'I'm just looking,' I said.

'Where are you going? Where are you staying? Where is your passport?'

'It's at Missamma's hostel, Wollander Revu,' I said.

'You must be carrying it on your person at all times.'

Tourists were thrown into gaol for this offence. Familiar Narsapur felt alien. I retreated to the bazaar.

This tale I'm supposed to have been telling, 'Three Men on a Plinth', doesn't really hang together. Connections are hard to make. The truth is too complex for us. The symbol is all. It's simpler to put characters on pedestals, and make them stand for what society venerates, than to examine what really happens. The climax of the story is the whole story. It's just this, that outside one of the more prestigious temples in small-town India three cement dummies, with whitewash robes, mushroom-coloured faces and glossy black hair, now stand shoulder to shoulder. On festivals and auspicious days they are respectfully garlanded with ropes of tan and brimstone marigolds. Rajiv, the Rowdy and the Philanthropist stand together in death. It makes sense.

BRICKS AND WATER

Muskepalem

THE FIRST time I took the wheel of Joy's Ambassador I drove out of town to the outskirts where Samelu lived in the village of Muskepalem. It was a process of learning and unlearning. I had to master diesel ignition, a near-dislocated steering-column gear-change, a kangaroo clutch and reluctant brakes. At the same time I had to forget the rules of the road, or rather interpret them as loosely and inventively as possible, which demanded great concentration. The first lesson was to hoot immoderately at ox-carts, rickshaws, cycles, pedestrians, pigs, goats, occasional cars, and lorries called Public Carriers which all carried the encouraging motto on their backsides, 'Please Sound Horn'.

At first I felt like a blundering English *sahib*, scattering natives to left and right, but all the other *sahibs*, driving with infinitely more abandon, were Indian. After an anarchic junction or two and some exhilarating zig-zagging along the main drag, my inhibitions ebbed. It was enjoyable. I crashed the gears and turned down a rutted track between palm groves and paddies. By the time I reached Muskepalem I wanted to be driving with aplomb, for Samelu was not only Joy's *peon* and right-hand man, he was her driver too. Down the twisting cactus-lined lane between houses people waved me in the right direction. They knew just where I was heading. I hooted hard and Samelu appeared. I parked where he pointed. He grinned broadly.

Samelu wanted to show me his new home. There weren't many brick-and-concrete houses in Muskepalem, and what there were were basic government-funded boxes with concrete lids. Samelu's small plot was all his because he had no brothers, but it was split by a path, or village street. On one side his ambitious unfinished house reared up on a high plinth; on the other smaller half, his mother was temporarily housed in a low palm-leaf shelter beneath coconut trees. I greeted her. Samelu's wife, Premaleela, emerged from the mud-and-leaf house which a neighbour had let them put up on his plot while their dream house was being built. They'd lived there for almost three years.

'Bedroom, kitchen, sitting room, all!' said Samuel.

I bent double to get inside without impaling myself on the palmyra thatch. There was a charpoy, rolled mats and cooking pots on the floor, clothes hanging and stuff stored above sagging rafters. Premaleela showed me the hearth and smoke-hole in a dark porch under the low eaves. She was a fine woman, shy but welcoming, broad-shouldered beside wiry Samelu. In her white widow's sari, Samelu's wiry mother squatted on her haunches plaiting palmyra fronds into square baskets. Her buttocks sat at her heels and the soles of her feet were flat on the ground. Her arms were gaunt and dark. Her spectacles glinted as she folded long thin parchment-coloured leaves. She and Premaleela could make twenty rupees a day between them, after the cost of the palmyra and the market man's commission. Mother often plaited all night.

Samelu made twenty-seven rupees a day at the hostel, six days a week, plus fifty rupees medical insurance per month and a five-hundred-rupee Christmas bonus. Solomon, the builder, made about twenty rupees a day for work on Samelu's house. He was also building himself a basic twenty-thousand-rupee house with government help. Through the village president and the *panchayat*, or parish council, Samelu had got a government loan of eight thousand rupees, later commuted to a grant, towards the seventy-five-thousand-rupee house that he'd been permitted to build. There were steps up to the plinth.

'High, high, very important,' Samelu said.

Their old mud house had stood on this site. Only its high verandah had prevented it being washed away in the floods of 1986 when so many houses throughout the delta, had collapsed and dissolved. There were two pairs of rooms with wrought-iron window grills, cavities ready for built-in cupboards and cement ceilings with mouldings and star-within-star motifs. From a pile of timber Samelu extracted a pair of doors, panels carved with lotus blossoms, that he hoped to hang soon.

'Here, kitchen,' said Samelu.

There was no chimney, and they'd never afford bottled gas; cooking would still be done outside under the eaves. There was no latrine and no piped water, though white PVC channels for wiring anticipated the new electricity supply being extended from street lamps to dwellings. One day. Outside the kitchen door stood a bathroom like a sentry-box. Cantilevered steps embraced both it and a palm trunk as they climbed to the roof. Up there Samelu could breathe deeply. He had reason to be very proud.

Below, Premaleela and Samelu served onion *bhajis*, sweet-meats and tea from a thermos flask. I thought of the expense. They insisted I sit on a chair balanced on hardcore awaiting cement. It was a delight to share their pleasure, to witness the respect in which the village held them and to know it proved by the *panchayat*'s confidence in their industriousness and integrity.

Samelu led me through the village. On a white patterned mud verandah a little girl in a dress decorated with mirrors, Banjara gypsy style, pirouetted on one leg beside her shy brother; they sucked at bananas while, on the *muggu* below, a chicken scratched amid a flotilla of chicks. We gazed over a cactus hedge into a palm-fringed field Samelu had rented. Where he'd dug brickearth, there was a pond. In his spare time he'd trodden clay, moulded bricks, laid them to dry in the sun, built them into a clamp or kiln fuelled with paddy-husk, and fired it. The project cost him just five thousand rupees; the bricks sold for twenty-five thousand. He made a handsome profit, and himself ill. Nearby, other men's kilns crumbled away brick by brick, like the ruinous footings of great pillars.

We slipped through a small gate in a cactus hedge and found ourselves in an orchard; here the woman who'd rented Samelu his brickworks grew her aubergines and herbs beneath trees laden in their season with sapotas, mangoes and tamarind beans. Samelu dug up a peaty clump of palmyra nuts with their spring-ing shoots: tender *thagalu* that are sold roasted in every bazaar. A man in a white *panchi* and thick spectacles left his drinking companions in his courtyard, lurched after me and caught hold of my wrist.

'Photo, photo.' His breath, laden with palmyra toddy, smelt like smoky urine. 'But, please, a little out of focus.'

At the woman's substantial mud house, with its palmyra-frond roof, her son brought out a wooden throne for me and an aluminium folding chair for Samelu. They asked me about English houses.

'Oh yes, we have roofs like this,' I said, 'not *thati* fronds but straw or reed that we call thatch.'

'For poor people,' said Samelu.

'Not any more,' I struggled. 'Thatch is for the rich.'

I did try to explain. The price of reed. Fire insurance. Luckily, their incredulity was cut short. The woman's son swung down from the topmost branches of a tamarind tree and presented me with pods like khaki velvet broad beans. I broke one open and sucked brown pulp off the seeds: it was stringy and gooey, sharp and fragrant, astringent and sweet. *Tamar-i-hind*, 'dates of India', used in cooking as we use lemon, and for polishing brass.

The paddy-fields were excruciatingly green, luminous in the dusk, as we approached Shiva's temple at neighbouring Lakshmanesvaram. I drove, Samelu navigated. There was nothing but a temple there, set in a green space. Shiva's seven-storey *gopuram* climbed – multi-layered stucco like sedimentary rock, exposed brickwork like scars – to rampant lions on its barrel roof. We entered through this towering gateway, but could not climb it because the dangerous stairs were blocked. In the womb-house a *Shivalingam* decked with fresh blossom sheltered beneath a brass cobra's hood. Durga Devi gazed from a second shrine with mother-of-pearl eyes. Small gods in saffron silk, *nandi* bulls, pale Ganesh and a dish of *kumkum* powder all looked lost in the twilight, abandoned to decay. Paint peeled from wooden horses riddled with worm.

'Six weeks,' said Samelu, 'big festival.'

It didn't seem possible. The priest's son showed up, just to check that good Christian Samelu had shown the Englishman all the sacred things. Samelu's postman was the boy's uncle.

'Government has taken it also, as monument,' he told me, 'but is salary paid? Not a rupee.'

Palm swifts flew up and down palmyra trunks and threaded between fronds, sniping at insects all the way.

'Much work to be done,' the boy said, 'idols to be found.'

Gold images of Shiva, worth *lakhs* of rupees, had been stolen from this place not long ago. But sure enough, within the month, they were recovered, held in police custody and bailed out in time for the big festival, Shivaratri, night of Shiva. The grey *gopuram* was the fairground's hub. After holy dip, folk traipsed across paddies from the river and queued to see the golden gods. Women had their heads shaved. White chickens with red wattles waited for the chop. Lakshmanesvaram was alive, or putting on a good act. Balloons rose between the palms.

But this time Samelu and I left a ruinous pagoda silhouetted against an apricot sky. A boy ran in front of the car. I shouted. He put his hands together and bowed in contrition. A toddler picked up a puppy and swung it round like a stuffed toy. I dropped Samelu in Muskepalem and drove in high style to Joshi and Santhosham's house. Colin had just got home from a general knowledge test in Rajahmundry. The bus had overturned on the canal bank, between new roadworks and oncoming lorries. He'd been crushed by school-mates and bruised down one side, but no one had been badly hurt. He'd seen six accidents that day. One driver was killed when his lorry careered into a shack shop.

Here, there were so many levels of vulnerability and danger, risk and enterprise, poverty and wealth. I thought of Samelu and his bricks, of Muskepalem and the flood waters. I looked at young Colin's surroundings, at the fridge, the television, the doll's house, the texts on the walls, the flush toilet. Which India was I visiting? Which India could I feel? Which India did I trust? Can any traveller enter into a full-blooded contract, for more than a few intense moments at a time, with what he's passing through? Over a meal, Joy told us about a village hostel funded by Germans. The sponsors paid it brief visits from time to time to see how their money was spent. They were feasted, but consumed only biscuits, peeled fruit and bottled drinks. A bathroom had been specially built for them with all the right porcelain, but they never bathed in it. They used wet-wipes.

19

THE BIRTH OF TIME

Tanuku

MY REVERIE was quietly interrupted by Joy, with a man and his two grandsons in tow. She whispered at me. She'd mislaid her voice several days before. She was sure I'd love to talk to grand-dad and take the boys up on to the hostel roof to see the view. I didn't want to talk to anyone, or move anywhere, but I could see she was determined to offload her visitors. I tried to smile, and bent my mouth like a strong man bends an iron bar.

'Namaskaram,' I said, getting to my feet.

I'd been sitting in the shade on Joy's balcony making notes in my journal. Earlier that morning I'd noticed that the *muggulu* at every threshold in town were *rathas*, chariots or god-cars. Not only were they the same, but each *muggu* was linked to the next by parallel chalk-dust trails along the street or round corners so that, in theory, the whole community was joined together. Had all the gods rolled into town and hitched their wagons?

'By this,' Sita Lakshmi told me later, 'all the evil in the town will be carried away.'

Some wagon-train. I'd been making notes about it, before being distracted by the view: not the river and the far bank, but girls sweeping the compound, washing, brushing hair, singing or languidly leaning to one another's mouthed intimacies.

The ideal female is 'slim, youthful, with fine teeth and lips red as bimba fruit, attenuated at the waist, with eyes like those of frightened doe and deep navel, slow of gait because of the weight of her hips and slightly bent forward due to the pull of her full breasts.' So wrote the fourth-century erotic poet Kalidasa, whose name means 'slave of Kali'. Many of these girls were upright slender beauties. Some were full-bodied enough to

grace a pagoda. A few might be alluringly bashful, but more
had bold eyes. But then Kali is no frightened doe, with her
four arms, her garland of human heads and her belly full of
blood.

My meditation on beauty, on sanctified chauvinism and the
conflicting expectations these hostel girls might choose to reject
or fulfil had been broken by Joy's hoarse introductions.

'Namaskaram, namaskaram,' said the man and his grandsons.

'This man is an expert,' Joy rasped in my ear, 'on
trees.'

'I am examining Missamma's coconuts,' he said and listed all
his qualifications, followed by those of his daughter the lawyer,
his daughter the doctor and his son the engineer.

This proud expert had a vermilion mark on his brow, white
stubble, white shirt and *lungi*. The boys, bright with pent-up
energy, fidgeted while he talked of poetry and photosynthesis.

'We must talk to plants,' he wobbled his head, 'for child is
father of the man, and genetics, journey of seed to seed, is indeed
very mystical, man being the multiest-cellular creature, in
whom the bounds of imagination lead us to higher horizons.'

'Let's go upstairs,' I suggested, and the boys lit up.

'They wish to see nature,' he said breathlessly. 'Ah, see,
all rivers meet and flow into the sea, souls into the super-
soul. So Krishna and Christ are one, the cowherd and the
shepherd.'

'Does Christ play the flute?' I asked, to remind him of all the
full-bodied milk-maids Krishna enchanted and ravished.

'Nine holes it has, the flute,' he explained. 'Ears, eyes, nose,
mouth, they are seven. And two below makes nine.'

It made sense. And just then a pair of house crows flew up
and transported the coconut expert to a still-higher realm.

'Ah! Skylarks!' he blurted.

That afternoon a young Muslim at the wheel of Joy's Ambassador drove me and the Brahmin auditor, Sita Lakshmi's father,
one and a half hours north to Tanuku where the National Cadet
Corps camp was reaching a climax. The auditor was pleased to

ride in a car. Better than his scooter, or a bus. He ordered the driver to stop at a roadside shrine. He made brisk *puja* for a safe journey and poked hibiscus into the radiator grill. We drove beneath the Calcutta—Madras road and made two right turns to get on to it and go west, driving on the left of course. It made sense. At the dogleg a truly gigantic image of Hanuman the heroic monkey-god towered in technicolour high above houses and shacks.

'It was biggest in India until this year,' said the auditor. 'Now there is bigger.'

After a few miles of good tarmac we turned into big bustling Tanuku. At the auditor's wife's sister's house down a cul-de-sac we washed hands and fed on rice-flour cakes, *sambar* and vegetable curries. Sita Lakshmi, self-possessed in jeans and T-shirt, soon came to conduct us to the Multipurpose School's parade ground.

At the gates the camp commandant, in crisp khaki bisected by a black cummerbund, welcomed us with a 'jolly good show' and extolled Sita to her father. She took me upstairs to a dormitory and washroom. A damp deputy commandant draped in a towel sallied in and retreated apologizing through double doors. Sita propped a small mirror by the window and made up eyes, cheeks and lips, and planted a jewelled *bottu* above the bridge of her nose.

Mascara made Sita's big eyes melt, lips red as bimba fruit framed fine teeth, hands quick as water wove a cascade of hair and finished off the heavy plait with gilt pom-poms that swung behind her knees. A tall glittering comb held an orange garland, with red, white, purple and blue flowers behind; chains of pearls and stones glimmered in her hair, a pendant rested on her forehead, ear-shaped ornaments were pinned through her lobes and hooked into her hair with, above, each side of the crown of her head, a shining sun and a crescent moon.

Sita withdrew next door to change into the tight blouse and sewn and pleated sari-trousers worn by Bharata Natyam dancers. She returned clad in scarlet and purple and gold, folds softly flowing or flaring like fans. She hung strings of coins, pearls, links around neck and waist. She massaged each hand through a dozen gold bangles, secured silver anklets and pinned a fine gold chain down the length of her plait. She had long since stopped explaining what she did. I might not have been there. She was deeply absorbed in the preparation of herself. She was complete.

She smiled at me then and we descended to the parade ground where the show had begun. Precisely on time. It didn't make sense. I aimed for Sita's beckoning father, but was hijacked by the C-in-C and ushered along a line of dignitaries in the front row, past West Godavari District's MP on his throne, to a seat between two Sikh majors. Their turbans might have been carved in ivory. I felt shabby, unexpectedly a guest of honour. Why? Because I was the one white man? Because I was Sita Lakshmi's friend? I should have felt at home on such an English occasion, but I've never much enjoyed garden fetes or gang shows.

Song followed dance followed recitation linked by a mistress of ceremonies in a white party frock who topped each act with her eloquence: 'We hope India will take note of your timely words' or 'That was excellent – and elegant' or 'You have transported us back to the willage'. During the turns the stage manager, an NCC officer, learned at last to switch the PA system on, moved mikes so that feed-back howled as agonizingly as possible, or wandered on to replace smoking mosquito coils beside the musicians. His devotion to duty upstaged everybody. When a boy made an entrance by knocking part of the scenery, a vertical table-tennis table, on to the head of the tabla player, he barely restrained himself from punching the offender in the mouth.

After unscripted dramas, break-dancers, dervishes, mimes and Michael Jackson impersonations, Sita Lakshmi came on. Then she stood still until the stage manager got the cassette player going. The Sikhs beside me grunted appreciatively as she began to dance. They revelled in the consonance of step, gesture and expression, in her disciplined fluidity, her sensuous precision. Dance steps combined with drum language, *jatis*, with the language of the hands, *hasta mudras*, and with the complexions of the gods. There are twenty-eight single-hand movements and twenty-four two-handed ones, each with its own colour, guru, caste and deity. Now she was Sita, ideal Hindu woman,

now flute-playing Krishna, incarnation of Vishnu, now Shiva
Nataraja, lord of the dance. As she moved, she moved us.
Abhinaya Darpana says:

> Whither the hand goes, let the glance follow,
> Whither the glances lead, there should the mind follow,
> Whither the mind goes, there the mood follows,
> Whither the mood goes, there is real feeling born.

Nataraja dances through ignorance into supreme harmony, and
as he dances a bell spins from his anklet; it rises high into the
air, falls, strikes the lord's shoulder and drops to the ground
making the sound, 'tha-thi-tham-num'. In that moment of eternity is conceived the first drum phrase, or *jati*, and in that phrase,
'tha-thi-tham-num', time and rhythm were born. And Shiva
struck his drum, and brought forth sound, *nada*, the first element
in the universe, that spawned all music, language and poetry.
Sacred OM resounded throughout the three worlds. The people
quaked with fear. So Shiva broke the drum in two, joined them
side by side, and their sweet sound drew the people close once
more.

The MP was introduced with details of his date of birth, his
education and honours. Standing on the stage in his fine lawn
panchi, he recalled the circumstances of his youth and the quali-
ties which had brought him thus far to represent the people.
Even his perspiration had the scent of wealth and power. A girl
almost presented a garland which was intercepted and passed
to the man who was there to present it. A squad of boys carried
a draped table, with a model boat on it, to the platform's foot.
One carried the plastic boat on stage and tried to present it,
before the proper presenter intervened. The platform party
tripped over themselves and their etiquette until at last the MP
received gifts from the right hands.

I was a sideshow to be garlanded and photographed too. As
soon as I decently could I escaped from the MP and the commandant and chit-chat over the buffet and drove away with Sita and
her father. Huge Hanuman reared into the night sky. A cowled
and cloaked driver slept on his creaking ox-cart; at the tiller of
his canal-boat a shrouded helmsman slid through darkness; a

gaunt woman squatted in the road, caught in the headlights of a mighty Tata truck. Once, perhaps, she was slow of gait and slightly bent because of the weight of her hips and her full breasts. Sita Lakshmi and the auditor slept. The Muslim drove brilliantly over pitted roads. Miles rewound miraculously. Back at Narsapur Joy greeted me like a mime, in a time before sound was born.

20

A GREEDY GODDESS

Hyderabad

Sita Lakshmi happened to be seeing a boyfriend off on the same train to Hyderabad as me, but in First Class. She slummed it in my compartment for a few minutes and wished me well. The whistle shrilled at 5.40, ten minutes late. The setting sun touched palm trunks and palm-leaf roofs with flame. Boys led buffalo through the dusk and tethered them in lean-to byres, birds roosted, women reached out from dark interiors and placed small lamps on mud verandahs. It was a landscape possessed by the languid rhythm of rituals that complete the day. I was thundering through it.

A man got to his knees, grovelled at my feet, grasped at my ankles, calves and thighs; it was the way to ask a blessing, but felt as if he was greedily assessing the meat on my bones. He wouldn't cease his importunate supplication. I couldn't suppress my revulsion. A student lifted him from me very gently and put twenty paise in his hand. I felt stupid and guilty.

The gentle student, a woman from engineering college, a man with an unusually grubby shirt and *lungi*, an elderly couple with a smelly cloth bundle that leaked cockroaches and I all agreed when it was time to sleep. We swung seat-backs up to make middle bunks, stepped out of our sandals and got to bed. I climbed on top with my rucksack, and my shawl for a shroud.

The journey was scheduled for twelve hours. We made up ten minutes in the small hours, halted between sleeping bodies on the platforms at Secunderabad, then for three miles skirted Husain Sagar, a seventeenth-century tank that looked almost romantic in the dawn, and pulled into Hyderabad Nampalli station at 5.30 precisely. The grubby man had changed into a

139

crumpled clean shirt and trousers. We were ready for the state capital.

Of course I wasn't ready for it: taxi drivers stuck to me like leeches in the concourse, auto-rickshaws scrambled outside, and husks of people huddled at little fires queued for scraps behind food stalls, washed slight bodies scrupulously over gutters, slept under filthy blankets on broken paving or shivered in squalid doorways. I couldn't cope with haggling and being given the run-around at that time of the morning so I summoned up the street-plan in my mind and made for my hotel on foot. A man dogged my footsteps. No sign. I doubted my memory. The world's more complex and dangerous than the map. I stopped. He stopped. I asked him. Graciously he pointed across the street.

This city was never part of British India. It was the Nizam of Hyderabad's capital. Potti Sriramulu's 1952 hunger strike and death in the cause of a Telugu state forced prime minister Nehru to re-draw India's provinces on a linguistic basis. Half the princely state and the Telugu-speaking part of the old Madras Presidency were tacked together to make Andhra Pradesh.

By phone I'd booked a room in the Annapurna Hotel. I wished I hadn't. It was filthy, sordid. Water ran unstoppably in the bathroom. I walked out into Abids, the commercial centre; the shops were tedious, the beggars merciless, the traffic odious and the air noxious. Dubious characters sidled in and out of liquor stores and discreetly gaudy prostitutes lurked in the shadows. I would enjoy it all enormously after a good night's sleep.

A good night was not to be had at the Annapurna. That first evening I checked out and into the Jaya International, which had a room free at the second attempt. It was comfortable, airy and clean. Cheaper too. My room was on a corridor with a balcony at either end; from one I could see high-rise, traffic-clogged hell through blue haze; from the other I looked down upon a delightful decaying mansion in white stucco; from my tiny balcony I studied the natural history of the side street.

Each morning a young mother and son swept the road, sorted valuable litter into bags and made small bonfires of rubbish at intervals. By the time Anand's *paan* stall opened the street was spotless. On Anand's right was a smithy where bits of cars or scooters or ox-carts were welded. On his left pineapples and local grapes were set out on handcarts. One day a man with a brush stood above the skyline all day on bamboo scaffolding and turned a forty-foot hoarding blue; by the second afternoon it was full of slogans and painted TVs. Next morning a man and his sons jangled past on four camels with bells at their knees; coolies stopped mixing cement to watch. They didn't stop for anything.

A two-mile walk down Jawaharlal Nehru Road and across the putrid Musi river took me to the old city. I'd seen the famous Charminar many times: on cigarette packets, on *navas'* sails at Narsapur, drawn in coloured powders across the breadth of a side-street in Palakol, but here it was in stone and stucco, four-square, its four-pointed arches crowned with lotus buds, its four one-hundred-and-eighty-foot minarets linked by pierced screens and decorated bands, ringed by graceful galleries, and topped by domes rising from lotus petals to finish in tall finials. This masterpiece of Qutb Shahi architecture was built in 1591, two years after Mohammad Quli Qutb Shah founded the city and thirteen years after a still-surviving bridge, the Purana Pul, first spanned the Musi.

'Nothing in this town seems so lovely as the outside of that building,' wrote De Thevenot in 1656, 'and nevertheless it is surrounded with ugly shops made of wood, and covered with straw, where they sell fruit . . .' Above those stalls, tangled skeins of telephone wires and electricity cables festooned the square; traffic swirled around the monument; a beggar woman on a low trolley paddled herself between rushing tyres. I stood on the Ayurvedic Hospital's raised forecourt and looked over the street to the twin domes and expansive courts of the Mecca Masjid, the biggest mosque in South India. A small boy stood at my side.

I threaded a way through surging traffic and watched a well-dressed man stop at the foot of one of the Charminar's minarets; he rang a bell, did quick obeisance before the idol, sipped holy water and dabbed vermilion on his brow; the tacked-on shrine was a Hindu cuckoo in an Islamic nest. The boy watched me watching. I retraced my steps to four monstrous arches called Char Kamaan between which the Qutb Shahi bodyguard used to be stationed. The western arch is known as Mitti-i-Sher, a corruption of Sihir-i-Batil or 'land of dreams'; it once led to palaces, now I passed through it with the boy still at my heels.

In the land of dreams a small boy dogs me, stares as I stare at herbalists' crammed with jars and wooden drawers and scents, pearl dealers' glistening trays, men rolling hot *lakkah* or lac for bracelets, silversmiths' and goldsmiths', brocade and antique sari dealers', and a man with a white beard and fez behind ranks of fluted phials of *aththaru* or attar of roses. At a stall I buy the mother and father of a *paan*: spices, quicklime, red katechu, areca nut, syrup and gold leaf wrapped up in a heart-shaped betel leaf. Oh, sweet narcosis, oh, nirvana! In the maze of alleys, cows sit at colourful carved Hindu doorways: vistas of cool court-yards and further archways. A woman eases her sari over her head and watches me pass with frank eyes. The boy has gone.

Outside a primary school a woman sold drinks off a handcart. Seeing me, she lifted her own child up into the arena of orange, red and green bottles. The child's hair was tied in a top-knot to show off her ear-rings; she grinned and raised braceleted arms above her head; her dress lifted and showed off her penis. What was I seeing? Why, in a culture that values males so far above females, are small boys dressed as girls? To avoid the evil eye. No self-respecting evil eye bothers with little girls.

A huge 'meals' in the Anwar café near the Charminar cost me eight rupees. An auto-rickshaw to the station cost about the same. Now I didn't want to leave, but I had to book a return train ticket in advance. I didn't dare join the much shorter queue at a window labelled 'Ladies, Senior Citizens, Orthopaedically Handicapped Persons and Freedom Fighters'. My next auto driver ignored my cry, 'Meter!' and wouldn't take less than fifteen rupees for a short trip to the foot of the twin hills that overlook Husain Sagar and the city. I put five rupees down on his seat, a fair fare, and walked off. Then I thought, What am I doing? Trying not to spend more than one pound sterling in a day? I'd spent about half that so far.

It was dusk. I climbed between shacks which were homes, and shacks which were shops selling religious necessities such as coconuts, and luxuries like plaster Ganeshes and pictures of Jesus. I imagined Catholics mounting this hill on their knees. At the top the poor shanty town gave way to hanging gardens and a glorious new temple, or *mandir*, of white marble built by

Birla, one of India's richest industrialists, to complement the Birla Observatory and Planetarium. The temple of Lord Venkateshwara is known as the Birla Mandir. I exchanged my sandals for a token. The temple bell clanged as each devotee rang it, but behind its irregular chime was the sound of women's voices, the drone of a *sruti*-box and the intricate rhythms of *tabla*.

I'd already seen the day's panoramic views from the temple's terraces. Now lights were reflected in the ancient reservoir below. Workers erecting a golden statue of the Buddha in Husain Sagar had recently gone down with it and drowned. A row was in progress over a police ban on an annual procession to bathe huge idols of Ganesh there. Hindu feelings were hurt, and sculptors and idolmakers outraged. A scion of the Nizam of Hyderabad was battling with Andhra's Chief Minister over palace lands and vast tax debts. There was continuing scandal over the quality of rice supplied to subsidized ration shops. That very day in the prosperous Banjara Hills a young woman had doused herself with kerosene and burned for shame at being raped by her landlord's son. That afternoon in Abids, close to the Jaya International, a man had been stabbed to death and robbed of thirty thousand rupees.

Night hid the landmarks, the corruption, the pain, the blood. Marble was sun-warm underfoot, chill where it had been in shade. Men and women held hands; people ascended and descended stairs from level to level, pavilion to sanctum, past walls rich with reliefs; flying floodlit fruit bats turned black and white against marble and sky; the women sang Lalitha Subramanyan's devotional music, enshrined in all the exquisite beauty of a rich man's temple poised on an ant-heap above a cesspool. When the music stopped I walked downhill and went for a good dinner in the Broadway Restaurant. It cost me a modest one hundred and thirty-eight rupees. On the way back to bed, in shaking off persistent beggars, I almost garrotted myself on a low-slung power cable.

Sunday was Republic Day. At Srinagar, in disputed Kashmir, Dr Joshi and a posse from the BJP *ekta yatra*, or so-called 'unity pilgrimage', were permitted to raise the national tricolour, but not their vermilion banner, as militants and military exchanged fire. In New Delhi, live on TV, floats and tableaux, folk dancers and shock troops, pantomime ships and helicopters, tanks and wind-surfers, missiles and fantasies followed each other as though Sandhurst was in procession through the *Mahabharata*.

On Secunderabad Parade Ground the Governor of Andhra Pradesh reviewed his forces. Novel tableaux embellished with portraits of the Chief Minister glorified state programmes for scheduled castes, tribals and women. The Sericulture Department won first prize for a giant silkworm. The South Central Railway celebrated its Silver Jubilee with a life-size model of the Nizam's saloon pulled by a steam engine whose stack puffed real acrid smoke.

The Governor called for unity in society. He mourned the year's two hundred and sixty-five assassinations and victims of caste war.

'Why, in the land of Buddha and Gandhi, has money and muscle power come to acquire a vital say?' he asked, quivering. 'Why is reason in flight against forces of unreason?'

'You should know,' some muttered. His words, at least, were an attack on petty interests, big money, status and force.

'Violence is a greedy goddess which consumes all whom it touches. Violence will make our own future an awful nightmare.'

'Beyond the land of dreams, Governor,' I thought to myself, 'the future's already here.'

That afternoon I meditated upon tigers, and wept. Nehru Zoological Park, on the Bangalore road out of Hyderabad, is the largest in India. At one rupee a ticket it was full of Republic Day crowds. Keepers and watchmen threatened a wildcat strike and were not much in evidence. Visitors stepped across the barrier above the rhino's pit, threw stones and whipped it with sticks. At snakes' dens they dribbled vermilion and saffron powders, and reverently dropped coins on to the hood of a patient cobra.

21

THE OLD KINGDOM

Golconda

QULI QUTB SHAH was a Turkoman adventurer from Persia who rose to be a governor in the service of the Bahmani kingdom on the Deccan plateau. That dynasty's disintegration into five sultanates let him rise higher. As sultan of a new Shi'a kingdom he began in 1512 to build his capital on the site of an ancient Kakatiya fortress: a granite outcrop standing four hundred feet above the plain. It was known as 'shepherd's hill'. *Golla* means 'shepherd', *konda* means 'hill'. Both capital and kingdom took the name Golconda.

It is a name resonant of exotic riches. Golconda became a synonym for a mine of opulence. Gold and silver, horses and spices, silks and wines flowed in to pay for Kunasamudram steel, diamonds, painted cloths, gold brocades and exquisite muslins. 'Golconda' fired the imagination of Scheherazade, fabled teller of *The Thousand and One Nights*, and still glitters like the great stones once dug in the kingdom and cut in the city. All the diamonds known in ancient times came from India; the mines were dubbed 'Golcondas'; some of the richest were found in the south of the kingdom near the Krishna river. Golconda's wealth dazzled travellers such as the Frenchmen Tavernier and de Thevenot and seduced the Mogul emperors Akbar, Shah Jahan and Aurangzeb.

I took a five-mile bus ride from Hyderabad to Golconda. The bus swung in through the Fateh Darwaza, the mighty gate by which Aurangzeb's conquering army was treacherously admitted in 1687. It is one of eight gates in an outer wall fifty to sixty feet high, six to seven miles around, and punctuated by eighty-seven semicircular bastions. All is built of massive granite blocks and topped with battlements like solid gothic arches framed by sky. My guide Michael arrived on his Enfield Bullet. His mother had brought him up within this fortress city and now he worked out of Hyderabad for the charity, World Vision. A childhood in a place like this would equip anyone with a sense of perspective.

Aurangzeb is said to have returned to Delhi laden down with the treasures of Golconda, including the 'mountain of light' or Koh-i-noor diamond which became an eye in his peacock throne. Eventually, after adventures that only such gems have, it was cut down almost by half, at Empress Victoria's command, to give it more sparkle, and installed in the British crown jewels. It always brings ill luck, they say. Now the British have lost an empire, Golconda is a ruin and Kohinoor is a brand of condom.

'See sharp spikes,' said Michael, 'to prevent elephants.'

We were not talking birth control, we were standing within the cordon wall that protects the fort's one entrance, the Bala Hissar gate, admiring teakwood doors studded with iron prongs vicious enough to stop any beast used as a battering ram. Above a finely wrought arch were machicolations from which molten lead or stones or boiling oil could be emptied upon invaders' heads. Inside the grand portico Michael stopped and clapped three times.

'Look,' he said, pointing at the hilltop. 'Listen.'

On the summit, above layer upon layer of palatial ruins, huge cut stones butted on to natural granite outcrops. A man looked over a parapet outside the durbar hall and briskly brought his hands together. Only after he'd dropped them to his side and turned away did we hear, clap-clap-clap, loud and clear.

'If you clap with one hand, what sound will come?' Michael asked, quoting an old Telugu proverb. 'But two hands are as good as telephone, and from here messengers shout direct to the throne.'

We passed between the barracks and the armoury, leaving the camel stable on the left, and on the right the small aloof mosque of Taramati, favourite concubine of Abdullah Qutb Shah. Here was the harem, the king's palace, the queens' palace, and here the tank where the sultan's women were expected to drown rather than surrender to conquest. I stood in a great courtyard surrounded by desolation and intricate detail, by ruin and precise proportion. I felt at home here, as one feels at home in a fresh but familiar dream. Archways were echoed by windows, and windows by ranks of niches. Steps led to platforms, doorways to domes, passages to vaulted chambers, and majestic arcades to pungent darkness filled with the shimmering gossip of a thousand bats.

Sunlight threw fine masonry and cut plaster into relief, and picked out relict encaustic tile and mother-of-pearl. But in the dark I could dress the stones and see the Turkish baths, dressing rooms tiled with mirrors, silk-hung bedrooms, carpeted halls and lamplit chambers glimmering with enamels and pearls, that opened on to fragrant gardens set around fountains.

Persian wheels raised water from canal to tank and from tank to tank to reservoir; as we climbed stone stairs between heaped rocks and masonry Michael waved at remains of clay pipes that let it down again to feed taps, fountains, baths and flush latrines. By the time we got to the top I was parched. No one sold drinks in the Baradari, or general assembly. Its first-floor durbar hall was dry. Beneath it Michael showed me the shadowy entrance of a secret underground passage. It was blocked with rubble.

'It leads', he said, 'to palace at the heart of Hyderabad.'

From the throne on the high terrace I surveyed Hyderabad and Secunderabad, domed tombs and hills, the rocky landscape of the Deccan, waterless but for great sixteenth- and seventeenth-century Sagars or tanks built to supply the old and new cities. Michael pointed to the small house within the walls where he grew up.

'It is too hard to find good men in India,' he said. 'Our skin is dark, so are our hearts. Money and women are currency of temptation. I ask myself, have I really escaped this taint?'

He held my hand and looked me in the eye.

'It's hard to find good men anywhere,' I said.

He explained how women are exploited by men and suppressed by other women, how mothers-in-law have great power. He talked of the great waste of women's potential.

'Women, mentally, are often so much better than men. My own wife, she can do everything, she goes out to buy vegetables and all herself. Is unheard of. She calls me by my name, Michael. A Hindu has one wife. A Muslim has four and can divorce easily.

147

He pays no attention to birth control. Hindus do. My wife is sterilized after two children and gets increment on her salary.'

He let go of my hand and sighed in the direction of the houses of the rich on the Banjara Hills.

'Even with good salary I cannot afford car. A person may eventually buy car for show, but not use it much. He may buy medical or legal qualifications. These command high dowry. If he cannot buy he may study, but for status, for rich wife, not for vocation. To raise three thousand rupees for wedding, a man may sell his son into bond to landlord for two years. This is how we are.'

Beneath the parapet a few gigantic granite boulders balanced one upon another. This weatherworn outcrop had been appropriated as temple of the goddess Mahankali or Durga Devi; in its shelter a pillared *mandapam* stood before a small sanctum. The sacred syllable OM was blazoned on raw rock above a dwarf *shikhara* tower flying red flags. Below, the rock face was whitewashed, ground for polychrome paintings of many-armed Durga on a tiger, Durga on a lion defeating the demon, Kali trampling Shiva, a caparisoned elephant, the sun and crescent moon and, in cruder line-drawing, a vulgar deity flourishing *nagas*, sacred snakes, or whips.

While Islam might move mountains for the sake of luxury or austerity or power, Hinduism so easily daubed native rocks with lurid gods. The goddess's temple was relatively new, it seemed temporary; in spirit it was the oldest thing in all Golconda.

We climbed down from the temple to the mosque of Ibrahim Qutb Shah. Twin minarets looked down upon a store for grain or gun-powder, depending on who you believe, and a small gaol where everyone agrees Ramdas, a government official, was confined for siphoning off revenue to renovate a temple to Rama in his native town of Bhadrachalam on the Godavari river. It was as dark and dank as a gaol should be, but just inside the door a gypsy woman in a pink sari strummed a lime-green *veena*, or simple sitar, shook bells and sung devotional songs. I went into the dark to see the idols of Rama, Hanuman and Lakshman that Ramdas carved in the gaol wall. Kumkum and turmeric thickly anointed them and, with the music, wound a scented garland about me there.

'In this tank crocodiles wait for the enemy,' said Michael.

Strange horsemen might have been deceived by the twisting ascent and plunged into the reservoir he indicated; it was deep. So was Badi Baoli, the big well at the bottom of the steps, where water once cascaded over stones beside a balcony; shahs and ranis strolled here and listened to water music, or relaxed upon swings in Nagina Bagh, the garden of late Mogul layout where the hero Abdul Razzack Lari is said, anachronistically, to have engaged Aurangzeb himself in mortal combat. The mortuary baths are conveniently sited, with antique plumbing and cisterns for hot and cold, by the fort gate and the road to the tombs.

Michael and I ate second-rate 'meals' in 'Picnic Spot' just outside the Bala Hissar gate. He guzzled water, but I topped up with much too much Citra and Limca which effervesced alarmingly in guts full of clotted rice and cold curry as we bounced along on his Enfield Bullet, winding between walls carved with mythical beasts towards the Banjara gate and the royal necropolis.

A film crew was at work there, staging yet another punch-up of melodramatic proportions. As usual the hero was the plump one with the smarmy moustache who wanted the light from the giant reflectors on his best profile.

'Where do you come from?' asked the assistant director.

'England.'

'You were already here for two hundred years.'

'Not me. Only a hundred and fifty.'

'I joke,' he said, thinking I'd missed the point.

Tombs were his backdrop. They were set, like Taj Mahals, around mortuary baths in flint gardens tended by coolie women who wanted rupees for decorating the foreground of my photos. Each onion dome grew up from a calyx of lotus petals upon a square base surrounded by a one- or two-storey gallery of pointed arches decorated with small domed minarets. On each tomb stern signs said, 'Dwelling in tombs is strictly prohibited.'

It was not an unattractive prospect, and must have been even more appealing in the days before Aurangzeb desecrated them. In 1645 Tavernier describes the daily dole of bread and pilau to the poor here, and says, 'If you would see anything that is fayre you must go to view these tombs upon a festival day for then from morning to night they are hung with rich tapestry.'

I explored the tomb of Mohammad Quli who was enthroned in 1580, aged fifteen. He was a poet and patron of the Telugu language. He laid out Hyderabad city on the east bank of the Musi in 1589 and gave it the Charminar and its other seminal buildings. He erected the first tomb of gigantic proportions for himself here, with a double terrace, octagonal columns and domed minarets linked by arched and crenellated parapets. High on the dome three tiny figures, perched on a frail platform hung from ropes between the north pole and the equator, leant outwards wielding paintbrushes. A third of the globe was mushroom coloured.

Inside, I saw the Persian inscription on Mohammad Quli's memorial stone of black basalt. I descended into the dark to find the grave where he was laid in 1612. It was a shadowy forest of pillars. A group of women chattered nervously as they approached the centre. We reached it together. Suddenly I must have loomed, tall and wan, out of the darkness in front of them. As one they shrieked and ran, feet padding and saris rustling, for the light. At my back Michael was bursting with laughter.

'These are village women,' he said, 'and you, you are the ghost of the Sultan Mohammad Quli Qutb Shah.'

In sunlight, the women and I had a good laugh. Then I rode pillion to a wide waste of dust where buses stopped between shops and building sites. I waved Michael farewell and boarded a double-decker, number sixty-five. It had terminal mechanical failure. With holy cows I waited an hour by a tiny watch repairer's shack, 'New Yark – Sales and Service', and a bus shelter in which a body lay, bundled in stained rags and thick with flies. It stirred at last, eased itself with painful slowness, lifted a matted head of hair and rolled a thin yellow cigarette.

POLITICS AND HONEY

Narsapur

AFTER HYDERABAD, Narsapur felt very much like home. I realized how comfortable it had become. Even the trinity on their plinths – Rajiv, the Rowdy and the Philanthropist – seemed to have arrived at some sort of understanding. By the gate to the temple in which the Rowdy had been cut down, a white-haired saffron-clad *sadhu* stretched out his hands to me; he had big beseeching eyes which hardened like those of a spurned woman when I passed him by. Of the two of us, he was the stranger here.

Tinsmiths, who made crazy percussion outside their shack, waved and grinned. The wild-haired mender of *chappals* or sandals greeted me with 'Good morning' as usual, though it was afternoon and his *namaskaram* was one-handed because he was speeding off on his bicycle. The man in the transparent polythene loincloth was still sitting at the roadside, plucking every last hair out of his scalp; it was all he did and he wasn't bald yet.

Across the canal, I strolled between the basket-makers' wares and houses, all woven biscuit and gold. Boat builders gnawed with adzes at skeletal timbers. *Dhobi*-wallahs, several with elephantiasis, worked at laundry beside a big rectangular tank in which all the rippling colours on the washing-lines were reflected. Beside the tank was the beef butcher's wooden hut: offal in heaps and hanging carcasses with tails that labelled them cow or buffalo. Back on the bazaar side of the footbridge was a shack where plucked chickens the colour of tallow, leaking vivid lites and crowned with crumpled combs, hung up before a smirking salesman in revealing juxtaposition with the poster pinned at his back, pale Samantha Fox in all her grotesque adipose glory.

Beyond the advertisement for 'Go Bonkers' ice cream was the State Bank of India where I sweated for my money under slow fans. Opposite that, a new three-storey building was going up. One of the coolies wore a canary-yellow sari; its top end was tucked in at the waist so that her breasts stood beneath taut cloth; the rest was tugged up between long legs. She carried a basket of cement on her exquisite head. No doubt a *harijan*, she embodied nobility, poise, eroticism. She'd have taken Europe's catwalks, or the cover of *Vogue*, by storm.

I had almost forgotten to notice these everyday sights. At Vishnu's temple, set within ochre-and-white-striped walls beyond a tank studded with lotus blossoms, I saw something more unusual. I'd thought it a decrepit, poor-looking place; its *shikharas* were shrouded by palm fronds hung from bamboo scaffolding. In fact, it was an old rich temple, related to the famous pilgrimage site of Tirupati in southern Andhra Pradesh, and it was being restored to glory. A man crouched in palmyra shade, high up on poles lashed together with cord. He was moulding the goddess Lakshmi's voluptuous torso in cement. Her head was a brick.

Fine-featured images of gods and demons stood against white stucco, pale at the base, dark at the artist's feet where the cement was fresh; for now, it was a monochrome pantheon. Above his head the shelves of stucco, like a weathered rock-stack's sedimentary layers, were bare. On his laborious climb through time and up the mountain the sculptor was populating the worlds. It took time to see this, to attune myself to the subtlety of his work. He smiled down at me. Through his black-rimmed glasses I observed the lively but contented eyes of a craftsman able to see without pain, to see and to create from within his own darkness and light, creatures monstrous and serene.

'There are all too few men with this skill,' said a man at my side. 'He is from village near Palakol. He and his team work seven months on this project.'

My informant introduced himself as a history teacher at the college. Two grandchildren romped at his feet under the anxious kohl-black eye of a very young servant girl. Her master was on the temple committee and lived in a house in one of the rows that flanked the temple tank. Before he took me home for tiffin, we walked and talked about the airy temple courtyard.

'This tall one,' he pointed to the usual copper temple mast at whose top bells hung from three cross-members, 'this is called *Dhwajasthambham*; it stands between temple main gate and sanctum; *dhwaja* says temple is here, *sthambham* means pillar.'

I followed his white-clad figure from shrine to shrine around the cloister. We crossed paving-stones engraved with donors' names. He beckoned me towards the *vimana* or sanctum and showed me a screened peep-hole in its outer wall. I peered deep within where glittering Vishnu and his consorts stood.

'These idols were brought here from Sriperumbudur, where Rajiv Gandhi was assassinated. They must not be moved one inch.'

He took me in, across a floor of black tiles, through white pointed arches, to the marble womb-house. The priest who greeted us carried a *thali* or plate of leaves and coins. He lit camphor and wafted the smoke, like pungent mist, towards idols of worked silver and gems. Between goddesses Sita and Lakshmi, Lord Vishnu held in one of his four hands the lotus that is the goal of perfection; in another, the conch whose unearthly note calls folk towards that goal; in the third, the mace that disciplines their passions; in the last, the *chakra* or discus that annihilates sensual man. Vishnu's body was gorgeously tooled silver; his face was of deep blue signifying infinity; his precious crown stood for unquestioned sovereignty over the world of plurality.

The priest, in saffron *lungi* and sacred three-strand thread, had the humble devotee's *nama* on his brow, a white V painted in with vermilion. But many diamonds framed Vishnu's third eye, a magnificent ruby. Suddenly I wondered if the Bowdens saw these stones. I doubted it. Joy never had, I knew that.

'A century ago,' said the teacher, 'this ruby cost two thousand rupees.'

'Brahmins and Kapus used to be the wealthy ones,' he said over tiffin. 'Today, Khammas and Reddis are the big farmers and landlords. People like me' – meaning Brahmins – 'have sold our land and bought properties which we can rent without trouble; we cannot deal with *ryots*, I mean peasants, nowadays.'

I thought of the saying, 'The famine came to the village the same year as the landlord.' And again, 'Property is the strong man's, not the poor Brahmin's.'

I talked politics later that day with the history teacher's colleague, another Brahmin. He rented the house where he lived. A retired professor of politics, he showed me a photo of his eldest son with 'leading British socialists' Neil and Glenys Kinnock. He wore a white *khurta* and *panchi* with an embroidered burgundy shawl which he adjusted as he talked. The reception room was full of mosquitoes and the hysterical fizz of the radio. The professor's middle son, a big man with wasted legs, squatted on a hard bed with a zimmer frame beside it, listening to India's one-day cricket victory over the West Indies.

He turned it off in jubilation. If he assumed every Englishman to be a walking Wisden, I was a severe disappointment to him. Failing cricket, he asked about Ireland and the IRA, about Wales and *Plaid Cymru*. He and his father were sympathetic, but the older man warned me against too much tolerance in one direction.

'Socialists in England are being silly about Islam.'

'But what about the BJP here?' I asked, thinking, who better to give me an enlightening opinion on the fanatical Hindu party that aims to pull down mosques and build temples on their ruins than a liberal Brahmin professor of politics?

My mind flew back to a teacher who lived in terror of hardline Hinduism. She and her husband were Christians, sure that her school and all his projects for the poor were as good as dead if the BJP got into power. While he was abroad the Rashtriya Swayamsevak Sangh, she said, had planted an undercover agent as her night watchman and sent a false telegram in her husband's name in order to get her to open the door. That story of the RSS kidnap attempt had moved me. Terror, loss of voice, tears caught her unawares once more. She despaired of corruption, of women still torched for dowry debt, of *sati* or widow-burning, and of the ritual temple sacrifice of young boys. Most of all she wept for the poor who must live in a society warped by the ultra-Hindu BJP and the secretive RSS, which, in M. J. Akbar's words, is 'not so much an organization as a state of mind . . . in its heart it is still taking revenge against Aurangzeb, the Mogul Emperor.'

'In India,' she had said, 'the common man cannot live.'

The professor, I hoped, might cast cool light on the state of mind she feared. The Bharatiya Janata Party's leader had made his ambition plain: 'I would like the words Hindu, Bharatiya and Indian to be synonymous.' His opponents were united in hatred of BJP tactics. Devi Lal caricatured them as crooked political traders: 'First they adulterate, then take the weight, set a rate and finally calculate.' V. P. Singh put widespread fears into words: 'The BJP is spreading religious venom like a drop of lemon juice that spoils the whole milk.'

'You see,' said the professor, lifting his glass of tea, 'we are teetotal and vegetarian. We live simply, in heartfelt opposition to materialism and the consumer society that threatens India.' He rose and beckoned, 'Please come.'

His son stayed where he was, but stared passionately after us. In the inner room his mother was doing *puja* before pictures of the sage Sai Baba, or rather, both of them: the white-bearded ascetic Sai Baba Shirdi who died in 1920, and the Afro-haired plump Sai Baba Puttaparthi who was born, or reborn, in 1926.

'I have spoken with Sai Baba on three occasions,' said the professor of politics. 'Now we await next incarnation.'

His wife turned from the domestic shrine and greeted me.

'Only today there is miracle,' she said.

'Yes,' said the professor, 'this morning this appeared.'

He pointed at something like a bird dropping oozing down the glass of Sai Baba's picture.

'It is honey and ash,' he enthused, 'and has fallen in five strands. This locket also, it has appeared on the tray.'

He opened both sides of the newly manifested silver locket to reveal back-to-back Sai Babas. He snapped it shut, replaced it beside joss sticks on the *thali* and drew me into the garden.

'We are a polytheistic culture,' he said. 'Hinduism has many gods like the Greeks. Like the Greeks we value richness of life and toleration. Appeasement of fanatics is madness.'

Away from in-house mosquitoes and the stench of incense and honey it was calm and fresh. Sacred *tulsi* or basil grew on an altar. Hibiscus bushes and damp vegetable beds, watered from an old well, scented the evening.

'Narrow fanaticism destroys. Moguls tried to destroy our culture. Muslims still do. We support the BJP, though all media and Congress paint it as extreme. The BJP *ekta yatra* is unity pilgrimage and many Muslims have joined. Unity in diversity is strength. All rivers flow into one ocean. This we always say in morning prayers. Our great sage Sri Ramakrishna was devotee of goddess Kali, but he saw visions of Christ and Mohammed also.'

Ramakrishna was born the year the Bowdens reached India and died in 1886, a year after riots at Ayodhya. Muslims in their fortified mosque fought off Hindus who wanted to build a temple there. It was, they claimed, the birthplace of Rama, king of Ayodhya and seventh incarnation of Vishnu, whose wife Sita had been kidnapped by the demon king of Lanka while her lord was in forest exile. As I talked to the professor of politics in his quiet garden, the BJP, wielding saffron banners and tridents, were still trying to take Rama home after more than a century.

At dusk the man I'd seen that morning was still plucking hair out of his head beside a temple decked with fairy lights and full of Indo-jazz from a glittering turbanned band. A bent woman at the temple gate grasped my sleeve and begged for alms. On the river, fishermen leant over their gunwales to leave oil lights floating near the far bank before sculling home. Joy didn't know why.

Later demonic drumming throbbed in the air, and paused. Santhosham and Shanth supposed it was some form of exorcism. We rushed down to Holland Wharf. Two boys were playing draughts there by candlelight. A man and his heavily pregnant wife beat little drums and ordered their infant son to dance for us. He cried and I paid them to stop. It was pathetic, not demonic.

Then wild drumming started again. Its crazed pulse plucked at inner and outer darkness. But it was not the dangerous Hindu ritual that Santhosham had expected. It came from next door to the hostel, from the old Dutch House where the Bowdens and Beers first lived. Mrs Beer eventually bought it and its

compound of almost three acres for a trifling forty rupees, worth
£4 in 1861. I'd stood beneath the high tiled roof that offered
shelter to holy fools, and been shown around the complex by
the charismatic Christians who now inhabited it. That had been
in daylight. In darkness they pounded out praise, intoxicated by
the Holy Spirit. In darkness I feared every kind of fanaticism.

What worlds one could walk through in this small town. The
teacher of history and the professor of politics had taught me
much. I had seen honey and ash. By now I knew without telling
that the symbols were more important than the sticky mess. A
grandmother might dip her finger in honey and write OM with
it on the tongue of the new-born child. That was the beginning,
'I am.' Ash was the last word. In between was the dance. But
what kind of dance? The sublime dance of self-realization. The
frenzied dance of delusion. A child's desperate dance for *paise*.

The symbols were all. They made sense of it all. By them the
Brahmin and the *chappal*-mender were held in their places. By
them mere circumstance was annihilated, as matter is refined
to ash. By their light we were illuminated, and blinded. There
and then I decided that, however sour the real world was, I
preferred to take my politics without honey.

BITS OF BUSINESS

Madras Presidency

THE TAJ MAHAL is closed and boarded up. Has been for years. The Taj Mahal restaurant in Barnstaple, that is. Across the road, at the end of Butchers Row, jewellery glints behind the high arched windows of premises where for half a century Bowden's Indian Balm Co. manufactured and marketed their celebrated ointment.

One day in India William Bowden found a fakir prostrated near his compound gate. He was almost naked, with hollow cheeks and a husky voice. Continuous retching and rice-water diarrhoea confirmed first impressions: he was dying of cholera. His skin was blue, his pulse imperceptible. William brought him into the compound and settled him into a grass hut. There he nursed the man with all his skill, dosed him with what remedies he had, kept him clean and slowly, gently rehydrated him.

Cholera was an old enemy. Soon after William first reached Narsapur, famine and the Pushkaram festival were followed by an epidemic. Fevers and liver diseases were rampant too. Local doctors would not attend outcasts or defiled castes such as Christians. William was forced by circumstance to repair his ignorance of medicine which 'has pressed very much upon my mind, as well as taxed my time, and I have had some anxiety from not having on hand the proper medicines indicated by the symptoms.'

In 1843 Elizabeth gave birth to her fourth boy, Frederick Henry, in the care of the doctor at Machilipatnam. A fortnight later, William felt impelled to return home to Palakol, although smallpox was raging there. He shut up Elizabeth's palanquin so that she should not see the disease's ravages. They found their home surrounded by hundreds, and people in the compound making offerings to two stones, gods who would protect them. William remonstrated, broke the stones to pieces in full view and buried them. 'Your baby, and all your sons,' the holy men prophesied, 'will die of this sickness.' But the goddess's anger did not touch them, theirs the only house in town to be passed by.

For us, remoteness spells vulnerability. William's concern was practical: 'We are more than three hundred miles from a druggist's shop, our nearest being Madras, and at that place medicines are highly priced and post charges are also high.' He taught himself homeopathy and, during bad outbreaks, travelled the district to tend the sick and dying. 'It is absolutely useless to prescribe for them,' he wrote, 'unless you nurse them also.'

How did the conditions compare with home? When the Bowdens left Barnstaple, the year before Victoria came to the throne, the town was proud of herself. She had an idyllic walk with 'lofty and umbragous trees, the river rippling round it, sometimes to the very edge'. She had an infirmary, a recent dispensary, and brand-new Salem Almshouses bearing the motto, 'He who gives to the poor lends to the Lord.' The Lord, presumably, repaid with interest. As a source of her wealth, and object of a little of it, the poor were always with her.

Item: Poverty, more pigs than people in some Barnstaple streets, eighty-one licensed houses and tiddly-wink shops, violence, electoral corruption, open sewers, polluted drinking water and a recurring susceptibility to outbreaks of cholera.

How exactly William treated the fakir, and for how long, I don't know. He may have prescribed camphor or prussic acid, and perhaps carbo vegetabilis or white hellebore, all of which in homeopathic doses counteract the extreme collapse and sluggish heart characteristic of Asiatic cholera. This was long before the pandemic of 1871 spread from India to Europe via Egypt and provided the German bacteriologist Robert Koch with raw faecal material from which he cultured and isolated the small, slightly curved bacillus now known as *Vibrio cholerae*.

The fakir recovered from his near-cadaverous state, regained sound heart function, colour and warmth. As he walked from the compound he overflowed with words of thanks.

'Sahib,' he said, 'I am wanting in a most suitable manner to repay you for all your very great kindnesses to me.' He pushed a dirty sheet of paper into his healer's hand. 'Sahib, there is a fortune in this for you, really.'

William thanked him, put it into his desk and forgot about it. Months later, when tidying up, he examined the paper for the first time and, seeing that it was a prescription in Sanskrit, had it made up. It might, conceivably, be efficacious.

In 1851, after fifteen years in India, they needed a fortune — and £500 was a fortune to them — to pay for Elizabeth's passage to England with five sons, aged two to fourteen. William would wait another six years for his first furlough, but it was time to think about English schooling and apprenticeships for the boys. Though Bowden finances were at rock-bottom, Elizabeth began to gather clothes for the voyage's torrid heat and Atlantic cold.

A few gifts arrived, but the total seemed paltry until news came from Bengal that, because of some scandal on the outward voyage, one of the best homeward-bound ships was being boycotted. A passage was theirs for a nominal fare and, what's more, the ship would put in at Coringa especially to save them the long journey to Calcutta or Madras. It was like loaves and fishes.

At Cape Town mother and boys were to stay aboard; all other passengers were booked into costly hotels. But a state barge met the ship with a letter to Mrs Bowden from the Governor offering hospitality at Government House. The Governor, it turned out, was the brother of an army officer in India who admired the Godavari missionaries. His barge rushed them ashore to beat a storm which kept everyone else marooned aboard.

Storms at Plymouth prevented anyone landing. But, after six months at sea, Elizabeth was in a hurry. The captain dared not allow his men to attempt a landing by boat. Elizabeth insisted.

'If you and your sons *must* go ashore in such a sea, Mrs Bowden,' the captain said, 'I must take you myself.'

He landed the family safely. Without delay she took a bumpy stage coach seventy miles to Barnstaple and hurriedly settled into the small terraced house Robert Chapman had rented for them there. She gave birth the next day. Welcome, Louis Arthur.

Item: some months before Arthur's birth there were seventy-two cases and twenty-four deaths from cholera in Barnstaple.

Chapman had engaged a young woman, Matilda Mary Gilbert, as mother's help. Fourteen-year-old William fell in love with Mary at once and, by the time he and his mother and little Arthur embarked upon the *Afghan* for Madras in 1854, they were betrothed. Mary and four Bowden boys – George, Fred, Edwin and Frank – remained in England for the next six years.

Item: 1857–58, the Rebellion or so-called Indian Mutiny.

Item: 1 November 1858, Proclamation at Narsapur of Queen Victoria's assumption of the Government of her Indian Dominions.

Mary and William were married at Narsapur in 1860. He was twenty-three, she thirty-four. When William the man welcomed her home to his farm colony, was she still the Mary that boy William had fallen for? Three years later their only child, Bessie, was born. Mary readily took to dispensing and kept up the tradition of triumphant diagnosis and cure for which Bowdens were renowned.

Item: The fakir's recipe – which included oils of cajuput, chaulmoogra, origanum and terebinth, unguent of althae, castor oil and camphor – proved to be profoundly efficacious.

George Bowden went to work for the Government Electric Telegraph Department. By 1864 he was 3rd Inspector, Bangalore, and the next year, Inspector, 5th Division, Calicut to Cochin.

At the same time William junior left the farm colony and the mission for employment with Line & Co., Black Town, Madras, as an insurance agent. Soon he progressed to become the British India Steam Navigation Co.'s agent in Cocanada, now Kakinada.

Frederick Henry joined him there in about 1867 to establish Messrs Bowden Brothers & Co., insurance brokers. Then he moved to Madras and set up F. H. Bowden & Co., agents for the Scottish Fire Insurance Co., with Louis Arthur as his assistant.

Item: 26 February 1869, Elizabeth Beer died.

Item: 2 October 1869, Mahatma Gandhi was born.

Item: 17 November 1869, the Suez Canal was opened.

The following year Edwin, my great-grandfather, described as 'Commission Agent resident at Barnstaple', married Martha

Oatway of Bideford, five years his senior, in Worcester register office with his father as a witness. With Martha he returned to Madras and then Kakinada to be partner in Bowden Brothers, working until 1874 with his younger brother Frank, who was an agent, merchant, and freight and produce broker until his death.

Item: 26 January 1876, William Bowden senior died.

Three months later Edwin, who was by now manager of the Perseverance Ice Co., Calcutta, shrugged off business ambition and took on his father's mantle for the next forty-eight years.

Meanwhile, F. Henry set up Henry's Thilum Works in Madras. Thilum was a remarkable liniment: 'As an emollient, anodyne, and detergent application, it is one of surpassing virtue,' testified W. J. VanSomeren, MD, Surgeon-General, Madras (Retired), in July 1881. 'In Rheumatic affections, its efficacy, when well rubbed in, cannot be questioned.' It so happened that Van-Someren was Frank Bowden's father-in-law.

Item: 9 January 1883, Elizabeth Bowden died.

The next year Henry and his wife returned to England and opened offices in London and Croydon to market Thilum, Hippacea veterinary liniment, Jvara-Hari or 'fever-destroyer', and Omum-Carpoor, a remedy for cholera, diarrhoea and dysmenhorrhoea.

Item: Vienna 1886, Thilum and Hippacea gained gold medals.

They were noticed too at the Colonial and Indian Exhibition in South Kensington. The Court Circular enthused: they 'have been proved to be so marvellous in their effects that we are fearful, if we enumerate the many complaints for which they will be found to be efficacious, our encomiums may sound too strong'. Henry was not shy of encomiums and took eight pages in Madras's *Asylum Press Almanac* for advertisements, testimonials and a list of one hundred and fifty agents, from Agra to Umballa and from Calcutta to Cochin, for Henry's Great Indian Remedies. Thanks to the fakir.

Poor health, ironically, brought William, Mary and daughter Bessie back to England. The fakir's recipe was the basis for W. Bowden's Indian Balm which they began to manufacture at Rackfield House in Barnstaple in 1889 to much acclaim.

Item: London 1896, W. Bowden's Indian Balm, silver medal.

There was Bowden's Veterinary Balm too, Sandalwood Dust, Balm Soap, Indian Bitters and Bowden's Alpine Corn Plasters.

Item: 23 January 1924, William Stanger of Rackfield House bought an unconsecrated plot in Bear Street Cemetery and erected a headstone in loving memory of Matilda Mary Bowden, died 1908, also of William Bowden, 1907. Later, on the obverse: William Henry Stanger, 1926, also Mary Elizabeth his wife, 1949, better known as Bessie. Great-aunt Bessie.

Item: 23 April 1924, Edwin Bowden died, Coonoor.

Item: 1974, Manufacture of W. Bowden's Indian Balm ceased. 'It was such an agonizing decision to have to take.'

Win Platt wept as she told me how she and her husband Jack had to stop making ointment. They were soon to retire, and it was impossible to get ingredients at an economic price. Letters kept coming from all over the world, begging for Balm. They lent them to me, and all the testimonials dating back to 1889, glued into crumbling scrapbooks they'd inherited with the business.

Thomas Ridd extolled the stuff in 1891 for ending ten years' suffering from piles. Orphanages and homes for the destitute proved its value against eye inflammation and ringworm. Two of William Aze's prize pigeons were mauled by a hawk, one with its liver exposed, but the ointment healed them good as new.

Robert Chapman, the remarkable Barnstaple patriarch who'd sent the Bowdens from Ebenezer Chapel to India with his blessing, praised Indian Balm for mending an injury he sustained in his carpentry workshop in 1897, when he was ninety-four.

Mrs Gosse, wife and mother of *Father and Son*, Philip Henry and Edmund Gosse, fell heavily in the Torquay Street and struck her temple, but 'a lady in the house used some of the Indian Balm, rubbing it well into the forehead. The next morning instead of the part turning black as was expected, there was no visible bruise nor pain'.

Pharmacists and doctors sent case histories confirming its efficacy. Tyrolean peasants cried out for it. It healed the stumps of frostbitten Chinese beggars. It cured dermatitis in Bahamian sponge divers and Faroese fishermen. It eased leprosy and cancerous ulcers in Africa, from Algeria to Natal.

G. W. Ray wrote in 1901, 'In my long pioneering journeys into the far interior of Paraguay and Brazil, where sickness, disease and death faced me at every step, I found the Indian Balm to be invaluable. The savages looked upon me as a great healer when, with your preparation, I was able to cure their festering wounds . . . I always found the Balm to give instant relief and effect a speedy cure. I hope never to be without it.'

Win's memories revolved around making and selling Balm, from the day in 1923 when her father took on the business, and the Rackfield Mission, from William and Mary's daughter Bessie and her husband. The next year he moved Bowden's Indian Balm Co. to the heart of town. Rackfield House, the original Balm depot, was only recently bulldozed and overridden by a new road. Now cheap jewellery glitters in the premises where Win sold W. Bowden's Indian Balm, made above the shop to a fakir's recipe passed down from my great-great-grandfather. Win passed it on to me.

Directly opposite, the Taj Mahal is closed and boarded up. Curries are served in Barnstaple's old railway station, now the Ganges restaurant. Before I travelled to Narsapur, I sat there in the Ganges looking out at the chilly River Taw in which Robert Chapman baptized William Bowden so many years before. That Taw was the starting point for William's journey and, in a small way, for mine. With the scent of Balm in my nostrils I could imagine it flowing east, not west, a tributary of the Godavari.

SHADOW OF THE PAGODA

Palakol

WHEN I FIRST saw the pagoda at Palakol I knew that I'd come home to somewhere strange. My ancestors lived in its shadow. 'Built by one of Palakol's merchant sons in the heyday of its prosperity as a supposed act of piety,' wrote E. B. Bromley, 'it might well have been dedicated to Mammon, the real god of the town.' Set among fruit gardens, Palakol had been a wealthy trading centre renowned for its cotton cloth. Narsapur was its port. Tradition says that the builder-architect who erected the pagoda or *gopuram*, one of two brilliant *maistries* of the time, was distressed to find that it leant a fraction to the north. He consulted his fellow *maistry* who, after a thorough survey, proposed that a tank be dug a short distance to the south; his prescription was precise as to size and position. Once the soil was shifted, the *gopuram*'s masonry settled just enough to bring its pinnacles to the perpendicular.

It loomed large and sepia in old photographs. I recognized it well enough. The topmost storey, with its lions and mythical beasts, was bright; the ground floor was freshly limewashed; but the ten storeys in between, and all their gods and demons, were sepia in life. It was the biggest *gopuram* in the region.

'Why do you come here?' said an inquisitive man, almost before I'd got off the bus. Standing in the bustle by the bus-station fruit stalls, I produced my tin of Indian Balm.

'Hmmm, but here,' he said, 'there is nothing to see.'

I came to Palakol a few times. On a good day it took twenty minutes by bus from Narsapur. On a bad day it took twelve. I timed it. Not long before I left Narsapur for the last time I drove George here in Joy's Ambassador. By then I knew the worst ruts and potholes so I was speedy too. George – or T. K. George, DD – ran a radio studio in Narsapur, 'Living Waters', where he made weekly Christian programmes in Telugu, broadcast from Sri Lanka and the Seychelles. He'd showed me his messy house and studio, his ageing recording gear, his musical instruments and the correspondence courses he mailed to some of last year's three thousand one hundred and thirty-one enquirers. He'd beamed most broadly when he preened his pedigree pigeons' breasts. Now George clutched at his chest and breathed stertorously. He had a heart condition, he told me, among other things; I thought it suited him, he was a natural hypochondriac.

I slowed down all the same. George pointed across the canal to a place called Penkulapadu. William Bowden once built paddy godowns there, roofed with terracotta tiles. When his granaries decayed years later, the ground, thick with fallen tiles, was allocated for a settlement. Penkulapadu means 'tiles village'.

In Palakol we crossed the humpy canal bridge and turned off to find Emmaus Chapel, on the site where the Bowdens rented a house from 1840. The district was still called Christianpeta. In the airy church the watchman scrabbled for his clothes. He was decent when Jonah Moses, aged eighty-five, tottered down the street in a white *panchi* with a carved stick and a hearing-aid. Somehow he'd heard that William Bowden's great-great-grandson was in town. His eyes filled with tears as he shook my hand.

Around the corner we found George's family house. It was neat and small and yellow, dated 1911. The dilapidated building next door was where, George said, the Bowdens first worshipped. I looked and, yes, I saw. But that was all. Back in town, close to the pagoda, he showed me the Girls' High School, built on the site the Bowdens bought in 1845. Their rented house had been very small, too small for Europeans, friends said, and William offered two hundred rupees for the old Dutch factory. The Governor in council refused, ruling that it must be sold by auction. It was knocked down to William for thirty-five rupees: a compound of eight thousand four hundred and forty-five square yards with buildings and gardens in the very heart of town.

George posed stiffly in front of the tiled house where the D'Bras family had lived. One of the few Indo-Portuguese families left after the Dutch ceded Palakol to the British in 1804, they were early converts. George led me to the old Dutch burial ground hard by the temple wall, used by Christians until Hindus opposed funerals there in 1904 and chased mourners out. For five years Palakol Christians had to be carried to Narsapur for burial while the case dragged on in the Machilipatnam courts and until a fresh graveyard was provided off the Bhimavaram road. The old cemetery was a dishevelled heap; everything had recently been disinterred by the Archaeology Department. Including Elizabeth Bowden's bones? Someone said that when she died in January 1883, at the age of seventy-one, she'd been buried here, not Narsapur. But no one was sure, and I was no longer looking for the dead.

In their first six years, the Bowdens saw no converts. For seven days in 1842 William and Elizabeth fasted and prayed. In that week a woman from the caste quarter, who had been a white man's mistress, embraced Christ. Embariyam, a shoe-maker of the Madiga or lowest outcaste 'caste', was converted at the same time. He and his wife, with four of the D'Bras family, were the first people William baptized. Embariyam continued to encourage the missionaries until he died of rabies in the hot season of 1878, by which time churches had sprung up all over the delta.

George and I drove from the temple to Embariyampeta, the leather-working, or chuckler quarter perched beside tanks on the edge of town. Bloated skins hung like pale balloons beside huts where hides were cleaned, and de-haired in liming pits. Powerful ghosts of prejudice haunted George's mind; he was disgusted by what he showed me and wouldn't take me to where carcasses were flayed. When the Bowdens took James, a leather-worker's son, into their house as a servant, the other outcastes walked out. But in 1854 William described how attitudes had changed:

Whenever a carpenter or other man of a caste was working at our house, he would not touch water . . . from the hands of any of our servants . . . Now a worker in horn is sitting

not far from where I am writing, making some crochet
needles required for Mrs Bowden's girls' school. James has
brought some water to clean some household furniture;
the horn-worker says, 'James, give me some water for my
whetstone to sharpen my plane iron.' Eighteen years ago it
would have been as readily concluded that men would have
wings to fly with, as that a caste man would take water
from the hands of one who had been a chuckler.

It was among chucklers that William Bowden junior worked in
the 1850s. He turned the waste burial ground that formed the
Christian *peta* into tanning pits and shacks. He enabled Madigas,
untouchable both because they dealt with carcasses of cows and
because many of them became Christians, to take charge of their
lives and labour and achieve a previously unimaginable dignity.

I looked and, yes, I glimpsed the challenge young William
faced. Within a palmyra-leaf shelter three poor pinched men sat
on the ground, torsos glistening, cutting and trimming triangles
of leather. In a brick and *chunam* shed a young man with eccentric eyes and wavy oiled hair fed triangles into a press, while his
mate stood and spun the heavy flywheel that closed the mould;
behind them on the floor was a growing pile of bicycle saddles.

Were these men independent co-operative workers? They
seemed demoralized, victims once more of an oppressive system.

'Why does he want to see us?' one asked incredulously.

'They are suffering,' a young boss-man wearing a gold watch
told me. 'Now caste Hindus invest in leather business also.'

I translated this in my own mind. They'd fallen into the hands
of money-lenders who wouldn't be seen dead near them or their
unholy work but gladly took the profits. Men worked in full
sun on the narrow street. Women and children crowded round.
Here, of all places, no one asked us in. Was it because George
emanated distaste, or because they'd lost their self-respect?

Their old houses were simple but substantial. Set a little apart
by a tank was a limewashed chapel among palm trees. The fabric
of William's vision survived, but its inwardness had fled. At last
we drove out of the crush. A puppy ran under the wheels and
squealed horribly. George urged me to drive on. We were sucked
into a rush-hour jam of handcarts, pony traps, rickshaws, lorries,

buses and ox carts. We extricated ourselves and crept away along the banks of irrigation ditches to the village of Tsundaparru, the Bowdens' farm colony for Mala outcastes, where in 1860 young William welcomed Mary his bride.

On my first visit to Palakol, the Palakol where there was nothing to see, I passed between beggars in saffron and white and through the *gopuram* gateway. Within the courtyard I propped my sandals on a rack and sat on a plinth to watch a bruiser of a *pujari* burn joss sticks and pronounce Sanskrit texts over a brand-new Kinetic Honda scooter, as the owner sprinkled *kumkum* on its speedometer and on limes hanging from its head-lamp. I couldn't sit for long. Priests urged me to see everything and pressed me for the price of my camera in dollars. Beneath the sepia *gopuram* and the white or rose-tinted *shikharas* the world was dark and colourful.

Shrines round the court held blue-black stone images of gods garnished with vermilion and saffron, marigolds and flickering flames. Under the *mandapam* or pillared hall before the sanctum, a big garlanded Nandi reclined, sticky with juice and wreathed with flies. Pillars bore mythological scenes in technicolour relief. The way to the womb house was flanked by guardians. A silver snake god, Nagendhrudu, glimmered in inner darkness.

An acolyte led me to touch the feet of an imposing *sadhu*. I didn't touch them. The old man spoke of the need for reverence, of the Father-Mother within, and of the All. When he mentioned 'wife of Shiva', I said 'Parvati'. When he said 'Nataraja', I said 'dancing Shiva'. He beamed. It was like passing an exam.

I made for the canal. Outside the State Bank of Hyderabad I photographed the statue of Gandhi kneeling by ranks of bicycles.

'Join me for a coffee,' said a young man from the bank in a tone that could not be disobeyed. He was the manager. His desk was remarkably clean. He had been appointed two months ago. 'We are moved on every two years to avoid vested interests. Now I am on leave, just killing time.' He looked quizzical. 'I invited you because I wished to talk and wondered what you were doing. We are all too aware of security. Coffee,' he called to a *peon*, 'sweet and black as the devil himself.'

I explained myself, then asked for the lavatory.

'Normally I would say just follow your nose,' he smiled, 'but here it is better.' And it was. I was relieved.

'Forty per cent of people have accounts,' he said. I raised an eyebrow and he added, 'Of course, coolies cannot bank during working hours; shopkeepers and merchants can, all secondary and tertiary layers, landowners also. There is land ceiling. One man may own so many acres only. So land is divided between sons and grandsons, or "owned" by stooges paid to keep the lease.'

Coffee came in small green glasses. I traced where I'd been walking on a big planners' map of Palakol stuck to the wall.

'It is long out of date,' he chuckled, 'drawn at the time of your ancestors, I think, otherwise I might find out where I am. As it is, I can only hazard a guess.'

A clerk dropped a letter on the desert of his desk.

'I was educated by the Jesuits in Bihar,' he confessed, 'but I am not a Catholic. No, we have an excellent understanding, my maker and I. I don't bother him and he doesn't bother me.' He opened the envelope. 'Ah good, a complaint.'

He grinned as he perused the flimsy typewritten tirade.

'A *dalit*, man of the scheduled castes, has paid a writer to address this to my superior. Money, he says, granted under the Reservations scheme for the purchase of milch cows, has only been part-paid despite him having been made, I quote, "to roam the bank hundreds of times". I am, as you can see, a wicked man.'

A man shat in the canal behind a line of cement politicians. How could I weigh ornate anger against urbane cynicism? A boy sat among tin funnels and cans of oil in a shack between the legs of a hoarding: 'No ban. No challenge. No competition. Onida TV.' Everyone trod around a pig, disembowelled in the dust.

'Which bus for Narsapur?' I asked at the bus station.

'This one and this one,' said a man in a *dhoti*.

'Which one goes first?'

'Only God above knows,' he said, clutching his briefcase.

I had to choose, and was blessed. We left first and got back to Narsapur in no less than twenty minutes. Phew!

25

TIGER PRAWNS

Kakinada

MY GRANDMOTHER had no birth certificate, it seems, but her 1924 passport confirms her place and date of birth: Cocanada, India, 21 April 1872. At Nidadavole, close by the school she started at Chettipeta, I boarded the Circar Express for today's Kakinada.

'Please sit down here,' said a compact man in casual Western clothes and trainers. He made room for me to join his family.

'Thomas Kadavill,' he said. The four of them had been on the train twelve hours from Madras, and nine hours from Cochin before that, but looked the image of the ideal Indian family as glimpsed spreading golden margarine or spilling from a glistening Maruti hatchback in TV commercials. The children were crisp. Beena's sari was uncreased. Thomas's creases were sharp.

Joy had never been to Kakinada and had no contacts there. I'd made some, it seemed. After staying with relatives in their native Kerala they were returning home to their adopted town. Cocanada had rivalled and overtaken Masulipatam as main port of the Northern Circars, the richest parts of Andhra Pradesh ceded to the British in 1765 after extended rivalry and struggle with the French in the Carnatic Wars. Although Kakinada was in turn superseded as a port by Vishakhapatnam's protected harbour, it took Rajahmundry's place as district's chief town.

An elderly beggar with protuberant eyes like peeled red grapes gripped a tin cup of coins and the hand of a boss-eyed simple boy who led him passenger to passenger all up the train.

'It's so difficult,' said Thomas, 'to know when to give to beggars and when to refuse.'

We teetered across the Rajahmundry railway bridge. I wanted

171

a long balancing pole. Nothing below but big Godavari and small islands with dry-season shanty shacks and pink-arsed monkeys in the paddies. On the east side dark red dishevelled areas rising from fields. Lumpy hills beyond. Lush rice around Dwarapudi, rich orchards. Rice mills at Samulkot, a distillery and sugar factory: giant industrial plants with ox carts queuing at the gates. ONGC's gas pipeline freshly scored across country to the stacks and silos of a fertilizer plant beside the ocean.

A curvaceous concrete office block was being constructed to the left of the track as we entered Kakinada; to the right, tents of tattered sacks. I had no idea what this place would be like or where I would stay. My ticket was for Kakinada Port.

'You must not alight there,' said Thomas, 'that is end of line. Alight at Kakinada Town. I'll take you to a good hotel.'

Not too good, I hoped. We all alighted and I hurried after Thomas. His car, a white Ambassador with a driver, was waiting. I waved an inadequate farewell to Beena and the children.

'I'll fetch them in some minutes. My Christian name is Thomas,' Thomas added, 'but please to call me Mohan.'

Not such a Christian name, I thought. We obeyed the green right filter at the first traffic lights I'd seen since Madras, while a policeman marshalled halted traffic like a steward at a starting grid. Of the town's three parallel main roads, two were one-way with a fast lane for motor vehicles to the left, and a slow lane for bicycles and rickshaws to the right. We cut across the slow lane and swept up a steep incline to the reception area of the tall pink Hotel Manasarovar. A path curved down past smart shops to the Yeti, the hotel's vegetarian restaurant. Another dropped behind the main building to the non-vegetarian Glacier. Mohan had a word in reception. It was the coolest place I'd been for a long time. And the most expensive, full of men wearing gold and immaculate linen. More than five pounds a night for an air-conditioned room with TV.

'You will come to dinner with us. We will arrange on the phone. And to my prawn factory. Here is my card. Just ring.'

Manasarovar's managing director was Mohan's friend. Lake Manasarovar lies just south of Mount Kailas, paradise of Shiva and centre of the Buddhist universe. Its waters, higher than Titicaca's, are turquoise and crystal clear. The hotel room was good enough for me. I lay back and enjoyed it. The Yeti and the Glacier could wait. A colonel with a snowy moustache talked polo, pukka chukkas, on TV. Room service brought me sumptuous chicken curry garnished with fried onions and fresh coriander.

From my balcony I surveyed the balcony of the Tirumala, one of the twenty-three cinemas in town. Men loitered there, gazing at stills of pale heroes and diaphanously clad devas. Beneath, a woman slapped wet cloth on the cinema's paving slabs and tended a cooking pot on a bucket of fire; she poked sticks in and fanned the embers with a tin lid. At the show's end, couples burst out of the darkness laughing together; one man slipped his arm around a girl's waist; boys hung on one another's necks. Shutters swung open to reveal gleaming projectors and a small projectionist who leant on the sill and stared at me for a long time.

As I descended the slope from the hotel into the real world, a drum orchestra clattered up Subhash Road against the traffic, one man swinging a smoky incense pot, another carrying a bowl of petals, a handful of which he flung backwards every few steps to drift over bearers and a garlanded corpse on a bier. Across the petal trail goats picked their way along the pavement outside car showrooms and boutiques. Down the road it was like Christmas or sale time. There were makeshift stalls and cramped premises, big plate-glass-fronted discount stores and ready-made clothes shops, balloons and banners high above the street, people crowding to buy finery and fancy goods for the next festival. In days to come I'd get to know the place, but for now it was just any old enchanting squalid mall, with added beggars: relentless children who pleaded monotonously, saffron-robed *sadhus* who whined, and a pregnant woman who pursued me, with breasts and belly protruding enormously from a skimpy sari.

The shopping street edged nearer the river bridge and an aroma of roasting coffee mixed with diesel fumes from a tight lorry jam. I squeezed between vehicles and the world changed again. A lad in a loincloth with beautiful buttocks and rippling torso manhandled a diesel drum into his fishing smack, *Sree Devi*, from three men in shirts and *dhotis* on the deck of a barge. A two-hundred-ton black barge with a billowing sail sewn from white sacks ploughed a deep furrow upstream. A line of them was moored, wide sterns to the wharf, unloaded by coolies whose turbans and T-shirts and shorts and arms and legs and faces were white from the flour sacks they heaved into lorries. At the broken-down end of a red-brick wall plastered with cinema posters two men leant, chatting, while a Brahmin cow craned its neck between them to be scratched behind the ears and caressed beneath the chin. All three gave themselves to this casual pleasure.

Beyond them stood port buildings and tiled godowns. Through flour haze, on the other bank, there were stolid Dutch-gabled houses, stucco confections with porticos and balustrades, palmyra huts and a temple. I made for the bridge. Halfway across, a cracked water main piddled into the river. Upstream, it became the Cocanada canal that ran all the way from Cotton's barrage at Dowlaishweram. On a mudbank men struggled to shove a propeller shaft up a fishing boat. Downstream, I sniffed for the sea; it was close, but seven miles offshore to the roadstead where ships and barges swapped cargoes. With late sun striking oily water, black hulks, bright boats and crazy buildings, I wanted paints and a broad canvas. I wanted to be Kakinada's Canaletto.

Butch women with bitchy cries jostled folk at the far side of the bridge. They carried firewood, demanded money. Their kohl-rimmed eyes were dramatic, their oiled hair coiffed, their features masculine, breasts small, narrow hips swathed with saris. A gang of transvestites, they bore themselves along in a cloud of pent-up hermaphrodite fury. They harangued stall holders but passed by leaving me unnoticed and unscathed.

The south bank was different again, gentle, small scale. On the north side people stared and stood off. Here they waved and beckoned. There were palm-leaf houses, chandlers' shacks, coils of coir rope, fishermen mending nylon nets, blacksmiths, welders repairing winch gear, perilous twiggy jetties to fishing boats of green or blue or red, a bloated dead dog on foul black mud and men wading in it to root the upright poles of a new catwalk. A boy squatted to do a Mr Whippy while a dog the same height sat beside him. When the boy stood, the dog licked up the orange cone with relish, leaving nothing for pigs.

Beyond a small temple I breathed a resinous scent. Timber was stacked high. Shipwrights drilled holes in new ribs with electric drills. Boats' skeletons were pinned with wooden pegs, clad with ruddy boards and caulked with pitch. High on a raw ochre barge carpenters hammered at superstructure. A demon scarecrow protected it, a temporary figurehead. Others shaved at a fishing boat's timbers with adzes. Beneath one of many new hulls, two men twisted an auger hand over hand, biting a deep hole in the keel for the propeller shaft. Already the unpainted cabin was decorated with a picture of the Holy Family.

The road veered away from the river through the quarter of Kakinada called Jagannaickpur, built on the south bank by the Dutch from 1628, acquired by the British in 1825 and destroyed by the cyclone and tidal wave which swept the coast from Narsapur to Vishakhapatnam in October 1839. Thousands died. Some ships were carried four miles inland. Merchants' godowns collapsed. Houses blew away. Far inland at Rajahmundry, the big house Judge and Mrs Thomas had just vacated was unroofed. Cattle and crops were devastated. Land turned brackish. Wells filled with salt water. Cholera followed. It was the climax of the chapter of disasters that welcomed my relatives to the delta.

I came to St Joseph's church and convent school. The white gothic church was dated 1840. It made sense. I crept inside. Ribbons streamed from the apex of the roof like ribs of a rainbow tent. Girls in pale blue were singing. Garish figures of Jesus, Mary and assorted saints stood in sympathy with Hindu tradition behind the altar. My Protestant ancestors would not have entered here. But somewhere close by, about 1867, the brothers William and Frederick Henry set up their business, Messrs Bowden Brothers & Co. Later they'd return to England to market W. Bowden's Indian Balm and F. Henry's Thilum respectively. Meanwhile they handed over the Cocanada insurance office to Frank and Edwin, my great-grandfather. That's why Lily, my grandmother, was born here.

Mohan was a Roman Catholic. Thomas was his Christian name. Office doors in the factory he managed, Fish Products Ltd, were surmounted by icons of Shiva and Jesus. From his window I looked on to a boatyard by the river. I was still in Jagannaickpur, but in yet another world between salt pans and the fishing village of Etimuga by the sea. The fishermen there sold Mohan their catches of prawns. He exported them, mostly to Japan.

Fishermen's wives and children squatted behind heaped trays all round the walls of the shelling shed. They grinned at me but didn't stop plucking heads and legs off crustaceans. The floor was sluiced down. In the ice-making plant water was sterilized with ultra-violet light and frozen into blocks four feet by one. The microbiological laboratory, a tool of quality control, was pristine. Women in the grading room wore white hats and plastic aprons; they stood at benches sorting seriously. An assistant scuttled round taking samples and arraying them before me on a bed of ice: pale orange shrimps, grey ones, and black-and-white king tiger prawns from thirty miles offshore.

'These fetch twenty-two dollars a kilo,' said Mohan. 'But the Japanese pay a better price still for Indonesian blue-shelled prawns.'

'How are your marine stocks?' I asked.

'Decreasing,' said Mohan. 'They are not meant to fish during the breeding season. But farmed stocks increase. In ten years I predict seventy per cent of our production will be farmed.'

A heavy door clicked to. I was in a dim, cavernous cold room full of ice, pallets, crates, packets labelled 'Monarch Pond Fresh Black Tiger' and 'Coromandel Quick Frozen Shrimp'. Edward Lear's nonsense lines fitted well, with their underlying chill:

> 'On this Coast of Coromandel,
> Shrimps and watercresses grow,
> Prawns are plentiful and cheap,'
> Said the Yonghy-Bonghy-Bo.

I wanted to laugh my head off; I'd never been so cold in my life.

26

TEETH AND TROUSERS

Kakinada

WHEN ELIZABETH BOWDEN welcomed enthusiastic new colleagues ashore at Kakinada, a few months after William's death, the first advice she gave them was, 'In this land ye have need of patience.'

I hired a car to take me to the beach. At the hotel door it wouldn't start. Rama the driver disappeared under the bonnet several times. Nothing happened. His gleaming smile was not at all reassuring. His boy prepared to push us off down the slope but the engine fired unexpectedly, the boy jumped aboard and Rama sped off, almost mashing a slow-lane rickshaw before meshing into fast-lane traffic with consummate impertinence.

The outskirts felt seaside-suburban. Then soggy. Beyond an employment project for cured leprosy patients, the road became a causeway across flooded land. In one of the frail villages that flanked it, women with buckets and *bindis* queued and fought for water from a tanker lorry. A vast chemical plant, fed by ONGC's natural gas pipeline, loomed like a vision of industrial heaven.

Rama relaxed as we cruised Beach Road, sheltered by conifer plantations and bursts of bougainvillea. We halted close by a moustachioed white figure with his hands on hips. Three men sat between his feet; if they'd jumped, they might have touched his knees. At his side, a broad flight of twenty-six concrete stairs climbed to hip level and an unfinished temple porch, spiky with reinforcing irons. He had ten heads, one on his neck, five to his right and four to his left, like a line of corbels staring from beneath a tapering *shikhara* topped with Shiva's *trishul* or trident. It didn't make sense to me, but he looked like Ravana, demon king of Lanka, who took Mount Kailas, Shiva's paradise, by the roots and shook it, and who also abducted Rama's wife Sita.

Rama wasn't telling. He padded after me across the broad sands, leaving his boy to guard the car. Crabs scuttled into holes. Lateen-rigged *navas* found plenty of wind in the bay. A man carried nets in through the shallows, wound on the ends of a pole, a sagging dumbbell. A lazy curve of beach led away to the fishing harbour, its huge market house and moored boats on the north side of the bay. Big ships were ranged along the shelf of the horizon. A lighthouse marked the end of a sandspit punctuated by palms and dwindling southwards to mangrove swamps. Barges moved against it like black beetles with glinting wings.

After that, Beach Park's delights quickly wore thin: climbs and slides, picnic tables with pastel-painted metal seats and sun-shades, a dry paddling pool and a bandstand with a roof full of rainwater. It was deserted but for two disconsolate sweetmeat salesmen. Like the barges, Rama and I made for the rivermouth. Before we reached railway tracks, freight wagons, godowns and dusty stevedores, I took a long look back at the line of hazy ships. Mynahs screamed and a Brahminy kite hung overhead.

One day in August 1855 a ship's boat brought Thomas Heelis and his sea chest ashore here. Heelis was a twenty-two-year-old officer on the *Malabar* who'd taken three days' leave to accompany William Bowden to Dowlaishweram. What he'd seen there convinced him of his missionary calling. He'd returned to the short-handed ship, knowing that his master wouldn't let him go. But the *Whirlwind* was in port, able to transfer men to the *Malabar*. He was free. He hired coolies to carry his chest, bought himself a palm-frond umbrella and walked fifty miles and more to Palakol. Thereafter he lived in the sun. He married and out-lived two wives, eschewed mere hot-season holidays in the hills and visited England just once before he died, a legend, at Narsapur in 1911.

Babu Rao was an enthusiast, brimming with energy and com-mitment to the cause of melding innovation and tradition. What excited him was the best of both. He was assistant general manager of A. P. Fisheries Corporation's boat-building yard. He showed off model *navas* and trawlers used to demonstrate buoyancy chambers, retractable engines and rudders to conservative local fishermen.

'Indigenous craft were surveyed and developed in 'fifties,' said Babu Rao, 'and this thirty-seven-foot trawler was built, the first ever designed by an Indian and constructed in India.'

'How do the fishermen like your boats?' I asked.

'It is hard at first,' he said, 'but now they see.'

Outside were stacked the giant tree trunks I'd seen from Mohan's office window, timber shipped from the Andaman Islands: pyinma and tungpieng wood used as substitutes for teak.

'*Nava* built from teak cost forty-two thousand rupees; from these, thirty-one thousand five hundred rupees.'

I thought of Bowden and Heelis buying teak upriver to build Heelis's first sea-going *Harbinger*. She was wrecked in a cyclone the year my grandmother was born. The Bowdens sailed on her successor's maiden voyage from Narsapur to Kakinada. I thought of William's canal boat *Echo*, and of Edwin's *Water-Lily*.

The stench of resin spun my head in the shop where *navas*, catamarans and cyclone relief boats were moulded in fibreglass. Subtler scents of sawn timber and tar permeated the air where men worked with chisel, adze and caulking hammer on wooden hulls in a neighbouring shed overshadowed and festooned by a banyan tree.

'My very good wishes to Mohan,' Babu Rao called after me.

I passed his greetings on at dinner, together with a green-and-silver paper-covered cardboard box of candies from Ranesh Kumar's tiny shop. The box looked thirty years old, I hoped the sweets weren't. Mohan's driver and the children had picked me up in the Ambassador for a fifteen-minute drive to their suburb. We sat in the reception room drinking brandy. The heavy inner doorway was of dark and honey-coloured wood with a chain pattern of pale inlay. The outer door was open and the fan spun. Was the chill in my honour? I described where I'd been.

'You have seen many things here also,' said Beena.

I was glad. She'd hardly opened her mouth on the train. I told her how at Quality & Co. where I'd bought instant coffee the proprietor sent his son out for an instamatic camera to snap the customer. Well, I was the only white man I'd seen in town.

'It makes a change,' I said.

'I don't think I know that shop,' said Balan in a languid, well-bred English voice. Balan was a tall, slender cricket-playing dentist with wavy, carefully brushed grey hair. I couldn't imagine him shopping in Quality & Co.'s neighbourhood. His wife, also called Beena, drained her brandy. She had an intelligent eye and a kindly toleration of the world, that included her husband. The first Beena called us in to a richly dressed table. We sat down to fish steaks, Tandoori chicken, *sambar*, grated carrot, rice, *puris* and bread. It was warmer inside, though there was hardly a flicker of chilli in the food. Was it cool in my honour? I asked them about things I'd seen.

'You have seen too many things here, I think,' smiled Balan. 'These transvestites, as you call them – I have written a modest article about Indian sexuality which I shall lend you – they are in reality transsexuals who live as anal prostitutes and beggars. They are Hijrahs, a caste to whom babies of indeterminate sex are given. Their curses are feared, so folk pay them money even before a word passes their lips. When a boy is born they are called in to dance and paid off on the child's behalf. It's a cock-eyed blessing based on the fear of homosexuality.'

Listening to Balan was like reading dated English prose. An immodest article. He was very proud of it.

'I met some government officials, in Lucknow for a wedding, who asserted that Hindi was the language of Hindus and should therefore be the language of India. If there were any truth – I use the subjunctive advisedly – in those statements, they had quite forgotten that India was only ever unified under British rule. English should of course be the national language.'

'My family is from Cochin,' said Mohan, 'we speak Malayalam. But grew up in Bombay, so Hindi. Then I work in Madras, French and Tamil. Now Andhra Pradesh, Telugu. But master of none.'

'My father was from Kerala also,' Balan resumed, 'but I was

brought up here. I understand and speak Telugu when I must, but I read and write nothing but English. We are Syriac, or Thomas Christians. I trace my family back to the eleventh century, and my faith to the first. St Thomas came to India long before Europe adopted a Palestinian Jew called Jesus. Those Hindi-loving civil servants had forgotten that too.'

The saint was nicknamed Doubting Thomas, but I nodded hard. Balan smiled, an advert for immaculate teeth, and plucked with long fingers to give his sharp creases space at the knee.

'I asked them, "How do you know Rama was born in Ayodhya?" They got angry,' Balan chuckled, 'red in the face if that's possible for us Indians. "And where", I said, "are the archaeological remains of the great battle of the Mahabharata?"'

Balan flared his nostrils, sucked and relaxed his cheeks.

'You see,' he said, 'the Indian psyche is a way of coping with the unreality of reality. Krishna steals a ball of butter from his mother's cooking and, with it on his very tongue, lies to her, says he did not take it. Hunters chasing a deer ask a *sanyasi* which way it went; he points in the opposite direction, "Thatta way!" This is why our politicians can lie on the floor of the house. Only Hindu mythology glorifies mendacity.'

'Not Hindu politicians only,' said Mohan.

'Mohan, you can make excuses, give reasons, but is it or is it not true that all Indians are liars?'

'Tell me,' I said, looking for an answer I wanted and hoping to change the subject, 'how do you know what caste someone is?'

'We ask other people,' said Mohan, 'or ask point blank.'

'Make it our business to find out in the first few minutes, subtly if necessary,' Balan added. 'But nowadays, if you have professional qualifications, or if you have money, even Brahmins will not discriminate. With money you can get away with murder.'

'He has lost patience with this country,' said Mohan.

'I have not *lost* patience,' Balan pursed his lips and spread his fingers, 'I have thrown it away. Patience is death.'

We all took a deep breath. Balan smiled benignly.

'Though I've never been west of Bombay, I've always yearned to visit an English pub.' He hung 'pub' in the air as one might hang 'Louvre' or 'Lourdes', then grimaced, 'But I understand that the working class has spoiled it.'

I wasn't going to let him off too easily.

'Please expand on that,' I said.

'I would prefer', he grinned broadly, 'to be succinct.'

27

FRENCH BREAD

Yanam

AT 9.55 A.M. precisely I strode past guards with cartridge belts and rifles into the Subhash Road branch of the State Bank of India. The foreign transactions clerk, I'd been informed, started work at ten. He arrived, late, waved me to a comfortable chair in his office, switched on the ceiling fan and disappeared. While he pottered about outside, I sat and thought optimistically about the bus I had been hoping to catch to Yanam at 11.15.

At least I'd found the bus station in advance. On a Sunday morning I'd zig-zagged across town. I saw a milling crowd and pushed into it. It was a low-level market, muddy beneath the crush of feet. As usual most of the shoppers were men, most of the sellers women. They squatted behind baskets on which slats of wood made little counters for fish: fat black-and-orange scaly ones, long ones like silver straps, small mud-skippers, blue-shelled crabs, and prawns, mostly small and grey.

How many of these fishwives had resorted to money-lenders in order to buy their stock? It was common practice to borrow in the morning and repay the loan at the end of the day. Plus ten per cent. Or to put it another way, an interest rate of three thousand six hundred and fifty per cent per annum, a reasonable enough return for a man with a little capital.

Vendors displayed voluptuous fruit and vegetables in the shade of palmyra umbrellas. A man butchered a pig on a low block and weighed bloody cuts in hand-held scales; a wizened puppy wrestled with offal on the ground; as I passed by, flies rose as one; they left the carcass like a shadowy spirit.

Two little girls with red ribbons in their hair stood up, lifted red dresses and ran home to have their bottoms washed. A spiral staircase climbed to a shrine above the railway crossing; the elevated goddess gazed down the track bisecting a shanty town. A man raked together a little burning rubbish with one hand and dangled a scrawny chicken over it with the other.

The bus station was missing. I walked along to the flyover that took Subhash Road across the rails. A bony bundle of woman was curled up in its shadow before an image of Ganesh. Ragged children played around frail shelters between concrete stilts opposite St John's School, a rounded, prosperous building with stout doors and inscriptions on white walls: 'Lead Kindly Light', '"Children" Precious Jewels in this School', 'Experienced Keralite Teachers/Dedicated Management/Spacious Classrooms/Modern Teaching Methods/Parent Teacher Meetings/Excellent Education' and 'Better than the Best'. An ancient young mother begged *paise*.

I retraced my steps to the rail crossing, pursued by two dark, finely muscled 'Koyas'; they wore tiger-tooth pendants and brandished brass-bound black staves; peacock feathers sprouted from their leopard-skin headcloths. Until they saw me they were shouting through doors offering to tell fortunes, and to curse anyone who didn't pay. They were photogenic but demanded two hundred rupees. I escaped across the tracks and found the bus station. I was grateful. I checked out bus times to Yanam and bought a cut loaf, its wrapper printed with Hindu gods and the Eiffel Tower.

'French Bread' it was called. Getting bread from the bank was more difficult. The Foreign Transactions Clerk sat down at his desk, processed my traveller's cheques and filled in forms. He told me not to worry. The bank had been founded, he said, two hundred years ago as the Imperial Bank of India. But the cashier had not yet arrived. When he did, all would be well. Did I know that Kakinada's population was three lakhs? That in the Second World War its people ran to the country because it was a prime target? It was stimulating talk, but the clerk broke off when the cashier appeared, conveyed my chits to him in person and returned with my money. I was grateful. It had only taken an hour.

I just made it to the bus station in time. How familiar everything seemed in town, things that would have knocked my eyes out if I'd come straight from Barnstaple. Open drains were being cleared out with tools like hoes. The bus was half an hour late. I bought loosejackets at a stall in the bus station.

'Each one three rupees fifty,' insisted the boy. I got four for six rupees.

'But why so expensive here?' I exclaimed.

'Complex,' his head wobbled in frustration. 'Complex.'

Hard to explain, eh? I thought money-lenders, protection, profiteering. No, he meant 'complex' as in 'shopping complex'. Simple as that. Rents were high in a complex.

By the time the bus swayed and bucked out of town it was packed solid. The trim conductor squirmed up the aisle for fares. The fat driver had wild wavy hair and a vermilion third eye. In a treeless landscape we sighed past salt pans and salt heaps thatched with palm fronds. Tanks were protected with white cloths knotted on strings at intervals. Regimented egrets, I thought. Small bridges spanned water oozing towards palms and mangrove swamps. A sign, 'Coringa Nature Sanctuary', depicted an estuarine crocodile, a fishing cat and an otter.

Where was the port of Coringa where Elizabeth Bowden and her sons boarded ship for England in 1851? By the 1890s it was just an island, separated from the mainland by the Coringa river, running north from Yanam. On my maps it was not even a name. A girl in an orange-on-white, white-on-orange patterned Punjabi suit stared at me staring at nothing at all.

Ranks of houses like tombs were home to workers in poultry and salt-processing sheds outside the big village or small town of Tallarevu. The *revu* or wharf was still there, with skeletons of boats, chandlers and coils of thick coir rope. In every other house a man or woman treadled a sewing machine. Children chanted lessons in 'Sunshine Tiny Tot' English-medium school. The bus took the bridge over the Coringa river – small river or big stream – and stopped outside Yanam's Post Office. The orange-and-white girl shook her head at me. Not here. Not yet.

At Yanam's dusty bus station I eased battered buttocks and thighs. A *ratha*, or god-cart, shrouded with fronds stood close by a smart factory called Regency Ceramics. A pair of Brahmin cows, with silver tips and red tassels on their horns, drew an empty ox cart with a whole palm trunk suspended beneath yoke and axle, one end sticking forward like a battering ram, the other trailing behind and ploughing a furrow between wheel tracks. Poking around among street stalls I came face to face with Hanuman. The sacred monkey swung fringes of black hair, its crown was the sun, its lovely eyes glittered behind a mask. It collected money for the temple from stallholders, marking down each contribution in a cash book. It posed for me by a massive bunch of bananas.

Streets were exceptionally clean. Liquor stores were numerous. Sari lengths streamed from the first-floor windows of a cloth shop. There were antique ochre roofs, pillars, vivid tiled façades, mosaics, fretwork cement balconies. At the town's heart was a bust of Gandhi set in a lush public garden surrounded by a Neapolitan-ice-cream-coloured wall. A woman chose powders, yellow, orange and red, from heaps piled upon newspaper and sacking spread on the ground; the vendor packed what she wanted in twists of paper. A man selected garlands of jasmine at the neighbouring pitch. The market was patrolled by officers in scarlet peaked *gendarmes'* hats.

Police headgear and the Eiffel Tower on bread-wrappers were all the signs of French influence I could see. Until 1954, seven years after India's Independence from Britain, Yanam's six square miles comprised a little slice of France. Then, in combination with three other ex-French coastal enclaves, it became the State of Pondicherry. *Puddu cheri* is Tamil for 'new village'. This fragment of East Godavari where I walked was not Andhra Pradesh.

The Godavari river was what I wanted. After a brief haggle I clambered into a *jutka*, or two-wheeled sprung trap; the driver flicked a plaited switch at his pony's flank and we clattered out of town down a causeway between fields to the water. The Gautami Godavari. *Navas* with furled sails were moored at poles by the muddy beach. A launch was loading passengers for Polavaram Island; a frail silver-haired woman perched at the cabin's side, neither on the roof nor under it. It was very hot. The cabin roof was tin. A fisherman sat on a thwart in his boat mending nets. He plucked off his turban, unfurled and secured it around his waist as a *lungi*. A *nava* in full sail and dark silhouette slid across metallic waters, the flexed figure of a boy grasping the rudder oar above his head. A man stood in his boat near the bank and spun out a weighted net, gathered it, pleated it and spun it out again. It hit the water with a slight gasp, O!

No fish. I ate a loosejacket in the shade of a concrete shelter, in the company of a sleeping man, an elderly couple who did not take their eyes off me, did not stop smiling, and a calf who ate the peel. I walked up the beach among a growing crowd of friendly children and men. One of the children on the fishing boats, a girl in tangerine, watched us all, turning abstractedly after us as she combed her hair. I was in a foreign country for the day, staring homewards across a glorious delta. As Narsapur stood at a bend in the river a few miles up the southernmost Vasista Godavari, so did Yanam on this northern Gautami branch. This symmetry satisfied me for no good reason.

On my walk back to town I saw a man in dark glasses and pale-cream *khurta* and *pajama* unlocking an absurd padlock on a flimsy palm-frond field gate. I simply had to greet him. He replied in good English and invited me in to his land. He introduced himself, Sirajuddin, and his water buffalo which gave five litres of milk night and morning. His lemon trees were fragrant. His young coconut palms would yield after three years. Between them he grew cattle fodder and peanuts. A phalanx of women and three turbanned men squatted to weed the crop. They smiled at him and laughed with him. He seemed an unusual landowner.

William Bowden writes of a landlord whose Yanam house was said to be haunted. He tried all sorts to be rid of the demon. A holy man warned that it would do him no good, so a subtle plan was devised. 'A fine young girl, daughter of a servant, was taken and placed by his side while the witchcraft ceremonies were proceeding. At a certain stage . . . the girl screamed, and started out of her place in convulsions, and shortly afterwards died. Such is the report.' The police investigated. The landlord was sentenced but fled into hiding. I couldn't see the *gendarmes* chasing Sri Sirajuddin for anything. He was a Lions Club member and chairman of Yanam's Marketing Committee. He made friends.

Peanuts were a ninety-day crop, harvested in March. Fifteen bags per acre, three acres, a thousand rupees a bag: forty-five thousand rupees for an outlay of ten thousand. For nine months the river at Yanam was salt, for three months in flood it was sweet. Sirajuddin's land was flooded every year. He sat me on a stool; a café owner handed lentil snacks across the hedge and one of the men, with white hair and good legs, climbed for coconuts. I was refreshed when I left Sirajuddin's kingdom. It was called France Teppa.

The bus was very hot and ripe with chickens, fish baskets and men full of Yanam's liquor. At Tallarevu a puncture gave us pause. Then we argued with a lorry and almost rolled down a bank. At the bridge in Kakinada our luggage rack tangled with an overhead cable. Everyone peered out, laughing. Sparks cascaded to the dust. I made sure only my rubber soles touched metal.

Next day I took a rickshaw from Hotel Manasarovar to the station. A faded poster advertised the last Godavari Pushkaram: 'Special Arrangements made at Rajahmundry and Kovvur for Holy Dip and Security of Pilgrims'. A tiny girl in knickers with matted hair and adult eyes circled my feet, pleading monotonously. The fingernails of her begging hand and the *bottu* on her brow were scarlet. She crossed the line and picked up a brindled puppy; it escaped as she climbed back on to the platform, but she caught it and brought it to me. The puppy allowed us to smile at each other, as a man and a small girl may share smiles.

The train was late. The platform had filled up alarmingly with Ayyappan pilgrims in black with bare torsos and garlands and bundles in white cloths on their heads. These devotees and that little beggar, I thought, live in the same world as the dentist. On my last evening I'd taken a rickshaw to Balan and Beena's house in the Gandhinagar district of Kakinada. It was cool by then. People lay wrapped up on the ground outside the Computer Centre. In a tank, ghostly lotus blossoms rose above the stars. The moon was a tarnished sickle.

'Scotch?' said Balan. He proffered a bottle of Black Dog

Whisky. With a name like that I was unsure if it would cause or cure depression. Furniture and rugs were lost between cement walls. The high-ceilinged house felt half finished though they'd lived in it for seven years. It was large and very detached.

'We can live without neighbours,' Balan smiled, subdued now.

The verve he'd shown at Beena and Mohan's dinner party had been sucked out of him. Atavistic pride had drained away.

'We cannot have children,' he announced. 'But would you want to bring up children in this country?'

Beena drew her cardigan around her sari and nodded.

'We believed that when our generation came to power they would not be corrupt. They have, and they are worse than our parents.' He laughed. 'Rotten mouths can be filled with gold.'

They showed me out through the kitchen, laminates peeling from the cupboards, into the garden. It smelt good.

'This', said Beena, 'is a frankincense tree.'

Gold, frankincense and whisky, I thought. Three wise men from the east. I wanted to arrange an impossible meeting between the Indian dentist, Doubting Thomas and William Bowden. I could have listened to them for hours.

'Take no notice of me,' said Balan. 'I'm an old Indiaphobe.'

28

THE LIGHT HOUSE

Antarvedi

IT WAS St Valentine's Day, I realized later. At sunrise I walked to the *ghat*. The river was flame coloured. White powder had been sprinkled along streets and river bank. It was not some great chalk design to welcome Lakshmi, but disinfectant to ward off cholera. On this, the second day of the Antarvedi Festival, thousands of people continued to stream through Narsapur from the railway and the bus station to board boats for the mouth of Vasista Godavari. Launches had been throbbing downriver all night long.

Yesterday it had been like a strange town. All the pilgrims stared at me as locals had done when I first arrived. Police had been drafted in to marshal the multitudes; at the launch *ghat* an officer asked for my passport and, in its absence, took me for a little chat with his superior: starch, pressed khaki, shoulder-strap, belt, holster, well-polished face. He was deliberately cool but his shifting eyes looked for trouble. I took the seat he offered. Languidly he crossed his legs. A lieutenant stood one pace away absent-mindedly chafing his calf with the business end of his *lathi*. What followed had simply been an authorized, but threateningly polite, version of the eternal interrogation to which every boy with a little English subjected me: 'What is your name? What is your country? What is the purpose of your visit?'

At dawn, there were no police at Holland Wharf. Beggars squatting behind spread saris lined the road. Most of them looked healthy and well fed. A few cars waited near the bathing *ghat*, some with drivers aboard, while their rich passengers pressed down the steps with everybody else. They all waded in, ducked forwards into the river, scooped up water in their right palms, anointed their heads and made *namaskaram* to the rising sun. Wet saris and *lungis* clung to worshippers who crammed inside the raised balustrade around the base of the pipal tree. They sprinkled powder upon the stone gods leaning at its trunk and left small oil lamps flickering amongst its roots.

It was unusually calm and quiet. Some people modestly changed into dry clothes before making for home on foot or by car. Others gained maximum merit by walking home wet. Their *puja* was done. They would not swell the crowds beside the ocean. I went back for a quick breakfast. Suguna provided me with a tiffin tin of *puli hari*, tiger food, and a flask of water to put in my bag, and Joy walked with me to the embarkation point.

It was extremely orderly. After the lines of beggars a First Aid tent advertised information about vitamins and condoms and AIDS. Then it was like entering a maze: hand-rails, still covered in resinous bark and lashed to supports planted in sand-filled tar barrels, funnelled the flow of pilgrims beneath palmyra shelters and led us round to the ticket desk past a posse of police. I showed my passport and paid the five-and-a-half-rupee fare. The temporary timber jetty, one of several carpeted with fronds and a layer of sand, swayed and bounced underfoot as I descended into a waiting launch. As soon as the cabin was full we cast off, to whistles and shouts of command. Nobody was permitted to stand. Nobody was allowed to sit on the roof. I waved goodbye to Joy.

She had told me of less regulated times, of past accidents, of overloaded pilgrim launches capsizing in mid-river. A month earlier I'd hired a launch and made this trip with sixty hostel girls. Joy had waved us off then too, shielding her eyes against the sun and perhaps against the memory of the girls who'd drowned on a previous expedition to the same spot. Joshi had showed me the series of shrines raised on the riverbank to the fierce goddess Kondlamma after her image had been washed up at Narsapur in the floods; he'd pointed out the burning *ghat*.

The launch had been full of singing. Many of us had sat on top watching the liquid world go by, men in loin cloths with feet braced against low gunwales of fishing boats, bodies silhouetted against patched sails, the gulls that mobbed them, the embanked paddies and processions of coconut palms, the last village in

West Godavari, the last island, the cyclone relief shelter like a helter-skelter, the Bay of Bengal.

We'd beached on the eastern shore beyond the village of Antarvedi; I'd run down the plank into shallow water and cut my left big toe open. Santhosham had bound it up with a strip of sari. I'd secured it with a rubber band. A toe parcel. Not a good omen. I'd limped as I prospected the site of the marriage festival of the god Lakshminarasimhaswami that my ancestors first attended in 1838.

Then, as now, it had a reputation for wildness, for frenzy, and an understandable intolerance of non-Hindus. People at Narsapur, including earnest Brahmins, had warned me off. But it had been a significant initiation for the Bowdens and I wanted to see it all for myself.

'Of course you must go,' said Joy, but then she always said that.

The launch was remarkably quiet. My fellow-passengers were restrained, expectant. Some smiled at me. We disembarked without mishap on to one of several springy jetties and were channelled, with the throng from other launches, along a causeway between prawn tanks towards the temples of Antarvedi.

On my first visit we'd made for the lighthouse, across dry ground that looked like bog because it was so accustomed to inundation. Joshi warned me off the thorn bushes, introduced for some reason by the authorities. To stabilize the soil? To destabilize landing-parties? Each thorn was vicious, a vegetable nail. One toe parcel was enough. I could do without stigmata.

'Ask anyone what this plant's name,' he said, 'and see what he say you.'

I asked one of the girls.

'Government thorns,' she said.

The lighthouse compound was unlocked for us. We paid a rupee each at the ticket office to a man who spoke good English and almost no Telugu. He invited me into his bungalow. A radio played film music. *Indian Express* newspapers were piled high. He showed me through a wad of family photos. Wife and daughters at home in Calcutta. I asked to use his outside lavatory.

'I fear it is an Indian toilet,' he said.

'That's fine,' I said, fearing the worst, and wanting but not wanting to ask what else he thought I expected.

All stainless steel and a pail of water. It was pristine.

The lighthouse was a tall square tower painted from the bottom up red, white, red, white, red with a cylindrical lantern on top. A hundred and ten concrete steps and seven rungs of a glossy green-painted iron ladder took all who didn't suffer from claustrophobia or vertigo up to the lantern platform.

A big tin of Brasso sat on a shelf. Every cog of the brass mechanism, every segment of glass prism gleamed. The lamp itself had been polished into near invisibility. The light's range was twenty-seven kilometres. Ocean and sky were indistinguishable. At either side of Vasista Godavari's mouth a broad beach curved away into haze like the blade of a golden scimitar. Prawn tanks like square ponds glinted beside the river. Palm-leaf homes and pump-houses stood proud on mud banks. From the village, marked by white and technicolour temple *gopurams*, a solitary man pushed a tricycle laden with ice-cream in our direction through a dusty landscape of palmyra trees.

The lighthouse cast a cul-de-sac of shadow. We picnicked in it, on the tiger food – and hard-boiled eggs. Suguna showed me how to crack and peel the shell off mine. It was very helpful. For all she knew, there were no chickens or eggs in Britain. A bitch and her pups scavenged for scraps. A small boy flung stones at them, provoking pained yelps and appreciative applause. Here, one-upmanship is imbibed with mother's milk.

The ice-cream man did good business as we crossed the dunes and the wide, wide beach to the ocean's edge. Suguna draped a towel over her head and strode off over the burning sand like a robust Moses leading the children of Israel. Mirages stretched and squashed her reflection. The children lingered in the surf, saris hoisted, voices raised against the breakers' boom and sigh.

We skirted a lagoon and found the orange road which led into an idyll of palms, cattle, white egrets, tanks adorned with lotus blossoms and mud-and-leaf houses; in front of one a man who enjoyed our admiration was making a fence of palmyra leaf-stalks with whole leaves like spiky fans inserted at regular intervals; it was sturdy and beautiful.

'Yes, palmyra is very beautiful here, but very expensive in town,' said Santhosham as we continued our pilgrimage. 'And here', she announced, 'is the city of Antarvedi!'

A rectangular tank the size of two football pitches. A *sadhu*, with tiffin tin and water pot at his feet, folding up his meagre laundry. A goatherd and his flock. A hawker on a bicycle festooned with stainless-steel pots. A handful of houses and shack-shops. Beyond the tank, beyond houses and palmyra trees, a white temple and a colourful one. A bullock cart. A cream Ambassador full of passengers teetering along the causeway in the direction of the prawn tanks.

Out there I met a young couple sorting prawns on their mud verandah. Their small house's wattle ribs stuck out. Above its dark doorway the palm-leaf eaves were at waist-height. The walls were thick with white impressionistic fleurs-de-lis. The dense chalk pattern on the verandah – parallel lines alternating with scrollwork – flowed under the pair of squatting figures like a magic carpet.

Late-afternoon sun lit them. The sight is vivid and warm in my memory. Especially so. I don't know why. The decoration imbued their house with a mysterious lightness, it buoyed them up. Its neatness and exuberance was gloriously gratuitous. Sunlight shone off the handlebars of an old warhorse of a bicycle parked by the verandah; it glinted on upturned pots and drinking vessels, on the woman's silver anklets, her nose stud, her amber bracelets, and on the battered bowl in which four dark hands with pale palms sifted the vulnerable coral-pink prawns.

His hair was tightly curled and, when he turned an open smile on me, his teeth were blinding white beneath a black moustache. His shirt was puce and his shorts khaki. Her sari was saffron and her blouse vermilion. Her smile was modest and generous, her eyes grave, the bones of her face exquisitely carved. Her hair, unusually, was loose.

'They can, he says,' said Santhosham, 'make enough rupees to live, day by day, selling prawns to dealers.'

I loved this simplicity, this light house, these smiles. For a moment I yearned for it all, as sentimental travellers do. Then that word 'dealers'. I made myself see their exploitation, their position in society, and on this mudbank the frailty of house and livelihood set against cyclone and flood. I saw their necessary, foolish courage. I loved those smiles all the more; like limewash patterns on dried mud, they were gratuitous, glorious. I left their house sober, but with a light heart.

When I returned a month later, with the crowds that pushed along the causeway from the launches to Antarvedi, I almost missed that house. It was so tiny, and shut up tight with a door of rattan and plastic sheet. That day the view from the lighthouse was of streams and tides of people flowing from river to sea, from fair to temple. It was wild. It was St Valentine's day, the morning after the marriage of the gods.

HOLY DIP

Antarvedi

ANTARVEDI was utterly transformed. Hundreds of bicycles were systematically parked and guarded by watchmen within an enclosure beside the causeway. The *maidan*, or open space, in front of the technicolour temple was crammed with pilgrims, bazaar stalls, ox carts and pony carriages. The day was young and I aimed first for the beach where I hoped devotees would still be taking holy dips. A beggar, with stumps of limbs that might have been the result of leprosy or deliberate childhood mutilation, crawled on his belly with a plate of coins in the small of his back.

I lobbed a fifty-paise piece into it and felt worse rather than better as I passed the gateway of the white temple. Each sight, each sound, each face was an enigma that urgently demanded comprehension, judgment, appropriate reaction. The temple bell rang every second or so as each new pilgrim entered the sanctum. The pungency of incense and the sickly smell of libations reached me. All I could see was the *Dhwajasthambham*, the copper temple pillar, rising above the crowd that seethed around its plinth. People going in clutched garlands and coconuts, those coming out had fresh scarlet impressed between their eyes and white ashes smeared on their foreheads.

A slight mute figure stood in my path. He was covered from shaved head to bare foot in white make-up. He wore a *dhoti* and a tiny pair of yellow spectacles. He blinked up at me. I didn't recognize the boy. Not a deserving case. I glared at him and, only as he ran back to his parents, I saw exactly who he was:

Gandhi, of course, a pantomime Mahatma. With no hint of reproach the family watched me stride away. Humourless *sahib*.

A month ago, the priest in the white temple had prepared me for a pilgrimage not a carnival. As if you could have one without the other. He'd welcomed me, with sixty hostel girls and hangers-on, into the precincts of the Vedic storm-god Rudra, who is also Shiva the annihilator. Shiva's third eye is the eye of wisdom and destruction. He sits on top of the world, Mount Kailas in the Himalayas, in deepest meditation. Here, topped by a torrent of matted hair, the Ganges, his image sat upon the main *shikhara* or temple tower, with garlanded trident in hand and cobras entwined about arms and neck: Lord Shiva, in the lotus posture, poised between two placid Nandi bulls and directly beneath a fearsome demon with popping eyes, hooked beak and deadly fangs. In collision as always, the serene and the grotesque.

The *pujari* took me within. It was dark, thickly scented. A bell chimed. A camphor flame burned. In a further sanctum, I glimpsed the goddess Parvati, Shiva's consort, his *shakti*, his energy. She sat up above too, upon the second *shikhara*, flanked by images of her vehicle, the lion. But down here, in permanent dusk and garlanded with jasmine and marigolds, was the *lingam*, a squat stone penis marked with the three horizontal stripes of Shiva and wearing the *yoni* or vulva like a collar.

'Just as *Antar-vedi* means "inside-outside",' Santhosham did her best to interpret the *pujari*, 'so the temple holds the god; as the body holds the *athma* or pure spirit.'

I turned towards the light and found myself gazing into the eyes of the great Nandi outside, and of Parvati and half a dozen other girls who clustered round the sacred bull.

'The parts of the temple should be compared with the parts of the body. Thus the heart it is that loves the god . . .'

The heart wasn't the part of the body I was thinking of, in my crass Western way. Joshi too had something else on his mind.

'Have you seen, outside, at the back?' he said.

He drew me discreetly to the rear of the *vimana* and tentatively pointed out stone figures carved in relief on the wall that, yes, I had noticed. They'd been picked out in paint to make them noticeable. They were copulating athletically. Perhaps I ought to have looked shocked.

'Some places, the people worship this things.' His gesture had been vague, but unmistakably indicated genitals. 'And do not know what it is they are worshipping.'

I thought they probably did know, but that the spiritually minded among them meditated upon the power of the creator and the perpetuation of *prana*, life. Joshi's problem with the sacred and profane was different to mine, but he had one all the same.

Now I was surrounded by bodies pushing towards the sea for holy dip, or returning with wet hair and baskets crammed with sodden clothes. Each side of the road there were bodies performing *yagna*, feats of self-mortification. There were scarred and mutilated bodies, and there were bodies whose business was show business. Each beggar was stationed behind a spread sari. Each sari length touched the next. They were laid end to end for a mile and a half, all the way down to the beach, on both sides of the orange road.

A shape in a sack writhed and rolled to and fro moaning with awful regularity; stumps of limbs bound up with blood-soaked rags stuck out of the sack's mouth. A child lay prone across his mother's thighs with weeping sores, bloody and pustular, on face and limbs. Another sat pathetically with amputated arms bandaged in crimson. There were undramatic beggars too, with none of the groaning and the gore: a wall-eyed woman, a man with callused stumps instead of feet, a man with one tiny arm and a rudimentary hand.

Repulsed at first, I began to look carefully at the horrors. Some were genuine enough. Some handless arms were extra long, blood stains on bandages were preternaturally bright, limbs were folded back and carefully made-up, running sores were cunning masks of muslin, mashed banana and rouge. Some deformities told tragic tales, others were straight out of the amateur dramatics' dressing room. It made no difference.

Devout pilgrims trickled rice from their right hands along the continuous line of saris, or dropped coins now and then. One woman threw down a rupee and stooped to pick up change. Fraud merited as many alms as good faith. Holy men swathed in cloth of crimson or scarlet or saffron or mustard or sulphur or jasmine meditated upon *moksha* or money beside framed pictures of Shiva or Jesus Christ or Ganesh or Sai Baba. Some had palm-leaf sun-shades stuck in the sand. Others' collapsible umbrellas were autumnal, black subtly tinged with green and turning russet. One modest godman had erected a small palmyra hermitage to shade his fine head of immaculately coiffed white hair.

Hanuman, the monkey and faithful ambassador of the god Rama, image of the perfect man and real hero of the *Ramayana*, who has himself been raised to godhead, sat stock-still in full sun; he was smeared from top to toe with jade-green make-up; he held his mace with its massive head at rest on his right shoulder; his jewelled helmet and very human eyes flashed above a plum-coloured muzzle. He breathed deeply. A god was a cut above a *sadhu*, and probably much more profitable.

The orange road softened and became sand. The tide was higher than I'd seen it a month ago; the lagoon was swallowed up; but the beach was still wide, and now dense with pilgrims. Heaps of black hair in a line on the sand grew as the heads of fresh devotees were shaved. A bald boy followed at my heels, muttering 'Paise' every few steps. A group of students chanted mantras at the surf. A troupe of drummers wearing lemon-yellow turbans beat out a tantric tattoo. And always, competing with the ocean's surge, came the insistent chiming of bells and the intermittent moan of conch shells. And always the urgent hiss in my ear, 'Paise!'

Every holy man on the beach had a bell in his right hand and a conch shell hanging at his left shoulder. Otherwise, the variety of dress was extravagant, from the all-white ascetic look to sets of robes that embraced each shift of the spectrum between yellow and purple. Some costumes were unadorned, others were festooned with beads and bells and bangles. Some conch shells were naked, others had stems of brass or gold. Vermilion and ash were daubed on many brows beneath turbans of every shade from white to indigo. On one man's head a proscenium arch of drapes framed pictures of the gods. On another's five brazen serpents reared up above lotus blossoms set with semi-precious stones.

Two boys of about sixteen in jeans and shirts and baseball caps approached me with big smiles. One of the caps said 'Friend' in large letters.

'Excuse me, sir, are you bathing?' Friend said.

'No, I'm not bathing,' I replied.

'Please will you take care for our things if we bathe?' his friend said. 'If we leave unattended it will be gone.'

They reminded me of a Tamil boy from Solihull I'd met in the queue at Heathrow Airport. He'd warned me about Indians.

'You've got to keep an eye on these people,' he'd said.

Here everybody, it seemed, left their belongings on a towel or a palmyra frond and walked into the sea for holy dip.

'How long will you be?' I said.

'Oh, just about half an hour only,' Friend said. 'Thirty minutes.'

But why ask me, when miles of beach were crammed with their fellow-countrymen?

'I'm sorry, friend,' I said, 'can't you find someone else?'

Friend and his friend sauntered off, looking even more pessimistic about human nature.

'I'm sure someone will keep an eye on your stuff,' I called after them apologetically.

'Paise,' said the bald boy under his breath. 'Paise.'

My great-great-grandparents stood here more than a century and a half ago. I've discovered just one record of the first of their many visits to this festival in the letters of Mrs Thomas, wife of the district judge, who was staying in a bungalow beside the salt creek at Samuldevi, ten miles due west, early in 1838:

February 17th – Yesterday the old Braminee post-office writer came to pay a visit and chat. He had been to a great Heathen feast at some distance – thirty thousand people present. He told us that the Narsapoor Missionaries . . . were there, preaching and giving away books, and that they said,

'What use your feast? *arl* (all) too much nonsense! What for make noise, – tumtums, – washing? – arl that, what for do? pray to God, that *prarper* (proper)!' We asked if the people understood and listened, and if any of them believed the 'padre's' words. He said, 'Understand, very well; – listen, plenty; – believe, no, sar!' Then he went on to tell us that they could not believe now, no more could he, but that their children's children would all believe; that we were now in the ninth Avatar, which would last sixty years longer; that then there would be 'plenty too much great trouble,' and everything 'more worser' than it had ever been before; that all religion would be destroyed, and this state of confusion would last for some time, but that, within two hundred years from the present time, the tenth Avatar would take place, and Vishnoo would appear to put all in order; that he would not restore the Hindoo religion, but that caste would be done away with for ever, and all people be alike upon the earth . . .

So, I thought, doing sums in my head, if the Brahmin post-office writer was right and if I was very lucky I might just live to see it. Fifty years to go! In the meantime, a *pujari* squatted on the sand with a young family. He fashioned two small hulls from palmyra-leaf stalks, stuck sticks of masts with purple-paper sails into them, sprinkled powder and lit their cargo of small lamps. Man and wife left their children with him and carried the boats down to the water. They launched them with prayers for the husband's prosperity. At my back the boy whispered, 'Paise.'

The nearer I got to Vasista Godavari's mouth the denser the crowds became. It is said to be the seventh mouth on the delta, though it's hard to find them all on any map. Serious devotees are supposed to bathe at all seven, this one last. The waters of river and sea commingled here are the holiest of all.

'Here also once upon a time a brother and a sister came to bathe,' – was this myth or history? – 'and they bathed, and because of the currents they were sucked down in a whirlpool and drowned.' Santhosham had told me this. Fresh and salt water mixed was sacred, and deadly too, a recipe for awe.

Here, pilgrims might well consider the Telugu proverb: 'The

villager fears the cemetery, the stranger fears the water.' Men
and women changed out of wet clothes with dextrous modesty
and made their way back along the beach towards the orange
road that led to the village of Antarvedi. They had gained great
merit. Fresh clothes were crisp and bright. The hair of those who
still had any dried quickly in the sun. Holy hands held bags of
rice at the ready for beggars. Bare feet padded along in my
shadow, and 'Paise' slipped out of the corner of the bald boy's
mouth.

JUGGERNAUT

Antarvedi

SUDDENLY I was aware that the bald boy had evaporated. I was able to run the gauntlet of beggars and throw coins about without him. A woman, painfully contorted on the ground, smiled and sat up to have her photograph taken. The sun was high. I sat beside the orange road in the shade of casuerina trees. A faint breeze stroked me. I drank some warm water in peace and watched the world reel past. By a sari speckled with coins and grains of rice, a man continuously caressed and rearranged the coils of his python. His wife and ragged daughter caught my eye, roused man and serpent from hypnotic play and came between the trees. He proffered his pet. Its tongue made a tentative excursion. If it had been a puppy I'd have shaken its paw; hard to do with a python. It was cool and smooth, like lacquer.

A clacking bicycle bell announced a vendor with a rack of bottled water. The snake family retreated for refreshment. A man stopped his professional writhing and groaning; he jumped to his feet and strolled over to buy a bottle. A tough guy on a scooter drove at me, weaving between trees, and braked just in time. Dust, two-stroke din. His mates, on foot, surrounded me. Now what? Tough guy gave me an oily smile.

'What is your name? What is your country? What is the purpose of your visit?' It was time to hit town.

On the outskirts I passed palm shelters, tents, makeshift barracks and police posts with signs in polite English: 'May I help you?' Who here, apart from the illiterate and me, couldn't read Telugu? Where, apart from me, were the polite Englishmen? At the far side of the village's rectangular pond, or tank, there were fenced compounds where a variety of organizations and sects and pilgrim parties gathered for inspirational *puja* and holy picnics.

Dr Bhimrao Ramji Ambedkar, father of independent India's constitution, stood on a plinth at the corner of the tank in his glossy blue jacket and tie. He is called the modern Manu, after the first-century Hindu law-giver who codified the caste system. There's sad irony in that title. He considered espousing Islam in the battle against caste. He abandoned Hinduism for Sikhism and, with two hundred thousand untouchable followers, converted to Buddhism a few weeks before his death in 1956.

'We are in warring camps,' he wrote, but 'nothing in the world will prevent this country from becoming one, and with all our castes and creeds . . . we shall in the future be a united people.'

Ambedkar the untouchable dreamed of it, just as the Brahmin post-office writer from Samuldevi a century earlier foresaw a time when 'caste would be done away with for ever, and all people be alike upon the earth'.

Dream of the future, I say, and be sure that you do not live too long.

Ambedkar, hero of the Harijans, stood firm, a cement figure in painted Western clothes. In *dhoti* and headcloth a figure of flesh and blood lay on a bed of Government thorns; he might have fallen backwards into a bush; his legs were folded; his mild, black-bearded face was the face of a Pre-Raphaelite Jesus; eyes closed, he reclined in bliss, like an advert for Sleepeezee beds; beside his cruel bed, a framed picture of Sai Baba; beneath it, blood on the sand. I could see thorns piercing him.

It made me sweat. I drank a cup of tea at one stall and a bottle of Citra at another in quick succession. Nearby, a beggar with a white beard, withered buttocks and warped spine lay unmoving, doing the splits, chin and clasped hands grounded beside one foot and many coins dropped by the devout. Extreme and permanent splits. His position – physical, social, economic – was pathetic in its pointlessness. It made me angry.

The shadow cast by the technicolour temple seemed a good place for a picnic. I made for it through the festival bazaar. There was normality there. Kids pressed their faces into slices of watermelon. Then drummers came leaping between the ranks of stalls, wild and anarchic. Two staring unkempt women beat the hell out of double-ended drums. Three men with bushes of matted spiky hair, limbs and torsos sticky with sweat and blood, whooped and shouted after them. One cracked a whip, wrapped it around himself, raised bloody weals on arms and back and chest. Another sliced himself with a curved knife. The third threw a child of perhaps eighteen months to the ground. They dripped their blood on it. One picked it up by an arm and flung it into a stall. Intimidated, the stallholder handed it back with interest. They snatched at the child and the notes. For hours they came and went, drumming, whooping, whipping and making money with their dust-and-blood-encrusted baby.

The technicolour temple of Lakshminarasimhaswami at Antarvedi was built about 1823, fifteen years before the Bowdens first attended the festival. It was paid for by a rich member of the fisher caste from Banuamurlanka, an old East India Company post near the mouth of the central, Vainteyam branch of the Godavari.

The temple's *gopuram* gateway was surmounted by successive intricately moulded storeys painted with an increasingly metallic sheen as they ascended through brown, black, blue, lemon, sage, lilac, pink, lime and gold, all inhabited by a brilliant array of gods, up to twin lions standing proud against the sky, forepaws planted upon the heads of elephants.

Beneath this pile, devotees queued up in lanes of posts and rails under a palm-leaf canopy and vanished through the gateway to reappear after a time on balustraded walkways above the level of the temple's outer walls. Up there, the small figures seemed to glide between white *shikharas* standing like wedding cakes around a central court in which two polychrome pagodas reared up, tall and densely populated by the Hindu pantheon.

I had first seen the wonders of this temple a month before when a beaming *pujari* let the girls and me in through a side gate beside a squat *shikhara* upon which Hanuman, the monkey-god, pulled the flesh of his chest apart with his fists to show a pair of figures – one red and one white – standing where his heart should be. We had strolled around the inner court. At the base of each colourful pagoda, the outer walls of the *vimana* or sanctuary were of weathered masonry. The girls in bright saris had moved and mingled against this drab backdrop, craning their necks to take in layer upon prismatic layer of gods that towered above them.

'We, the human family, are not all philosophers. We are of the earth, very earthly, and we are not satisfied with contemplating the Invisible God,' wrote Mahatma Gandhi. 'Then I ask you to approach these temples not as if they represented a body of superstitions ... We have to approach these temples in a humble and penitent mood. They are so many houses of God.'

One God. So many forms of God. Many *devas* or gods doing the work of God. And many *vahanas*, or vehicles of the forms of God, each representing a positive or negative quality, virtues on which the gods ride or vices which they override. Ten *avatars* of Lord Vishnu. Nine *grahas*, gods of sun, moon and planets. Eight *dikpalas* at the points of the compass, protectors of the world. That's for starters.

Seven white horses plunged forward off the *shikhara*, drawing the one-wheeled chariot of Surya through a hoop of flame that is the sun. Up there also, stood two trinities: the gods Brahma, Vishnu and Shiva; the goddesses Saraswati, Lakshmi and Parvati. There was Garuda the man-bird, vehicle of Vishnu; Hamsa the peacock, vehicle of Saraswati; and Simha the lion, *vahana* of Parvati. There was Narasimha the man-lion, fourth avatar of Vishnu. And Lord Vishnu himself reclining upon voluptuous coils of the serpent Ananta, his head sheltered by the snake's five-hooded head, with Lakshmi seated at his feet, borne up by the ocean of milk.

Faithful Hanuman knelt at the feet of Rama, seventh *avatar* of Vishnu, while Sita, perfect woman and incarnation of Lakshmi, stood at his side. Lord Krishna, ideal lover and Vishnu's eighth *avatar*, sat playing his flute in the bliss of pure love with Radha, most beautiful of the milkmaids. She is the soul made one with God, the soul who has long forgotten the pain of separation, the root of all suffering. The girls and I had circulated around the *shikhara* staring up at these figures, and many more. Vivid, gruesome, comical, serene, it might have been a lesson in the theology of Disneyworld. It all made sense.

The *pujari* had led us to a locked room and let us in. It was packed, like a fairground in a box, with newly painted wooden demons and monkeys and snakes and horses and lions and *devas* with four arms, each mounted on a palanquin designed to be carried in procession by sixteen men. The elephant Vijendra struggled to release his foot from the crocodile's jaws. Krishna sat high in a tree gazing down at bathing milkmaids, one frozen in the act of pissing on the ground, and another red with menstrual blood.

I knew how kids at home would have reacted to this, to each lion and horse with its penis picked out in pink and red. These girls studied it all seriously, if warily. Vulgar was sacred, if wrong. One girl had been intent on putting me right.

'All devils,' she'd kept saying. 'All this are devils.'

The *pujari* had shown us around the pillared cloister where blue-black stone gods set behind grills were anointed with vermilion and saffron. They possessed a power which the painted idols had foregone. He'd taken me into the *garbha griha*, the womb-house within the *vimana*. There, in the dimness, in the warm glow, the god Lakshminarasimhaswami sat like a brass Buddha. The blank eyes in his mask-like face were mother-of-pearl, like shades in negative. Two doll-like goddesses attended him, one named Chenchu Lakshmi, the second with no name. She was mystery. She was the other woman. The *pujari* had wafted the flame and stench of camphor about them in broad circles. At my back the sanctuary bell, unexpectedly struck, had sounded very loud.

Outside the gate the *ratha*, or chariot of the gods, stood still on six solid wheels, with ropes like ship's cables coiled up on its lowest stage. It was a mobile pagoda of seven storeys, each supported by sixteen pillars, and surrounded by carved and curving flounces. That day I'd seen how the girls were dwarfed by its wheels. I knew that in the past devotees flung themselves beneath the juggernaut, that temple women's children were thrown down in its path, and that not long ago a boy Joy knew had fallen accidentally and been crushed to death.

A jeep drove headlong into the shady area by the temple where I sat on palmyra fronds with a crowd of pilgrims. Some had to leap out of its path grabbing at upset picnics. It halted and several grinning imbeciles jumped out. They were police officers. I wish I'd said, 'May I help you?' I only thought of it as I finished chewing my *puli hari*.

The *ratha* was waiting at the head of Antarvedi's sandy main street. The crowd offered fruit and coconuts, threw coins and notes. If money fell short nobody nicked it; someone picked it up and passed it on. Each storey was fringed with gaudy cloth; on the lowest, men clambered, hanging up bunches of bananas until it was stuffed solid; the next had a balustrade, lattice-work screens and a pair of four-armed guardians for the protection of Lakshminarasimhaswami and his brides. A larger-than-life-size charioteer held the reins of two garlanded horses that pranced over the heads of kneeling figures grasping swords.

The god-car's path was packed with people milling around stalls. Electricity cables hung above the road ready to garrotte the gods. The mad troupe appeared with drums, whips, knives and the bloody child. I retreated to join people lining the street.

Some crammed beneath a palmyra shelter. Some stood on a concrete roof. Some crouched in the shade of fences. Others found pools of shadow beneath palm trees. I leant against a verandah on which a number of dignified men sat in chairs.

'It will pass this way,' a Brahmin told me.

'Good,' I said, trying to look pleased that by following the example of thousands I had managed to stand in the right place. 'To the temple of Gurralakka?'

'Oh yes, that is quite correct,' he said gleefully. 'You have done your homework.'

There was so much I didn't know, and still more I couldn't understand, but it was a comfort to know that this Brahmin knew that I knew that Lakshminarasimhaswami was about to ride with his brides a mile up the road to his sister's temple. I started to tell him about my ancestors; but a sweaty unshaven man giving out leaflets interrupted us. I stared at unevenly printed Telugu.

'It is for savings scheme, make money,' said the sweaty man. 'You like some tea?'

He disappeared before I answered the question.

'Monthly savings plan,' said the Brahmin.

Three musicians came by with a dancing Brahmin bull in its finery. Two blew *booralu* reedily; the other banged a drum until the bull lowered its head and charged him into the crowd; it was a mobile bull-fight, though this beast was trained to stop dead and lift its horns whenever its tormentor fell to the ground.

'No tea, sorry,' said the sweaty man. 'I have not money.'

This was no advertisement for a man selling quick bucks. I didn't know whether he was explaining or begging.

'Don't worry,' I said.

'I have son,' he continued, 'but not money. You like to take my son? Wait, I will bring him.'

He disappeared before I understood the question. I didn't know adoption agencies worked so fast. It was time to move. The well-dressed bull snorted over the fallen drummer. I found a pitch on a modest hummock amongst Government thorns in full sun. At least it gave me a good view. Hot wind blew dust in my face.

Small children were driven along the road by their parents; dad threw them around and banged a drum; mum beat steel plates like frantic cymbals; two boys cartwheeled as a girl spun in the air and landed on top of the pole dad held. She looked like a speared fish. She hit the ground doing the splits and flipped over, poking her head out between her thighs.

Now my hummock's full; people stand anywhere thorns aren't. The festival president, a deathly pale high-caste man in red-and-white turban, black Nehru jacket and narrow white pyjamas, struts stiffly down the street at the head of a glittering band in crimson-and-gold turbans and tight-waisted jackets. The bandsmen almost keep step; they throb and bray. Nimble as a toddy-tapper, a man shins up poles, unhooks each power cable that spans the street, drops it to earth. The temperature rises.

The god-car stirs and starts forward behind a haze of raised dust. Men compete for places on the thigh-thick ropes. Scores of police keep step with them as they pull. No one falls under the *ratha*'s mighty wheels. Through air filled with music, dust, laughter, shouts and bananas thrown like confetti at the newly-wed gods, the ponderous pagoda rolls ever nearer. A man in a *dhoti* rides beside the charioteer and fends off missiles with a big steel dish. Another cowers under a prancing horse and rakes bananas and coconuts into heaps with his hands.

The god-car stops alongside my vantage point. We all sway. So do huge bunches of bananas and the men squashed between them on the *ratha*'s first floor. Through lattice-work above I can see the one thing that's still moving; the hammock of the gods swings forward and back. Attendant priests peer out. Perhaps they too have no idea why the procession has halted. Not even police bother to prevent boys caressing the stationary wheels. The hammock slows, and stops. It's quiet for an instant as if we all breathe in. Then men take the strain, ropes are taut, and the chariot jolts on its way with a riot of men and boys in its wake, pushing and chasing like revellers at any wedding send-off.

I realized how hot I was. How tired. How dry. Like half the crowd I made for a drinks stall. Maaza, ice-cold mango juice, was better than ambrosia. I worked the stiffness of so much waiting out of my limbs by walking the causeway, past the prawn-sorters' closed-up house, to the river and the jetties. No chance. The queues were long. Three hours long perhaps.

'What is your country?' said a man who stopped at my elbow. 'Why you are here? Where do you stay?'

I explained, just as a polite Englishman should.

'May I help you?' he said. 'Please come with me.'

He was a policeman in mufti. My new friend rushed me to the head of one queue. An officer with a face of implacable opacity sent us packing. My friend paid something to a colleague at another jetty. We embarked first. I wondered how much it would cost me. As the full but orderly boat churned upriver we chatted a little about Joy and her hostel, and ourselves.

'How many children?' he asked.

'Two hundred and seventy girls,' I said.

'Two hundred seventy!' he laughed in astonishment. 'You?' Then, after an hysterical pause, he waved a hand at our fellow passengers and solemnly said, 'You do not like these people.'

Was it a statement or a question? Accusation or command? Did he despise them? What caste was this constable anyway?

Lakshminarasimhaswami's *ratha*, with gods and priests and bananas aboard, rolling down Antarvedi's sandy main street.

Dancing with gods aloft at the bathing *ghat*, Holland Wharf.

Holy men with bells and conches on the beach at Antarvedi where the sacred Godavari river runs into the Bay of Bengal.

Civil engineering in progress: bridges and *dhobi*-wallahs taming the Godavari at Rajahmundry.

Sacred engineering on Kakinada's beach: Ravana who took Mount Kailas, Shiva's paradise, by the roots and shook it.

View from the harem to the Durbar hall at Golconda, 'hill of shepherds', the ancient fortress capital.

Deep in the 'land of dreams', Hyderabad, Andhra Pradesh's capital.

Fishing near the mouth of the Vasista Godavari.

Madimsingaya, a Koya toddy-tapper from Kokiragudem; the groove in his left hip is a wound from a bear attack.

Ascending the Godavari: the khaki river turned milky, then lilac and gold, purple and silver; the hills height-ened, thickened, foggy blue to bottle green to silhouette.

On the cockfight's fringe at Sivagiri: Sai Baba grinned up at me; cards and coins accumulated seriously; I made no sense of it.

Cocks with steel spurs, men circling, one crouched in his bird's posture as if sympathetic magic might help its cause.

Sannasamma, a Konda Reddi woman from Cheeduru.

Yuniah and Suvarthamma baptizing a new convert: she fumbled for her footing and, for a long instant, three figures were linked hand to hand in the mighty Godavari under the bulk of the Bison Hills.

The Horn Dance at Pedagudem: bison horns, peacock feathers, bow and arrows, drums' stunning pulse, women's raw song.

Konda Reddis: the sober watchman from Gedapalli, the tipsy headman of Cheymaluru and boy high in the hills.

The first TV ever to visit Sivagiri: it came upstream with the 'current'.

'I like the people here very much,' just sounded stupid.

I took his photograph on the springy jetty at Narsapur. He didn't ask for money. I was grateful. I quite liked him.

I sent him his photo. If I dream of that St Valentine's day now, it's crazy. No sound, just the sight of a pagoda-on-wheels trundling through rutted sand towards Gurralakka's place. It's as marvellous as a church spire running off down a country lane to join the circus.

31

THE SOLITARY REAPER

Mogaltur

JOY SLIPPED her sandals off, stepped down into a hole and paddled unsteadily, lifting her apricot-coloured sari above the muddy waters. It was early morning at the building plot next to Obanna and Gracie's home. Joy was there to lay the foundation stone of a house, the Christian version of the Hindu ceremony in which gold and other things are incorporated in the footings.

'When I go down into my grave I won't be conscious of it,' said Joy, 'so it's good to have the experience now.'

The day before, a 3 p.m. 'mango shower' had wetted the world for the first time since New Year's Day, raised earthy scents and filled the trench. The *maistry* handed Joy a trowel loaded with cement. She daubed a rock or two and laid some ritual bricks. The plot's owners were pleased. After prayers, Obanna and Gracie gave us coffee, Bombay mixture and bananas. Their adopted 'nephew' Ydidiah talked to me about books. On Christmas Eve he'd been excited to discover that my wife's name was Maggie.

'Do you know the poem, "Journey of the Maggie"?' he'd asked.

'Oh, yes,' I'd thought quickly, 'by T. S. Eliot.'

'Ah, now I am most pleased to know one who loves poetry.'

I'd met him again when Gracie laid on a delicious lunch of curried goat and black gram cakes and we celebrated the official opening of a new china coffee set, given to Obanna by the leprosy hospital in lieu of leave. New buildings are ceremonially opened here, but so are cars and fridges and TVs and cups and saucers. Joy teased Obanna about what he'd eaten on Christmas Eve.

'Weren't they good, those rissoles? Didn't Satyanarayana and his family say so? And none of you eat beef, do you? Mutton, chicken, fish, yes. Not beef. Ha! Not even beef rissoles?'

Obanna laughed with embarrassment. If cows were not sacred, they were not quite edible either, though his business manager's heart appreciated that mutton was nine times the price of beef. Ydidiah kept quiet and ate little. Obanna led me up to the roof. It was hot. Next door's palmyra-leaf roof was tinder-dry.

'Amma bought this plot for us in 1970 for five hundred and fifty rupees. Now, government price is in excess of one lakh.'

A lakh is one hundred thousand rupees. It wasn't poetry. It would be music if it wasn't inflationary. Obanna made some money from coconuts, two or two and a half rupees each. I reached out to stroke their intense ochre and green. The flat concrete roof and its surrounding balustrade were kinked to accommodate the coconut-palm trunks that had stood there since before the house was built. That was poetry.

Magi might have lived at Mogaltur, town of the Moguls. Ydidiah agreed to be my guide on our journey there. I picked him up in the Ambassador and we drove out of town past the leprosy hospital on one bank of the canal, crossed a crumbling humpy bridge and continued on the other bank towards the south west. Here and there the canal was clogged with water hyacinth.

'That is coconut tree,' said Ydidiah helpfully. 'That is paddy field where they grow rice.'

I couldn't seem to explain that I hadn't explored the delta with my eyes shut. Still, today he was my guide.

'Please stop here. Here I will ask.'

He leant out of the window to consult a milk vendor on a bike loaded with stainless pots. Ydidiah was an attractive young man of about twenty-three; he had good bones but his eyes were quietly desperate and his attention span was short.

'Straight, we go straight,' he ordered. 'I also have paddy near

Palakol, but last year floods destroy my crop.' His story was commonplace and tragic. 'Please stop. I will ask.'

He asked in the town with a cinema called Mogaltur. It was a small urban clot in the rural flow. We went straight ahead, or rather followed the causeway as it zig-zagged between fields. We crept behind a bullock cart. A woman with her sari drawn up between her legs waded in mud and bent to thin rice seedlings.

'Look here,' said Ydidiah, 'the solitary reaper.'

It was picturesque. We talked about Wordsworth and I asked if there were Telugu poets who had revolutionized the way people here looked at their world. Ydidiah wanted to discuss *Paradise Lost* and the epic muse. Or he wanted to mention them. Then he asked again and the answer was good. We were there. I parked in long grass beside high walls. A mason on a lashed-up ladder of bamboo was repairing a section. Through gates I glimpsed palaces of sorts. Beyond them was the citadel we'd come to see.

It looked like a chunk of Iron Age fort. It had the right smell too. Swelling banks stepped upwards. But a closer look revealed brickwork at the base of the ditches. I climbed to the top, with one eye peeled for snakes, and tramped the earthen walls. At about my height, a toddy-tapper fixed blackened clay pots beneath bleeding inflorescences at the top of a palmyra tree. Within ruinous walls of masonry across a silted moat I could see bathetically eloquent relics of grandeur.

'The houses of kings,' observed Ydidiah.

Kings – flick, Rajahs – flick, Razu caste – flick, Kshatriya class – flick, arms of Brahma, went the little card index in my head. Flutter went a crow-black bird in a bush on the earthwork bank. Binoculars: male koel, green bill, red eyes. Koels are cuckoos that fill the nests of crows with impostors: stone-coloured eggs blotched with ochre like their own. Ydidiah peered at it for an instant and handed the binoculars back.

'Enchanting,' he sighed.

The toddy-tapper, who I assumed was of the same Settibalgi caste as Obanna, Ydidiah's guardian, came to enquire who I was and what we were up to. His khaki T-shirt and gingham *lungi* contrasted with Ydidiah's crisp shirt and knife-edged trousers.

'It is difficult to talk with these people,' Ydidiah said.

It seemed they chatted easily enough.

'Difficult in what way? Because of dialect, or caste?'

'No, caste is division of labour, nothing more.'

Did he think I'd swallow that? I didn't pursue it.

'No, they have some words we cannot understand, but it is very difficult to talk with these people, that is all.'

It made sense. But I wanted straight answers in the vulgar tongue. A tetchy water buffalo shied away, lunged on its halter tied to a stake. I'd only tried to scratch its head. A high-crowned Brahmin cow glared at me haughtily. We left the cattle tethered by the fort and made for the archway in the brick wall.

Through it stood trees set in a paved garden before a country house, or modest palace. First-floor bays and a long balcony were embellished with balustrading and scalloped arches of intricate woodwork beneath an imposing roof of heavy many-layered terracotta tiles. Paint had long peeled. Plaster had fallen. It was near derelict. A stooped woman emerged from the ground floor. It still offered her humble family a substantial home. She was happy for us to look upstairs.

The outside steps had partly crumbled. It was a scramble. Floorboards were rotten. Weathered carving splintered. Through elegant silhouetted doorways there were glimpses of spilled light illuminating carved ceilings whose dense mouldings and bosses once burned crimson and gilt. There were crenate niches in walls of pink and blue, and delicate reliefs. I studied the panels: moulded pillars supported scrollwork surrounding vases of blossom and sinuous foliage in which parakeets perched.

'Marble,' breathed Ydidiah.

Maybe it should have been marble; it was clearly plaster.

'I think it's plasterwork,' I said, 'but very fine.'

'Very fine plasterwork,' said Ydidiah, 'not marble.'

The view from the bay was of other massive roofs, but what confused my eye were the windows' extravagant curves, frame upon overlapping frame, scene changes behind a proscenium arch. What was Aladdin's cue? I gripped slender pillars where the floor looked frail. Ydidiah wanted to talk about *Samson Agonistes*.

'Why don't you concentrate on your English studies,' I said. 'Obanna and Gracie want you to finish, don't they?'

'Yes, but there are reasons. My brother is problematical to me, my father is a vagabond, my mother is expired.'

Above the galleried balcony rats scurried along exposed joists and disappeared into darkness. An obese one ran down the ridge of a lower roof and into a hole in the wall.

Once upon a time a beautiful girl who lived in Missamma's hostel left because she was pregnant. The boy eventually married her but turned to drink. She left him and his beatings for another man. Then to support her children she flew to Kuwait to earn money like so many women of the delta. Some are enticed into bondage or prostitution. Some return to live grandly for a while, buying silk saris and gold and land. Their men, who might normally do coolie work, sit around like bank clerks. This woman worked as a chambermaid and became the hotel manager's mistress. He wanted her to live with him. She converted to Islam but he would not marry her. To punish him, she killed his brother.

A small report appeared in the paper here, but went largely unremarked because her new Muslim name was used. One of her sons read it but kept quiet. Then came news that she was returning home in a serious condition, a customary euphemism. When the coffin arrived folk queued to view the body that had been hanged, cut down and paraded through the streets of Kuwait City.

Muslims wouldn't bury her because she was a murderer. There was no question of a Hindu cremation. At last a small Christian church gave a plot. Her bones have long settled. Joy recently saw one of her sons in handcuffs at the police station. He's a thief, wild, always in trouble, and a drunk like his vagabond father. Problematical, as his brother said.

Life is problematical. How can Ydidiah mix? How can a wife be found for him? With his history, his pile of poetry and his paddy fields, he is a solitary reaper. Telugus say, 'Every man must dip in his own waters', but I felt fond of him and wished him peace. If only he could focus, persevere, get something right. He waved at a tree in the courtyard of the king's house.

'It is cashew-nut tree,' he said.

I took my rusty botanist's eye to it with interest, but it didn't look right. It had immature fruits, green and pimply.

'Or is it jackfruit?' I asked from within its green shade.

'Oh yes, it is jackfruit tree, not cashew-nut,' Ydidiah said as though I had made a foolish mistake.

There were no kings, no magi, no wise men. We drove on until we came to a shrine beside a tank. Deep pink lotus flowers seemed to hover above a silken surface. Ganesh, elephant-headed god of wisdom, presided here. He detaches his disciples from the distractions of the world, removes all obstacles and consequent sorrows. Devotees had placed dewy-eyed crimson hibiscus on his thighs, and let some drop with divine careless-ness. Ganesh's vehicle, the rat, lives on the floor. Once, when the mighty lord was thrown from his rat, the moon laughed and was eclipsed for her pains. Today folk gathered to smile and ask us questions but Ydidiah grew impatient. I turned the car for home.

'It is difficult to talk with these people,' he said.

32

EASTERN GHATS

Sakhinetepalli

IN THE LATE afternoon it was a pleasure to walk upriver to the
ferry point. Various combinations of roads and alleys led to it.
The riverbank was the direct route. Most of the way it was just
a narrow path between the wall at the end of someone's property and the steep slope to the water. The view of the river was
idyllic, but I couldn't look at it, I was watching my feet and
dancing between turds. Where the path passed a temple I'd look
up and breathe more deeply because there it was always clean.
The sacred and profane may be difficult to disentangle here, but
one thing's clear: it's not nice to shit by shrines.

Better to forgo the view. Watch schoolkids in khaki doing
army drill. Look at the straining rickshaw-wallah, his vehicle
stuffed with tiny homebound boys in tidy uniforms. Observe
the crow taking a leisurely ride on the piglet's back; the glittering
cock leashed by his leg, scratching before a threshold in that
morning's chalk design; women moulding huge pots in cement;
men beating coir with heavy mallets, ruddy rope hanging in
coils under dusty palm-leaf roofs; Durga devotees' red cloths
hung up to dry beside a doorway filled by a man in a crimson
lungi with a beard and a big belly, his wife in a sari of scarlet
and purple, and their well-muscled son, his brow painted gold
and vermilion.

Note the same colours sprinkled at the snake shrine's holes.
Watch the technique of the sweet-maker, pulling at a rope of
pale gold candy looped over a nail in the side of his stall, pulling
it and looping it, stretching it to aerate it, flies settling and taking
off to the rhythm, buzzing between his confection and the open
drain at his feet. Look how the road drops to the river. See

ticket-sellers beneath a shelter on the top step of the *ghat*. Take a long view of that word, Anglo-Indian out of Hindi.

A *ghat* may be a landing-place at a ford or a ferry-crossing, a place where laundry is done, where holy dip and many another *puja* is performed, or where corpses are cremated. It's simply a passage or flight of steps leading down to the river. The word was by extension applied to a mountain pass or defile in the hills. Such a *ghat* was to be climbed and, through English ill-usage, came by about 1600 to mean the mountain itself. So the mountain chains that flank the subcontinent were named Ghats.

I stood seventy miles downriver from the Eastern Ghats and seven miles up from the Bay of Bengal. Imagination had no need to stretch so far. There was too much to see. I leant at a railing and gazed at the mystery, a few hundred yards of sliding river, the subtle countercurrent, the far bank. From the hostel my view was of paddies backed by palms, solid or diaphanous according to the light. From here I could see huts and stalls at the landing and the yellow road running into Sakhinetepalli.

As a warning against relying on a mean person, the proverb says, 'Can you swim the Godavari by grasping a dog's tail?' Each dusk birds and fruit-bats flew across the river out of the sunset towards the night, towards the dawn. Most people travelled east too, filling *nava* after lateen-rigged *nava*, each detaching itself from the ruck and raising a patched sail blazoned with Liptons or Top Star or 3 Roses premium dust tea, or a nicotine-coloured one advertising Charminar cigarettes. A pair of boys sculled a pair of boats, permanently twinned by two sets of planks, to the slipway. Timber ramps were propped in position and a cumbersome Ambassador edged on to them. Everything rocked and one ramp fell, but the car was safely aboard. Its passengers sat in the boats and the boys propelled the whole thing across.

If Narsapur was my base, then the east bank was where I went to put my journey into perspective. A ferry ticket was fifty paise. I sat on the *nava*'s gunwale with my feet on the floor of bamboo canes. The first time, early in the morning, there was no wind and the young ferryman pushed us out, spun us round, walked from stem to stern along one dipping gunwale and began to scull with all the muscles in his body, twisting and rolling, the boat swaying.

A beautiful Brahmin sitting at the temple door watched us go as a man watches a conjurer's illusion. With suspended disbelief I stared back at Ganesh, Hanuman and Durga in garish shrines above the *ghat*. Soon the ferryman nudged us into the quiver of boats at the far bank. A bicycle at the prow toppled and trapped a man's leg. Another man struggled to wrench his motor-scooter out of the bow. I stepped into the neighbouring *nava*, into the water and on to the beach. The ferryman chased me for more paise. I flaunted my ticket, then saw that everyone with a ticket was paying him as well. If you short-change the ferryman you don't get back.

Away from the bustle, fiddler crabs semaphored a welcome and waved lazy goodbyes as soon as I approached. On the slimy banks of a creek mudskippers struggled along like fish out of water, which is what they are. The creek was bridged by a slippery log. I crossed it very carefully, followed by a woman who strode over with a brass *bindi* full of water on her head. At the bend in the river that eroded so much of old Madhavayapalem, I looked across to the deep pool where once famous teak ships were launched and East Indiamen were laden with fine madapollam cloths.

At my feet I found a human skull. 'Fate never fails,' says the proverb, it is written in the sutures. A small intact grave lay a few paces off. *Harijans* and low-caste Hindus bury their dead. Higher castes do it too if they can't afford wood for the pyre, though it's *papamu* – a sin. The outline of a boy in school uniform was drawn in chalk dust on the dried mud mound; twigs each side of his face had pegged a leaf over his mouth with food for a crow to eat and, 'crarkk,' pronounce the soul satisfied.

Back at the ferry-point, in a small unfinished brick temple, stood a black goddess and her consort with mother-of-pearl eyes. Leaf-roofed houses squatted on their mud verandahs beside brick-and-tile mansions. From low sheds came the wheeze and pound of diesel cane-crushing machinery, the smell of sweet ferment, and billowing steam from jaggery making. The road past was white, upholstered with waste pith. At the shrine of the white goddess, she of the red sari and the amicable attendant lion, I turned off down a track deeply rutted by ox-carts between coconut palms.

It was a paradise. Behind layers of trees, women in vivid colours walked through dappled light. Bullocks chewed cud, bells tinkling. A boy rode a buffalo, horns like drop-handlebars, and drove others towards the river with a long frayed cane. A man cranked water from irrigation ditch to paddy by Archimedes screw. I cut along field-banks in this, the Garden of the Godavari. The shocking green of rice shoots. Palmyra-leaf bases like burnished copper. Coconut-palms' elephantine trunks. Jade fruit. Fronds' filagree wafting and lifting like so many veils.

I luxuriated in the breeze off the river, and walked along the low ironstone embankment that mostly keeps the river out of the fields. When it really floods, Joy said, the palms go under. I studied her side of the river. Over there, just down from Narsapur's ferry *ghat* was the *ghat* from which launches set out for Antarvedi Festival. Now there were fishing vessels from Kakinada moored there five abreast, weathered orange, green, blue, with drying fish strung on the rigging like jewellery. Last night I'd watched a group of dark roguish fishermen mend nets, squatting on the slipway while a local man in a deep blue turban and baggy light green shorts waded in and repeatedly spun out a circular net with no success.

The next *ghat* down was Holland Wharf with its *nandi*, its shrine, its bo tree, its figures of Mother Godavari and the Sage Vasista, its ★★★★★STAR-HOT EL stall and Joy's old hostel. The ferry, *Vasista Godavari* in its fresh livery and loaded with tanker lorries, was setting out. I crossed on it one day, while it was being repainted. Men were still thwacking rust off decks with heavy hammers. I wondered how much steel was left. There were two 'bridges', two engines and two cabins with bunks, rumpled blankets, images of gods and remains of joss sticks. This side we nudged the slipway. Something jammed in the propeller, as the boss from Goa explained. A man stripped and went overboard with a rope and a crowbar. He hid in the opaque water for a disturbingly long time before extracting a concrete block.

One day Joy asked if I'd ask the boss to take a patient across who was far too shaky to climb in and out of *navas*. She was a doctor from East Godavari who'd been operated on in Narsapur

Christian Hospital. He was happy to help *gratis*, and provided the frail doctor with a deck-chair. From the *ghat* I waved her off, with Joy and the hospital's director of nursing.

'I live here one year already,' the director said, 'but not until today have I seen river; it is too difficult to walk alone.'

Each time I crossed to East Godavari and looked back to the west bank I considered my family's impact on the Narsapur riverscape. Joy's hostel buildings stood tall beside the Dutch House next door in which our great-great-grandparents first lived, its long red roof surviving at the heart of later grey additions. How long does anything last here that doesn't last for ever? Further downriver was a furious accretion of new shrines to the goddess Kondlamma and, beyond them, a stretch of embanked flood defences, steps for holy dip, and then the burning *ghat*.

There, in downriver Narsapur, I visited Kondlamma more than once; she was repulsive-seductive. Her image had floated down the river in the floods, 1986 I think, and been washed up beside the Sunshine School at the end of a lane of humble houses. At the *ghat* there, fishermen mended nets of blue nylon spread on the ground between shrines. They smiled at me and grinned at each other. One jumped up, startled, as something writhed and wriggled through the layers; a small high-stepping lizard made good its escape from the net. It ran towards what looked like a fairground sideshow. I laughed.

Gaudy images posed inside a big cement doll's house: Ganesh the elephant-headed, Vijendra the elephant, the lord Ayyappa and a warrior tugging an arrow from his eye, one foot braced against the tableau's centrepiece, the *vigraha linga*, a black phallus adorned with a pair of eyes and Shiva's third eye. It was set in a black *yoni*, or vulva, as a fat pestle might stand in a mortar. From its tip sprouted Shiva in azure, with trident and drum, snake at his neck, head crowned with the head of Parvati and the crescent moon. A big bright-eyed cobra twined around the lingam and peered out from behind as if to say, 'Hallo, folks!'

From the small temple porch I could see the river which bore Kondlamma here. Her vehicle, the lion, faced the sanctum. An old *pujari* beckoned me in. He thanked the flood with all his heart for bringing a goddess of such power. In the womb house it was dusk. Camphor and turmeric pricked my nose. Kondlamma's four arms held a conch shell, a trident, a sword impaling red bangles and a lime, and something else, an incense pot perhaps. Here, more than anywhere else, I found it hard to look at what was in front of me, hard to observe the object for the aura. It was hard, indeed, to see for sensing. Now it's hard to say why.

She was the Mother Terrible, swathed in a blood-red sari with a belt of gold. Scarlet, and much gold on her headdress, in her ears, around her neck, on her breast. Her nose-ring was studded with diamonds and rubies. Her face horrified. Gashed with features, fangs, tongue and huge hypnotic eyes, it was hard to focus on. Her foot rested, or rather pressed down, upon the back of a crawling figure of a man, dark brown, pathetic, utterly real. The mixture of nightmare and naturalism was terrifying. A bell clanged at my back. The *pujari* wafted a pungent flame about the goddess and gave me sticky jaggery and jasmine blossom.

I returned to see if I could see. A young *pujari* welcomed me. He thanked the flood with all his heart for bringing a goddess of such power. He ladled holy water from a brass vessel into his right palm, forefinger bent beside thumb, and sipped it. The 'man' beneath the goddess's foot, he told me, was Mahisha the all-powerful demon who dethroned the very gods. Then I knew that Kondlamma was Durga by another name. United against the demon, the gods' combined powers took a female form, *shakti*, embodied by the goddess. Mahisha might change into a bison, an elephant or a giant with a thousand arms, but the goddess astride her lion was invincible and pierced him with her lance. Man is imperfect, say the sages; he is bound and sad and has a thousand enemies within. He must invoke the goddess to annihilate with her bloody blade all false values, all weaknesses, all littleness.

Here, facing Kondlamma and Mahisha, I stood at the heart of the labyrinth, the fortress, the sacred city. I did not know if it was prison or protection. Amazement half blinded me. Beside the wooden image of the goddess that once sped downriver like flotsam from the hills, there was a black stone one, a little Kali also clothed in scarlet. Kali it was who fought with the chief of the demons, but every drop of his blood she spilt sprang up as a thousand giants. To vanquish him the Black Mother drank up all his blood and danced for joy until the earth quaked. Her husband Shiva begged her to stop. In her frenzy she did not see, but threw him down among the dead and trampled on him. So she is depicted, with corpses for ear-rings, a necklace of skulls, a girdle of severed hands, a garment of blood, standing on the lord of the dance. Kondlamma is Kali by another name. Is Shakti.

At the heart of the mandala is militant asceticism and every kind of frenzy. There duality is dead. Shiva is a thousand-petalled lotus at the crown of the head. Shakti lies coiled as a serpent at the lowest *chakra* of the body. Here in the Tantric mysteries they meet, by self-denial and discipline, by drink and drugs and meat and sex. Beside Kondlamma a brazen snake reared up from a dish, and in the sanctum's porch stood the cobra-hooded urns which I'd often seen on dancers' heads beside the *ghat* or passing across fire. A plastic shopping-bag with rope handles lay on top of them. Opposite was some ragged wiring, a turntable and a pile of dusty records. Here's wakeful-ness, I thought. The *pujari* gave me a sweet smile, a marigold and a banana.

A little way downriver I came to a new bathing *ghat* built for Pushkaram Festival. In a shelter sat Brahmins wearing white *panchis* and sacred threads. At the neighbouring burning *ghat* a party of mourners cheerfully watched me go by. They squatted in palm-tree shade upwind of the blazing pyre. The body on the sticks was well alight. It seemed very simple, very pure.

The skull cracked. A fish jumped. I walked away through palm-groves and paddies to the plod and sigh of cattle ploughing in green shade. In a ditch a ruddy crab scuttled for its hole. An otter – or was it a mongoose? – slipped across my path and jumped an irrigation channel. I crossed on a palm-trunk and emerged in town beside a lime-and-yellow house in the Gaumont style and the white minarets and green gates of a mosque.

There was drumming in the street on my very last night in Narsapur. With Satyanarayana I made for it, not far, at the corner of the alley that led to the shrine of Kondlamma. A woman sat in the dust beside a small palmyra shelter for the gods. The drum troupe developed shifting rhythms, sharp and deep. The *booralu* players skirled. Two dancers with god-pots on their heads pranced and pounced on the beat. Behind them a picture of the goddess, like a massive icon, was mounted on a rickshaw. Men were dressing her with garlands of marigolds and jasmine.

Drumming and trumpeting went on all night. I tried to sleep and succeeded some of the time. I was packed and ready to leave this Hindu place, these holy *ghats*. I was aiming for the Eastern Ghats, upriver to the gorge where the Godavari breaks through. From there the goddess had swept down on the flood. It would be quite another India, a fresh twist in the labyrinth.

At six the next morning I chased the raw music and met the devotees as they passed Rama's shrine on the way from the river. Musicians still pounded and blew. Dancers still pirouetted. But today they held *thali*, steel plates piled with white powder and, as they danced out of the dawn, they flung plumes of it in unison high into the air. Above the drums' salvo, it drifted across palm-leaf roofs like smoke from gunshot, *vibhuti* or sacred ash. It is *rupa-arupa*, with and without form. It is indestructible. It is the end of *karma*.

33

LUCKY BRAKES

To Polavaram

STRONG SUGUNA lugged provisions and cooking pots downstairs and deposited them in the compound. The heap there already held a primus stove, a fat bedroll, Joy's bags and my rucksack. Wiry Samelu took charge of packing it all into the Ambassador. Or would have done if the car had been there. I could see what kind of day it was going to be. The expedition was in my honour, but I didn't know what was going on. It was to have been an early start. Five minutes after we were scheduled to leave Joy drove off to make a dawn visit to the hospital. One of her girls, courageous Vasundara Rani, was dying of drug-resistant TB and Joy wanted to say goodbye in case it really was goodbye.

It was good to hear Joy blasting the car horn. Girls ran to open the gates. Six staff helped Samelu pack the car fast. It wouldn't fit. Everybody told the others how to reorganize it. Loudly. It's hard to do something seven ways at once. I knew just how I'd solve the puzzle – not a Virgo for nothing, so the astrologers say – but I kept quiet and watched. I'm good at that too, and I wasn't going to play the big white *sahib*. Joy came down like the wrath of God and ordered everything out. Loudly. She was right of course. Meths for the primus was already leaking from its can. The bedroll would air on the roof-rack.

Suddenly everything slotted in and we were off, not much more than an hour late. I did my best to drive out of the gates in style. To catch the upriver launch we had to reach Polavaram by lunchtime. Just sixty miles as the crow flies. God knows how far by road, half-made and unmade, between canal and river, over and round potholes. We were harried or held up by battered buses and rainbow-coloured public carriers with the legend 'Please Sound Horn Stop OK' on their tails. I threaded the hefty car between ox carts and water buffalo and goats and gave a wide berth to scooters and bicycles that zig-zagged across the pocked stretches. I wanted to catch the launch, but not to pancake the suspension, jar Joy's painful back or make Suguna sick.

By wilful amnesia I'd emptied my mind of the British Highway Code. Now I enjoyed driving on my nerves, and off the top of my head. I savoured moments of improvisation that untied knots of incompatible vehicles, sudden extemporary swerves that preserved both life and momentum, impromptu expedients made all the sweeter by the slackness of the gear-shift, the almost whimsical play on the steering, the exhilarating laziness of the brakes. The very lack of immediate response afforded by the controls made control itself a doubtful notion and immediacy an imperative one.

Perhaps it was nothing more than this, the looseness of the connections between cause and effect, the fact that everything here was artful rather than scientific, perhaps it was this more than all the religious notions in this world that made fatalism inevitable.

Joy unbent slowly and eased her spine as inconspicuously as she could. Suguna's dark skin almost disguised the greenness of her complexion. We left the locked car in the sketchy shade of a single tree, climbed an embankment at the side of the road and dropped down through scrubby land towards the river. It wasn't long past eleven when Joy had suggested we stop. We'd just driven through the town of Kovvur, from which road and rail cross the Godavari to Rajahmundry. I could hardly believe that we'd come so far, more than two-thirds of the way to Polavaram.

We sat on the high river bank in the shade of palmyra trees. Their trunks were plastered with hand-printed pats of cow dung drying in the sun. We ate our picnic while immediately below us a water buffalo flicked its tail and wallowed in brown scum. A few yards out a woman thrashed rocks with washing. As I relieved myself by a cactus hedge a man drove goats past; he deliberately did not notice Joy and Suguna squatting. Far across the sheer surface, the young foothills of the Eastern Ghats – young in geological time – had been plucked up like pinches of mastic.

We breathed deeply and climbed into a hot car. At Pattisema we saw a rocky island in mid-river, a clot of trees surrounding a temple's startling white *gopuram* and *shikhara*. By the time we rolled and bumped into Polavaram I was scratching around in my memory for an old story. William Bowden tells about a Brahmin landlord, with a house and a small fort here, who held a tract of hill territory on this side of the river occupied by Konda Reddi and Koya tribal people whose magical powers he feared:

After he obtained his majority, he wished, it is said, to obtain a counter power to that of the Koys, and commenced a series of magical rites in his own house. His mother residing with him, became alarmed, as it was said by the magicians that he would be unable to bear the power of the god whose aid he sought; she therefore interfered to prevent its prosecution. But he determined to pursue it, and repaired with his young wife to a temple situated on a rock in the river . . . Here he recommenced the rites, and one night, as he and his wife were seated in front of the idol, some Brahmins being in the precincts, it is said he touched the cloth which covered the idol when a squeaking noise was heard (probably that of a mouse, or other small animal). He started, saying to his wife, 'Don't be afraid.' She replied, 'I only thought you would be alarmed,' when he reeled and fell backward. He was taken up by the Brahmins and carried out. He threw up a lot of blood and in a day or two died.

A pastor, in white *khurta* and *panchi*, was waiting with his bicycle at the first junction we came to. He pedalled like crazy to the little church where Joy had arranged to park the car. He left his bike there and jumped in with us. His name was Abraham and he was breathless. At the end of the road to the beach we offloaded our baggage; I left Suguna and Joy haggling with bearers and drove Abraham back to the church compound.

'This way, please,' he said, waving at a small gate in the fence. I pointed to double gates at the side.

'No, no, no,' said Abraham. 'Is better this way.'

What could I do but follow his advice? I drove down a steep slope to the narrow gate and stopped. He got out and looked.

'Ah, dear me,' he smiled. 'Is not possible here. This way!'

He indicated the double gates I'd first aimed for. After complex manoeuvres which amused a gathering crowd, I drove in and parked in the lee of the church building. Abraham and I shrouded the Ambassador in its cloth cover. I hoped it would be safe.

Ten days later, when Joy, Suguna, a couple of girls and I came downriver again, Polavaram seemed a civilized metropolis full of filth, stink, crumbling buildings and pigs in gutters. On my way through it I walked past a surreal ruin beside a palm-leaf house: bits of arches, balustrade, fretwork hanging in the air. It should have been the Brahmin landowner's house. When I reached the white church I unveiled the car. All was well. It started first time. We loaded up and drove off across country on back roads to visit Koya plains villages and the town of Koyyala-gudem. I explored Puliramanagudem, 'tiger-god-town', while Joy preached at a communion service where bread was chapati and wine was Pepsi in a whisky bottle. At Itikulagunta, 'pit-of-bricks', I relaxed on a Koya bamboo bed while the girls picked jasmine and hibiscus. By the time I turned in through Holland Wharf's gates at midnight we'd been travelling for seventeen hours.

Before we left Polavaram that day, Joy asked a group of men at a coffee-stall where we could get air. I wanted brake fluid too, but that was too much to ask. They pushed a boy into the car and told us not to bring him back. He showed us the way to a roadside mechanic's where I pumped up the tyres for one rupee a time. The boy refused a rupee for himself and ran home grinning. Nearby men cut up old tyres and used the rubber to made sandal soles and other goods. Did new trades have a hierarchy like the old crafts? Did proud Michelins despise the remould caste?

The road was a high causeway across paddies. It narrowed as we went, until Joy decided we were on the wrong track. The surface fell away from crown to sides. It was like attempting a three-point turn on top of a crusty loaf. I backed to the edge and pumped the brakes madly. Nothing. I heaved the handbrake. Nothing. I crashed into first gear and stalled the engine. We stopped, swaying. Suguna got out into a thorn bush which grabbed at her sari and held her. Joy said that almost four wheels were still on the road. The girls looked quite happy. It was their first ever car ride. A passing tailor, with toddy on his breath, climbed into the passenger seat with lots of bad advice.

When rocks had been wedged under three wheels and the tailor ejected I let the clutch out, cautiously, and started up. The others pushed. A policeman materialized to watch us gain the crown of the road. Buffalo streamed past while everyone got in. I drove off in the opposite direction and a muck sweat. Rushes of a little film ran before my eyes: the car and all aboard falling, falling backwards on to its roof again and again.

'I couldn't pump the footbrake fast enough,' I said, 'and the handbrake didn't work.'

'Oh, that never does,' said Joy, 'never has, for years.'

Thanks very much, I thought, thanks for telling me. And a little voice in my ear reiterated my intuition about lack of control. It made sense. Loose connections between cause and effect were all it took to make fatalism inevitable.

That was much later. By then I'd gathered plenty of evidence to support the conclusion. For the time being I wasn't concerned with life and death, merely with catching or missing a launch. Abraham padlocked the church gates and pedalled off on his bike; I ran beside him and jumped, wedging one buttock on the bamboo rack behind his saddle and straining to keep my heels out of the spokes. Everyone watched as I passed by in pain. The street was rough. The bamboo was unforgiving. It was corporal punishment.

Abraham dropped me at the top of the beach and I waded downhill through sand. Flagrantly beautiful laundry flapped in a hot wind on line after washing line by the river. Saris were spread on dunes like pigments in a paint box. *Dhobi* women waded in the shallows and whacked colours against stones on stilts. The far hills were bluer, lumpier now. Beside a red and green boat Joy and Suguna were waving. The launch was waiting for me.

34

THE CURRENT

Via Porsammagandhi

THE LAUNCH was not waiting for me. It was waiting for its cargo. I sat on hot yellow sand and watched the *dhobi* women's children watching me. A crow perched on a washing line and swung in the breeze. Hills bubbled up moss-green and tawny across the water. When most of the sacks were loaded we climbed a springy plank and found places on the narrow bench that ran around the cabin. It was good to be in shade. With her generous lap and a blanket, Suguna made a bed upon which Joy could give her back respite.

I'd thought about this moment for a long time. Now I sat and savoured the delay. The shouts and grunts of coolies. The flump of rice bags on the boards. The fresh scent of *bidis* hand-rolled from tobacco leaves. The slap, slop, slap of wet cloth on rock. The stale sweetness of diesel and river water mixed. The discreet suck and gargle beneath my feet.

Following the hot season of 1853 George Beer penetrated further than ever into the hills on the west bank whose shadowy beginnings I could now see. He returned to a weavers' colony he'd started near Kovvur to find it gripped by fever. By late September, when he travelled to Narsapur, he was exhausted from nursing the sick and dying. On the way he suffered sunstroke.

Summoned from Palakol, William Bowden saw his dear friend's total collapse, touched his dry flushed skin, felt his bounding pulse and feared that his extreme temperature presaged congestion of the brain and deep coma. He did everything he could to cool him. When there was some remission, with Elizabeth Beer's blessing he accompanied him through the night

232

to Masulipatam. The physician there treated George for a few days. The patient's duskiness lightened a little, the pulse that had grown thready strengthened, and the doctor's prognosis was favourable.

Thus reassured, William left his colleague in good hands and set out to fulfil an appointment upriver. He had arranged to join Captain Felix Thackeray Haig, of the Irish family of whiskey distillers, to reconnoitre the Godavari's upper reaches. A protégé of Colonel Arthur Cotton who had 'never yet seen such energy displayed by any other man', Haig had just brought off the most exciting engineering coup in the delta, the Gannavaram aqueduct. It cost more than three times the original estimate, but was completed against all the odds within four months. 'An extraordinary feat,' exclaimed Colonel Baird Smith of the Bengal Engineers. Haig's aqueduct carried a canal for half a mile over the Vainteyam branch of the river. By it Nagaram Island was irrigated and transformed into 'the Garden of the Godavari'.

Even while at work on that mammoth project near the delta's mouth, Haig had dreamt of opening the upper river to navigation. What better fellow-explorer could he find than William Bowden? William was by now forty-two, and freer than usual because his family was in England for the time being. Work in Palakol and Narsapur could look after itself while he fulfilled a long-held ambition to discover more about the hill tribes' territory.

The bow wave was an arrow aimed against the current. We'd started out only half an hour late. In front of me a young man settled down to sleep on rice sacks with one arm under his neck and the other over his eyes. A man stowed a cockerel between his legs and let down his *lungi* like a screen; the bird and its clucking soon subsided. A woman with a cold face propped one foot beside her on the bench; her wrist on her knee, she plucked at the roll-up cigar she smoked with its lighted end in her mouth; she squawked at the smartly dressed granddaughter who clutched at her swinging leg, then caught my eye and filled her face with a warm smile. This surprising softness hardened as suddenly; she turned and spat powerfully into the river.

We passed an island with a glowing temple poised on it, like the one at Pattisema where the Brahmin made his fatal attempt to gain power over the Koyas. Its *gopuram* was overshadowed by a gangling electricity pylon. Ascending between peaks and cones and shoulders of hills covered with feathery forest, silver trunks and ochre rocks, ploughing a swirling wake between yellow-gold beaches through waters that so recently carried the hill-mother Kondlamma down to Narsapur, the electrification of the Godavari was an incongruous notion. Still, we made progress against the current. Why shouldn't progress make progress too?

Bowden and Haig made a useful reconnaissance, but William suffered a touch of sunstroke. Back at Palakol he learned that George Beer had died of it; the damage to his nervous system had been irreversible. William felt bereft. Elizabeth was in Devon. It was almost eighteen years since he and George had each married an Elizabeth in Barnstaple and sailed for Madras. It was six painful weeks before he regained sufficient strength to travel to Masulipatam and escort Elizabeth Beer back to Narsapur.

The hills, the sweeps of beach, the curving river grew increasingly brilliant. We pressed onwards, then zig-zagged from stop to stop. Passengers came up the flimsy plank with vendors of fruit or snacks or leaf tobacco. Close up, it was a world of pure light, primary colour, silica and water. It was prismatic, crystalline. Drops, from the leaden bucket hauled aboard for drinking, fell back slowly and full of sun before they smashed on the surface and slid away in a luminous body like the distillate from an alchemist's alembic. Further off, things vegetable grew fiercely behind a gauzy veil. Hills fumed. Huge boulders sat on the brink of wells of shadow in which creatures with hot breath were spawned. I wanted to travel here for ever. Men sitting in a rough circle on the cabin floor gazed at symbols on the cards in their hands, smoked, scratched, sighed and pushed rupees away, gathered them up with suppressed cries. Even here, glory and money. The slight young man laid out on fat hessian sacks might have been dead, the rice grains at his soft neck, maggots.

Our third stop was Porsammagandhi. A youthful father lifted up his baby daughter, vermilion *bottu* on her brow, and put her hands together to make *namaskaram* to the goddess who lived in the vivid temple high on the bank. An educated, high-caste couple, she in a rich sari, he with shaven head, disembarked together with humbler pilgrims. All carried chickens or coconuts. A family boarded, fresh colours daubed between their eyes. The goddess Porsammathalli had accepted their offerings, the milk of coconuts, the blood of chickens and goats. Both *amma* and *thalli* mean 'mother'. On the beach, a man disembowelled a chicken and washed it out in the river. Kites circled above, their harsh requests already granted by the great mother-mother.

After his expedition with Haig, my great-great-grandfather often came upriver on foot and by boat. Following his example, Thomas Heelis made several attempts, on board the *Harbinger*, to pass through the gorge in the Eastern Ghats, and over the shoals beyond, before in 1860 he finally reached the great Hindu festival at Bhadrachalam on the inland plains. Only just before he died, William was able to travel further still on business with his son Fred, to Dummagudem, the town that Haig had made his base. Such journeys were by then routine, though few people had William's habit of stopping off in the jungle on the way.

Our busiest port of call on the east bank was Devipatnam, 'goddess town'. High on the bank I could see a big hoarding with a picture of a tiger and the slogan, in English, 'Save Wildlife'. I was used to Indian hoardings but I still asked myself, one, how come hunters in the jungle were so well educated, and, two, was the tiger a film star and had it been democratically elected? TV aerials protruded from police barracks; colonial façades cracked; the rest was small-town stuff though I knew this was an important place because it was the last marked on my maps until way beyond the gorge, and because the launch made four stops at it.

At the fourth, a light-skinned man in well-pressed shirt and trousers stood out among dark bodies; police in starched biscuit-coloured cotton were planted on the sand with buffed boots apart. One impressed me enormously by bounding, unimpeded by the usual bribe-belly, to the top of the steep bank and back without heavy breathing. He was one of a new breed of mountain policemen.

Our steersman, perched on a shelf forward, spun his white

wheel to take us into midriver; chains crawled on the decking and turned the rudder at the stern. The engine thudded. This town of the goddess was the last place I'd see the law for days. It was a frontier town strung out along a crumbling cliff. Above it, the Godavari ran a full two inches across a blank on the state map. I'd tried to buy a large-scale one but it seemed impossible, or impertinent. At least mine didn't say 'Here be dragons'. Joy slept peacefully enough beside Suguna.

A banana-seller toured the launch; he had marked aboriginal features that I'd soon recognize as Koya characteristics. A young mother looked bored and slapped her quiet son for no reason at all; he cried for five minutes; she smiled. I climbed out on to the decking and up on to the corrugated-iron cabin roof. Up there with men and boys, tethered cockerels and prone bicycles, the journey was magical. Every so often we stopped, at the east bank or the west, before a backdrop of ever-building hills.

At one place a widow, with a stick and thick hair whiter if possible than her sari, struggled aboard. At another, naked boys stared, arms akimbo. Fishing *navas* decorated with zig-zags and chevrons were beached beside cloth shelters and cooking pots bright in the westering sun. Paths led from open beaches into shadowy palmyra villages beneath mango and tamarind trees.

Some play of light, current and bow wave turned the surface to a swelling chequerboard. Exhaust from the pipe sticking out of the roof mixed with heady tobacco. I wished I hadn't given up smoking. The engine chugged complacently. The khaki river turned milky, then lilac and gold, purple and silver. The hills heightened, thickened, foggy blue to bottle green to silhouette. For four hours I was transported. The sky was apricot.

'Here we are,' said Joy.

And there, waving wildly on the beach, was Sirra Yuniah. There was his wife, Suvarthamma, and friends. We walked the plank into their arms and garlands of marigolds. They didn't let us carry an ounce of baggage as we trudged joyfully up the steep beach. Across the sandy track that was the main village street, exuberant bunting flew between bamboo poles. Soon we could read a fringed banner that said a big 'Welcome' above our names and the date. After Joy's name, 'Narsapur' in brackets. After mine, 'England'. Both places seemed very far away.

My eye took in palmyra thatch, woven bamboo, government concrete, banana trees, palms and slender poles carrying wires.

'The current,' grinned Yuniah, 'here three days.'

SHIVA'S HILL

Sivagiri

ELECTRICITY arrived three days before I did. It was called 'the current'. The village was called Sivagiri, 'hill of Shiva'. Some Hindus and at least one Muslim family lived in it, but its natives were *girijans*, 'hill people', members of scheduled tribes lower in the social scale even than scheduled castes or *harijans*. If *harijans* were untouchable, *girijans* were unthinkable except as cheap labour. Despite a government that protested too much about improvement schemes, and associated scams, 'scheduled' was about the worst thing you could be. Scheduled for what, I wondered, extinction or, worse, demoralization and enslavement?

Untouchable Suguna, of the defiled Madiga leather workers, could if she wished look down from a great height upon the Koyas of Sivagiri. Their society and those of other Gondi tribes had evolved in fastnesses untouched by Vedic Aryan or Dravidian India. It was Haig and his kind who had opened up their world. Haig's ideals were noble, but land-grabbers and greedy officials came on his heels. Yuniah had come upriver in the wake of Beer, Bowden and Heelis with a Bible in his hand. When first he'd set out for these hills, Joy's mother, *Amma garu*, had given him an umbrella, a mosquito net, two bed sheets and her blessing.

Yuniah told me that tale when I first met him at Nidadavole. Then he was in the midst of tragedy. His daughter had just given birth at hospital in Secunderabad; an *ayah* delivered the baby boy while a nurse stood idly by; the umbilical cord strangled him to death; to release him they tore her apart. Yuniah didn't know whether she'd live, or die from loss of blood. He wept, but told me of my aunt's generosity. His daughter lived.

Now he was determined to give us all we could desire. He and his church sang a welcome under a simple shelter overshadowed by a tamarind tree. Suvarthamma and other women cooked us all a celebratory fish curry on the mud hearth beside her house. It was very bony but very good. Yuniah installed Joy and Suguna in a woven-bamboo kitchen on a mud plinth under a palmyra roof. I got the government house to which it was attached: mud steps, a high threshold into one small room, whitewashed walls, windows of perforated cement like magnified air-bricks, a curved concrete roof with chillies drying on it, double doors of faded aquamarine and a flood mark eight feet above the ground.

A paw-paw tree, a bean plant and a flowering gourd grew in our tiny fenced compound. The bamboo fencing was highest around the bathroom and latrine that Yuniah had constructed. The bathroom was a cement window flat on the sand beside brass *bindis* and buckets filled night and morning with cold water carried up from the river and boiling water fresh from Suvarthamma's hearth. The latrine was a pit plus superstructure: a high stool with a hole in the seat upon which Joy and I were supposed to perch. Upon which each did perch, for it was immovable, much as I wanted to crouch. Upon which each entertained the young of Sivagiri whose glittering eyes pressed at the bamboo slats. Through which we each had to aim with precision.

There is, I think, a myth abroad in the hills. That while normal people squat to crap and lose themselves in dreams, white folks like to keep their standing and demonstrate their mastery of both equilibrium and trajectory. The bathroom, though, was pure delight, mixing and pouring water over my naked self under big stars. The tiny brand-new street lamp couldn't compete.

My house was small and dark and stifling, a storage heater that drank in the sun's heat all day and gave it out, or inwards, all night. I extinguished the kerosene lamp fast, before it got still hotter. I didn't bother with my net, but lay under a sheet on the taut canvas bed Yuniah had requisitioned. I listened to the Christians laughing and singing, to their tambourines and drums, to pye dogs snarling and brawling and yelping at my door.

My pulse throbbed. Light sliced between the doors, lanced through the windows. Across the street a woman pounded *dhal* in a stone mortar. The heartbeat was hers not mine. A baby cried. Goats pattered past. I watched life through a slit. As an early morning dose it was digestible, but soon I grew hungry for more.

Beyond the last house, and the palmyra cattle shelters, ginger-and-black fruit bats hung furled in a tamarind tree. The path dropped to a broad shelf of beach above the river. Thistles and mauve-and-yellow flowers like deadly nightshade grew there. The last dawn veil lifted. Though the hills beyond were already hazy, the foreground was luminous. It was naked and beautiful.

It made me gasp. Chillies lay drying on the sand, raked into rectangles, carpets of crimson and madder and cinnabar, each composed of many shades, each with its dominant note. Every pod was a glistening stitch, fruit of the nightshade called Capsicum, hot heart of Indian cuisine since the sixteenth century when the Portuguese introduced it to Asia from South America.

Parchment-coloured palmyra fronds were stacked between them. Scales hung from a tall bamboo frame on which red-hot cargoes for downriver markets were weighed. A miniature *nava* pulled away from the shore full of tiny figures in *khurtas* and saris. It was an odd illusion. Beyond the scales, the beach dropped steeply, invisibly, and sloped down to the river. Close-up reds, parchment and old gold butted up against azure on which the loaded *nava* glittered like a brooch set with pearls and multicoloured stones. Azure reflected the far bank's sands, its sage and moss greens, the hills' cobalt and ultramarine.

The biggest hills had long straight backs. They were the first of the Pappikondalu, the 'Bison Hills', through which the Godavari breaks. The big village for which the *nava* was making across the river was called Kondamodhalu, 'the beginning of the hills'. I gazed at this view most mornings and drew breath. It was a new India, a new beginning. Past me, goats and Brahmin cattle and water buffalo were driven out of Sivagiri to graze.

After a breakfast of spicy doughnuts made from black gram,

Joy embarked on her Sunday duties. She addressed the Christians in their makeshift church; they gave back her warmth and laughter. Then Yuniah led the congregation in joyful singing, and on foot down past the red chillies, down to the water's edge. Saris billowed in the breeze; the march, charged with excitement, might have been to the brink of the Red Sea. Yuniah and Suvarthamma waded in and one by one six women, young and old, and two young men went down into the river to be baptized. Women made a sari screen behind which their sisters changed, and flew the wet lengths like banners as we climbed back up the beach.

Sivagiri's Koya headman had given the Christians land for a church building on top of a small hill beside the main street. Yuniah banged his drum and the congregation sang hymns as we climbed. Garlanded, Joy unveiled a marble plaque with a four-colour Telugu inscription and we all processed around the raw foundation ditches. Yuniah had collected enough money to build stone footings. Work started tomorrow. The *maistry* smiled and joined in the prayers. Walls and roof, doors and windows would come later. For the poor Christians here it would be a church and community centre; for the whole village it would be a sorely needed shelter in time of flood.

At the bottom of the hill, beneath the bunting and the 'Welcome' sign, Koya women in the congregation linked arms at Yuniah's instigation, made a circle and danced a Koya dance. At first they weren't quite sure about singing for the words spoke of the pagan hunt and the great mother, but soon their heels thudded round and round in the dust and their voices ebbed and flowed. We feasted and, when the church service resumed, I climbed back to my new vantage point.

I called it Jesus's Hill. From its flat top I could see Shiva's Hill rising solitary at the village's edge. I looked down on fenced compounds, palmyra roofs, official concrete. Furthest from the river government houses lay in ruins, burst apart by flood water. The tide mark on my house was at eight feet; that was in 1990; in 1986 the waters had risen above the roofs; this hill was the village's place of safety.

The river ran tamely in its bed. But it could spread across the beaches, climb the mighty dunes and flood the whole valley.

The volume of water was unimaginable. Down amongst the ruins I tried to imagine it. People carried and herded what they could up Jesus's Hill, but animals and houses and furniture and beds with bodies on them were washed away. It was unthinkable. Then I thought of the ruined head lock at Vijjeswaram, of flood marks on Joyce's buildings at Nidadavole; I remembered Joy telling me how coconut trees across the river from her hostel were submerged in 1986; if the Godavari could obliterate half the delta, it could certainly fill a few hundred square miles between the Bison Hills. It was hard to imagine it, but it made sense.

At Trimbak, near Bombay, the first trickle issues through the mouth of an idol. The stream communicates with the Ganges, they say, by a mysterious subterranean channel. The sacred Godavari's catchment area is one tenth of the subcontinent, fed mostly by the south-west monsoon. Here it rises in late June, about ten days after the rains set in at Bombay. 'During floods', wrote the engineer George Walch in 1896, 'it foams past its obstructions with a velocity and turbulence which no craft that ever floated could stem.' Yes, it all made sense.

One evening, as I contemplated the river in late sunlight that made colours hotter than ever, cattle stumbled uphill to their palmyra byres and Sai Baba, a boy I knew, came swaying home on a water buffalo. Sai Baba was named after the *rishi* that the Narsapur professor of politics venerated. Perhaps he was the sage's third incarnation. He liked to watch everything I did; while his small girlfriends sang and danced in our compound at night, he brought eggs or tomatoes to Joy's step and just looked. That evening he rode the buffalo, without whacking it, past a man on his haunches who caressed a puppy with one hand and preened a proud cockerel with the other. It warmed an Englishman's heart.

The very next afternoon Yuniah led Suguna and me between fields towards a dusty arena in the shade of a spreading tamarind tree. Men and women sat on the track selling *samosas* or *bidis* or drinks. One, a widow in black-framed glasses and a green-edged white sari, I'd seen baptized. Sai Baba squatted with other boys and men around a *kalamkari* cloth decorated with an elephant, a tiger and a horse. A ragged man dealt cards bearing those same symbols down by a pile of money. Sai Baba grinned up at me. Cards and coins accumulated seriously. I made no sense of it.

Beside the arena men sat on their haunches in opposing lines with cockerels between their knees. The birds blinked, crowed at one another, craned necks, clawed at the dust and twitched frenetically. They were psyched up. The scent was of toddy and tobacco. Men with curly hair, narrow eyes, broad noses and wide cheekbones sized up the enemy. One, in a purple turban, helped his friend lash a honed steel blade to his bird's right foot.

In the arena men offered cockerels beak to snapping beak, then retracted them and sucked at their tail feathers before launching them into the dust. Sleek cocks circled each other, then lunged and leapt, combs and ruffs erect, in a flurry of glassy feathers. Their masters circled too, one standing, the other crouched in his bird's posture as if sympathetic magic might help its cause. Spectators squatted or stood in a big circle under the tree, checking bets, urging birds on with an under-the-breath moaning that rose to a wild groan as combatants danced and slashed with claws and spurs, pranced and lurched, then staggered at the duel's climax. The loser pumped blood onto its feathers, onto the sand. Again and again. All afternoon.

We escaped from the bloody arena to a small dam that held a dry-season lake at the base of hills behind the village. The jungle began at the far bank and climbed to two thousand feet. Tigers and bears came down to drink at night, Yuniah said. Lotus flowers hovered above the surface. White egrets took off. A chestnut bittern froze, erect. An unidentifiable corpse in the shallows writhed with maggots. There were ways of dying. The sun dropped behind massive silhouettes; across the river, the Pappikondalu's long backs caught the last light. We sat. The swell of bloodlust still reached us, made it the more peaceful. Suguna and Yuniah took turns to stare through my binoculars.

36

JUNGLE JUICE

Takuru

THE MAN who'd stroked his puppy and cockerel still had the puppy when he greeted me next day, and the sweet-and-sour smell of toddy on his breath. Behind woven bamboo fencing, the mud plinth and walls of his house were smoothly moulded. As he led me through to the hearth on the back verandah and the buffalo in the yard, he proudly pointed out a tall cupboard or *almirah*.

'Very good,' said Yuniah when he saw it later, 'but much to carry up the hill when floods.'

Yuniah and Suvarthamma had nothing that was not portable, nothing to stow in an *almirah*, because they had almost nothing. They lived simply by choice. This man's daughter-in-law showed off her things, her wedding photos, cinema pics pasted on one mud wall and, most exciting of all, a single lightbulb in a socket. They had not been slow to tap the new street lighting. They weren't tribals, they'd come upriver to farm tribal land.

Opposite was the Post Office, though there was no sign to say so. The young postmaster, also a Hindu, invited me to sit on a verandah roofed with palmyra and screened with vine. It was cool beneath translucent green. He offered me peanuts. His wife brought tea. A heavily framed photo of a child hung by the door.

'Who is this?' I asked.

'He is my son, age of four only.' The postmaster's face clouded. 'Since ten months he is dead.'

Children played around our feet, but it was as if they did not exist. Both parents were devastated by their memories.

'He take nail into his mouth, we do not know it cuts him,

he is very sick. We spend two thousand rupees for doctor and medicine for diarrhoea,' he said hopelessly, 'but it is tetanus.'

'We did everything,' she said, 'but everything wrong.'

The postmaster squatted in the middle of his father-in-law's peanut field. Plants had been stacked, roots and pods exposed, to dry slowly. A shack of palmyra fronds and Portland cement sacks sheltered two beds; an oil lamp hung on a forked stick. The crop was well guarded at night. Coolie women thrashed roots against a wooden frame to knock pods off. The postmaster lit a small fire and roasted some in its ashes. I shucked them hot. The fresh nuts were exquisite. The women smiled at my delight.

A toddy-tapper strode across the field with his climbing slings of rope and old tyre; he wore a turban, a loincloth and a belt; a wood block on the belt had a hook for a bamboo flask and a slot for a naked long-bladed knife. The postmaster suggested I go with him. At the field's edge, where land fell away to the river, there was a line of palmyra palms, *Borassus flabellifer*, *thatti chettu* in Telugu, 'the tree of a thousand uses'. What Koyas called it, in their Gondi dialect, I never discovered.

Despite their stock in trade, not many toddy-tappers fall. This one swam up trees. With hobbled feet braced at the trunk he leant back in the sling, then swung forward, taking his weight off it for an instant, hoisting it up, legs following in unison, soles gripping the bark, up, up, up with all the awkwardness and grace of a man moving expertly, but out of his element.

Up there, beneath a crown of spiky fans, sections of thick bamboo stuck out at angles from cut leaf-bases. He unhooked one and replaced it with an empty. The full flask swung from his belt as he shinned down. He stripped fibres, fine cream threads, from a frond and stuffed them into the neck of a gourd. He poured palm sap from the bamboo into the body of this funnel and out through its fibrous filter into a glass. Mine was the easy task, the tasting. It was very easy indeed. The toddy, *kallu*, fermented in the heat of the sun, tasted fresh and deceptively harmless like cordial or sweetish cider. The toddy-tapper smiled at me with wide, burning white eyes. He refused money.

Kept for a while, *kallu* ferments further and evaporates to something more intoxicating still, like a liqueur. Either way, it fills the stomach. Coolies drink it to save them eating. Distilled, it makes a version of the spirit called *arrack*, a name derived, some say, from the Arabic for 'sweat'. It makes you sweat. Sometimes poppy leaves and marijuana, or *bhang* are added. Crude distillation produces liquor containing a high proportion of methyl alcohol and fusel oil, a poisonous cocktail of amyl alcohols. Newspapers frequently reported multiple morning-after *arrack*-shop deaths. But *kallu* was refreshing, delicious. Back in Sivagiri, I lay down to write up my journal. Soon I pulled the sheet over my face to keep off the tipsy flies.

Early one morning, wholesomely refreshed and less emotional, I set off with Yuniah and Joy to walk downriver along the fertile plain between the river and the hills, past the cockfight arena and the peanut plot, past fields of maize, chillies and pulses, through scrub and young teak plantations hung with enormous lacy leaves decaying on the branches. Some trunks had been felled and stacked ready, Yuniah said, to be poached piecemeal. We ate astringent berries with big stones. I sucked at my cheeks.

'Bears here for fruits at night,' said Yuniah. He prodded a small boulder with his foot. 'This is god.'

No shrine, no sanctum, no sacred colours. A rock at the side of the track. Pure immanence. *Konda devata*, hill deity.

Children chanted Telugu lessons at school in the neat fenced village of Cheeduru. The chant petered out and the subject became anthropology; they studied Joy and me intently. We took tea in the yard of a low house with bamboo-barred windows. A man with sparse silver hair and a white *dhoti* sat on his haunches under a shaggy palmyra roof. His name was Jogu Reddi, his gaze was gentle, his mouth was kindly, his skin was flawless.

An ancient crone joined us, adjusting a sparse sari over her withered breasts. Here was a woman, a real beauty, I thought. Sannasamma had sparks in her eyes, wisdom in her gappy smile. With Joy, Yuniah and Jogu Reddi she disappeared into the darkness of the house. I was left staring back at a boy who peered at me through next-door's fence. He didn't flinch. A pair of glossy black goats lay together beneath a circular shelter supported by termite-eaten posts. Fowls scuffled and pecked in between deep shade and startling sunlight. I was getting hot.

I walked on to find shelter in a mango grove. Tiny figures, man and boy, drove cattle from the river across a wide beach; they picked various routes through scrub but all came together on a steep path to the village, led by a yoked pair with big horns. Was life like that if you trusted it? In the shade with me a man honed an axe head on a wet stone and knocked it on to its haft. A toddy-tapper smoothed his curved knife on a thick stick.

'Cooo-oo! Cooo-oo!' Joy and Yuniah's rising cries roused me. I emerged from the grove and met them on the track. They'd been searching. We practised the summons together just for fun. 'Cooo-oo! Cooo-oo! Cooo-oo!'

The high alluvial ground grew flatter. Ahead, hills were a wall, backdrop for Takuru, a village distinguished by government houses of stone with red-tiled roofs and gardens of marigolds and rose bushes. Along one dirt street a series of these roofs had been vandalized by lads who'd come down from Cheeduru tanked up with toddy and jealous because Takuru got the current first. The tiles had been off for a month, and would be until the case came up. Repairs meant tampering with the evidence.

In his bamboo church Joseph the evangelist taught me to wash feet and sandals at once without using my hands. We feasted on chicken and rice. A young man, Bechinnadurgruo, promised to take me to see something by the road. Yuniah couldn't find words for it and Joy couldn't explain. They had church work to do. I followed Bechinnadurgruo because I was restless. Something was waiting for me here, upriver, that I hadn't seen yet.

It was very hot. The tobacco house was hotter. It stood at the edge of the village, a barn of bamboo plastered with mud to shoulder-height and decorated with white handprints; from there to high eaves it was wickerwork; a furnace tended by a sweaty coolie breathed smoke into it. I poked my head through a door. Full, fragrant. Layer upon dense layer of leaves hanging sickly yellow in the heat. 'Virginia'. It sounded very odd.

Fire-cured leaf wasn't what we'd come to see. We walked

between vibrant green tobacco plantations, through fields of yellow and black grams which we chewed as we went. In tree shade a man and woman were threshing *dhal* with sticks on a sieve like a bed, whacking pulses out of brittle pods. We marched to their rhythm even after it faded. A gaggle of guys off a jacked-up Public Carrier advised their driver how to mend a puncture. They looked out of place. But here was the new road edging inexorably up the west bank. Soon it would press past Cheeduru and on to Sivagiri. It wasn't what we'd come to see.

What we'd come to see were piles of stone half hidden by vegetation where jungle fell to the rough road. Coolies carried ironstone down from a quarry in the hills and lorries took it for smelting to Rajahmundry. Or so I gathered from Bechinna-durgruo's one-word English sentences. He posed for his photo, hot and smiling beside one of the heaps. I chose one gritty stone as a souvenir of something that shouldn't have been forgettable.

Back in Joseph's compound I couldn't stop sweating. A child playing beyond the bamboo fence glanced in and saw my wet white face. He burst into inconsolable tears. A pye dog limped in, one severed forepaw swinging from a flap of skin. When I moved towards him he hobbled off fast, yelping pitifully.

Joseph showed me a neem tree at the field edge. In its shade a pointed but badly weathered carved stone like a spearhead thrust up through the earth. It was wreathed with cobwebs.

'It is a god,' he said, 'called Portraj.'

On the bank's brink, forty feet above the river, a mighty tam-arind perched on a cage of roots. Floods washed this village away too and sent people running for the hills. A stone Hindu god with eroded half-human features rested against the tree. A diesel pump below us chugged and struggled to lift water up so far. The launch came into view, still half an hour downriver.

It would come, if we waited. Flood carried the great mother to the plains, but the twentieth-century current came upstream: motor launches, Public Carriers, new gods, land-grabbers, cash-crops, wage-slavery, forestry officials, money-lenders, the road and the current. And what flowed downstream in return? Chillies and pulses, for instance, ironstone, tobacco, teak and bamboo. And what leaked away? Language, self-determination, dignity.

A small girl clutched a bundle, a school slate and a smaller brother. They made their escape along the bank and clambered up and into a *nava*. Father loped after them. They fled, but gave up wearily in the end. Perhaps they should have kept running. On the launch a boy with stick limbs brandished a hand of bananas and two men stinking of *arrack* slapped cards down for coins.

Sivagiri had a power-cut that night. We were due to eat with Sathyavathi, a woman Joy had known for years, but no one came to call us. We breached etiquette and took the initiative, with a kerosene lamp to light the way. Neighbours gathered at her house to watch the fun as her husband, full of toddy, screamed at her son recently back from college that the peanut crop had been filched, that he didn't help his father, that . . . Son hit father. The crowd drew breath. We slipped away to the daughter's house. The son-in-law went for news. Father turned up and swore.

'Why don't you kill me?' he shouted in slurred Telugu. 'You're killing me anyway, slowly, you and your brother.'

We crept through darkness to a government house the family used as a store. We sat on woven mats and ate sublime curried fish and chicken off banana leaves. Sathyavathi was a serene hostess. Once proud, Khamma caste, things had gone wrong since they came upriver. They'd lost savings, eight gold sovereigns, lost all in the floods, lost self-respect. What could Joy do?

A lot. The daughter had once lived at Joy's hostel. She'd written many letters to a married man. He'd promised to take her to Hyderabad and get her a job in the Gulf. Old story. His wife warned Joy. The man had already bought the tickets. Joy locked the girl up. A near thing. Sathyavathi would never forget it.

37

HUNGRY SISTERS

Perantapalli

ON THE BEACH at seven in the morning, with an umbrella up against the sun, Joy lay back in a deck chair and kicked a leg in the air. She was thinking of England. Of the English at the seaside. Her sari of black and green and crimson was immaculate as usual. She was waiting for the ferryman. We all were, Joy, Suguna, Yuniah, Suvarthamma and I, with tiffin tins of *puli hari* and flasks of water. We'd booked a seven o'clock boat to carry us through the Godavari gorge. I laughed at Joy's parody. We all laughed.

Mists that still hung above the water evaporated. It was as though the air itself was being distilled, as though the light was the essence of light. Not a colour in creation could hide.

'By the way,' said Joy, 'Sathyavathi's peanut crop hasn't been stolen. Her husband was just too blind drunk to see it.'

The day was starting very well indeed. Soon two boatmen boarded a *nava* over at Kondamodhalu. Sheik Baji, Sivagiri's Muslim boat-owner had arranged this craft for us. By half-past seven they had beached at Joy's feet. We set the deck chair in the stern, with a cushion for her back; I sat on a thwart; the others preferred to sit on bamboos in the bottom of the boat. One lad stood on the pointed stern and sculled; the other, facing me at the bow, tucked his *lungi* between his legs, braced his feet and rowed with one paddle. We pressed against the stream.

An Indian great horned owl on a branch overlooked monumental boulders streaked black and ochre. Stout *jinni* shrubs grew half submerged at the river's edge. Bluetailed bee-eaters stabbed the air. Lemon-and-black waders I couldn't identify plodded long-legged in the shallows. A woman washed pots.

Another bathed and covered herself with her yellow sari as we drew near. Now and then there was simply the cry of birds, the plash of paddles, the purling of water along the hull, but mostly there was chatter and laughter and song after song led by Yuniah's melodious tenor.

Some way beyond the Konda Reddi village of Koruturu on the west bank, our bow-man exchanged his oar for a punt pole and we slid into the beach below the invisible settlement of Cheruvaaka. A woman appeared with many greetings and a flask of sweet spiced tea. I drank it standing on the steep sand. Our *nava* looked frail beneath the Bison Hills. Ahead, they fell steeply from two or three thousand feet and squeezed the Godavari to nothing.

The bank became desolate, rocky, beneath turbulent hillocks of scrub. Then the shore was all jagged boulders heaped at the jungle's fringe, landslips beneath taller forest, great rocks tipped into the river. A mountain had split in 1983, the lad at the stern said. Joy had felt the quake in Narsapur. After an hour we stopped at Theladhibbalu, another steep beach and nothing to be seen but castor oil plants and two men dragging bundles of eighteen-foot bamboos downhill and staking them in the water to soak, ready to be shipped to the paper mills. Suguna handed round *chapatis* sprinkled with sugar.

The sun hid beyond the black hills. But behind us it was like sunrise on the water. Upriver I recognized the view of peaks and meshing slopes from a photograph in a book at home: 'Gorge of the Godavari Looking Upstream' with a native craft at bottom right. I was here. On cue, a *nava* loaded with sticks, four girls and a boy slid downriver, oars flicking, with nervous glances directed at us. Official teak for the timber yards and bamboo for the mills was one thing, but forest sneaking to the plains for firewood was another. Smuggling was good business.

We entered the gorge. A sign on the west bank, as if anyone needed one, said, 'Andhra Pradesh Forestry Department. Papi-konda Sanctuary *Core* Area.' A long translucent snakeskin lay sloughed off on a rock. Steep gullies and ochre ravines opened up. A miniature canyon was reflected in the river and shivered by the stiff cool breeze that got up suddenly. A long high gully rose through jungle. It was supposed to be the track, said Yuniah, of a giant tortoise that climbed from the river and ascended the mountain long ago. This grandeur, this beauty deserved myths.

Until now, apart from old photographs, I'd had only the accounts of writers who, before the days of film and TV, tried to render the exotic both familiar and sublime. Henry Morris wrote, in 1878, that 'the gorge through which the Godavari enters the plains forms one of the most beautiful pieces of scenery in Southern India . . . I have never witnessed more exquisite scenery on the Neilgherries [Nilgiris] or the Shevaroys . . . Sir Charles Trevelyan compares the scenery to that of the Rhine between Coblentz and Bingen, but it lacks the signs of human life which adorn, and the historical antiquities which beautify, the European stream.' You can say that again.

After four hours afloat, the gorge narrowed to some two hundred yards. I thought of the four-mile-wide river down at Dowlaishweram. Yet again, I tried to imagine the floods of which this stream was capable, to conceive of a torrent of a million and a half cubic feet of water per second – three times the volume of the Nile – scouring these mountain walls. Watching them plummet, and seeing light vanish in the water, I felt the Godavari's depth. Unfathomable, people said. It made perfect sense, even though I knew the river was two hundred and fifty feet deep at most.

Deep enough, it was, to give you a touch of liquid vertigo if you thought too much about it. Jungle-clad walls tightened on the water like a vice. But they weren't the cold clashing rocks Scylla and Charybdis that Trevelyan and his kind, with their classical education, carried in their heads; they were stampeding bison with dusky hides and towering horns. In the depths beneath their hooves there was plenty of scope for darkness.

The *nava* was full of lowered voices, secretive talk about the people of the Bison Hills, gossip perhaps about their ritual offerings to the great mother. The Konda Reddis sacrifice to the hill goddess Beera meyah, the Koyas to the hungry sisters Sammaka and Sarrakka who may be nourished with the blood of chicken and goats but only satisfied with the blood of men.

Human sacrifice was banned in India in 1835, the year before my ancestors arrived. In the aftermath of the 'Mutiny', 1858, five hill chiefs were hanged, of whom William Bowden had known four. One, Subbareddi, whose appetite was for news of sedition from the north 'had been soured for a long time', wrote Bowden, 'through the Government cutting off a kind of blackmail which he claimed on all goods passing through the Gorge at the foot of his village.' His feuding and blood-letting was judged in court.

'May I be permitted to speak?' he addressed Judge Morris. 'I heard that Nana Sahib was advancing with his victorious army, and that whoever did most against the English would be rewarded most.' It made sense. Their reward was swift suppression. Of Subbareddi's village Bowden adds, 'Report says the officer rooted up the temple and destroyed it utterly, and that numerous human skulls were found there.' The place deserved its myths. 'Since four years,' said Yuniah, 'my neighbour, sacrificed.'

Yuniah and Suvarthamma lived in Kondamodhalu then. Their next-door neighbour, a Hindu father of six, was kidnapped; his headless body was given back to the river. Last year one of three men from Nellore, pot and pan sellers, was captured. His friends went back up hill to find him, but fled downriver in terror to the police. Nothing came of their investigations.

The victim, or *meriah*, would have been well looked after: fed, dedicated, shorn, anointed with oil, butter and turmeric.

'Head cut off,' said Yuniah. 'Is kept. New sari put with blood. For everyone.'

'For blood,' as the Kalika Purana teaches, 'if immediately consecrated, becomes ambrosia.' The severed head presented to the goddess on a *thali*. The blood-sodden sari torn into strips and divided amongst the clan. Each strip kept in a pot. In season, each pot buried with the seed. So blood fed the mother, the mother fed the clan, the crop sprang up and was good.

'About now,' said Joy, 'approaching the Telugu New Year, is when they say they catch somebody. A man, always a man.'

This, then, was where Kondlamma was born. This was where primeval Kali danced and devoured, laboured and brought forth.

After two miles the hills relaxed, the gorge opened and launched us into a lake-like expanse with, to the east, a glorious high beach below the mouth of the Koluru tributary. We followed the Godavari westwards and moored at last by *navas* in the shelter of scrub beside a shelf of sand. We climbed to a tamarind, and on up into lush jungle. Wild peahens strutted beside a stream.

Seeing a number of peacocks along the bank, I landed with my gun, in hopes of getting one for curry . . . But before going one hundred yards, a monstrous tiger sprang up close to me, giving three tremendous roars, with the intention, I suppose, of intimidating me. Through the mercy of God, Who alone sustained me, I did not lose nerve, but was enabled to face him with the gun, upon which, turning to one side, he very leisurely walked off, every now and then giving me a side glance . . . Praise the Lord, O my soul!

So wrote Thomas Heelis of his return journey from the great Bhadrachalam festival in 1860. What would he have thought of the pale apparition that now sat among jungle shadows in an unearthly island of sunlight? White walls, a sign above steps up to a narrow gateway, 'Sri Ramakrishna Hermitage', women ashramites at a stream washing clothes in dappled light. We crossed stepping stones, slipped sandals off and entered the compound. The white *shikhara* around which the hermitage revolved was austere, adorned only with symbols including the star, the crescent and the cross.

Among fruit trees and coriander beds stood the shrine or *samadhi* of Swami Balananda who established the hermitage sixty years ago near the tribal village of Perantapalli. *Samadhi* means both a holy man's 'state of ecstasy' and 'place of cremation'. In his youth Balananda had his right thumb cut off for forging money. Later, he taught that blood is energy; blood's source is food; food's source is land; land is ruled by politics; politics' sacred role is to provide food and to curb greed. Basil, *tulsi*, most auspicious of plants, thrived on the swami's altar.

Of the sisters who ruled the hermitage, one was grim, uneasy about us, the other was amenable. She led us into a hall, also the sanctuary, where an imposing Shivalingam was set amongst sparkling marigolds and crimson hibiscus. Water, from a brazen vessel suspended by chains, dripped unceasingly upon the stone *lingam* crowned with petals, seeped down into the *yoni* and flowed away in a channel across floor and compound to the stream. Amid so much moisture the odour of sanctity smelled very like sex.

The kind sister showed us photographs of Adam, an Englishman who had left home young and found paradise here.

'I see him,' said Yuniah, 'boy in bazaar, Kondamodhalu.'

That was in the late 'sixties. When Balananda died, Adam succeeded him. Last year he left for health reasons, though the women expected his return in three months. The sullen sister glared darkly, wished us away. I, at peace when we arrived, felt like an unquiet spirit being driven out. We walked from paradise and crossed a second watercourse into the wilderness.

Between tumbling streams we settled among boulders on a carpet of dust and fallen forest leaves. Good place for snakes, I thought. After our tiger food, *puli hari*, we settled down. Too curious to sleep, I soon made my way boulder to giant boulder upstream to where Adam's house stood perilously, part ruinous, part fallen away. I looked down upon sleepers between rocks, upon a hermitage that seemed, all at once, a whited sepulchre.

I clambered down beside the other stream. I caught sight of the others asleep. Something dark lay on Joy's arm. I stepped onto a boulder. Joy stirred. What should I do or say?

'Joy,' I hissed, 'don't move. Snake!'

She stirred, so did the snake. It slid across her upper arm and off, towards me. I stamped. It stopped, raised its head, busied its tongue, swayed and stared. It was at least four feet long, grey-green with black markings, ten feet away, between me and the others. I took a pace forward. It dropped, slid between stones with alarming speed, leapt the stream and slithered away.

If it had been that old enemy, the serpent, he could hardly have provoked more excitement, more terror, more rejoicing.

'*Girinagar!*' breathed Suvarthamma, wide-eyed.

'Hill cobra,' shouted Yuniah. 'Poison, no antidote.'

Suguna wept. Only Joy kept calm. I hugged her.

'Praise the Lord!' the others chorused. 'Praise the Lord!'

I felt like a Victorian traveller, with an umbrella over my head, as we approached the gorge. Suguna asked Joy if an ocean liner was as big as these hills. We stopped at Koluru, or at flimsy shacks below the village where two families lived on the beach. They lived hand to mouth by bartering their catch. We found shade in their shelter. From June to November, when the river was high, they'd return to their village below Rajahmundry. For seven months they lived here on the sand, with a woven straw tent and a kitchen of bamboo and dried bean plant. They invited us to eat with them and stay the night. I went aboard one of their slender *navas* to see where they slept under bamboo frames covered with sacks and plastic. At the prow, above stores in boxes, they kept a picture of Jesus and burnt candles before it.

They wanted their sons to go to a hostel and learn to read, to come back and teach them. It was one small daughter who caught my eye, half hidden among hanging nets, twisting her arms coyly above her head. Her mother, with heavy oiled hair and a scarlet sari, ground root ginger between a pebble and a hollowed slate-grey stone. She put it in the tea. It was exquisite.

I climbed the steep dune that was the beach and saw, above Koluru's palmyra roofs, high peaks of the Pappikondalu. Down to the left, the Koluru river wound its way out of emerald and lime lushness. Men chased floating teak planks and children scrambled up and down the crumbling sands. None of it was more memorable than the kindness of fisherfolk who offered all they had. I wanted to stay, but our food was being prepared downriver.

The gorge was in shadow. It was chill and choppy. Below, we came to a deserted village – just sandhills and tracks to water – haunted by the flickering wings and demented squeals and screams of a pair of Malabar pied hornbills. Terns and swifts tore through the dusk. Layers of hills were different darknesses below luminous sky, above flecked and flickering water. The first star appeared between puffed clouds. On a sand bar a fire was lit, then another, then four.

After three hours we stopped to eat at Cheruvaaka. There were fireflies and small oil lamps. The current had not yet come. The tastes of curried aubergine, fish, wood-apple chutney. The sound of eating, a dog snuffling and yelping when kicked, a cow chewing and breathing heavily in darkness.

The river's breath was cool. Clouds had come up. The lads

rowed and sculled us through pitch blackness. No stars. No moon. Even the songs had ceased. Just rhythmic splashes and the Godavari's buoyant embrace. Then, at last, Sivagiri's lights.

Suvarthamma did not sleep a wink that night. A cobra, once offended or denied, follows wherever its victim goes, follows with its restless tongue and gives its fangs ease in the desired flesh. She lay awake petrified that Perantapalli's *girinagar* was hunting us, hunting us down. She lay awake praying it would not find its victim's bed, that Missamma would be spared.

38

THE HORN DANCE

Pedagudem

OLD SANNASAMMA waded down into the river. Young Sai Baba swam and wrestled noisily with friends. Sannasamma, the Konda Reddi widow from Cheeduru, wore her skimpy white sari. She seemed about to slip beneath the water. She grasped Suvarthamma's hand.

'Can you swim, mother?' asked Yuniah.

We all laughed. He waded closer to the beach and took Sannasamma in his arms. After rain upstream, the river had risen in the night. Sannasamma was shorter than her daughter and the young Koya women from Sivagiri whom Yuniah had just baptized. All four had missed Sunday's service for some reason. For them, a quieter holy dip was in order. It was Thursday, and it would have been quiet but for Sai Baba's splashing and squealing.

'Quiet, boys!' said Yuniah.

Sai Baba crept from the water and sat on the sand to watch. He was as good at watching as playing. Sannasamma affirmed her faith in Jesus and renounced the devil and his works. Yuniah baptized her in the name of the Father, Son and Holy Spirit. She came up wet and smiling, eyes and gap-toothed mouth just visible behind a streaming veil of silver hair unloosed in the water. Suvarthamma, up to her waist in the river, reached out as Yuniah handed the old woman over. Sannasamma fumbled for her footing and, for a long instant, three figures were linked hand to hand in the mighty Godavari under the bulk of the Bison Hills.

Back on the beach, in a dry lemon-yellow sari, Sannasamma was a new woman. She was joyful. Until then I hadn't noticed the tattoo marks that divided her forehead and spotted her chin, the stud holes that pierced her broad nose. She didn't stop smiling. Nothing could have been less solemn or more serious.

'We will see man cut by bear also,' said Yuniah that afternoon as we crossed the river by *nava* to Kondamodhalu. Where fishermen furled nets in boats we disembarked and traversed a broad beach in the wake of women with *bindis* of water on their heads. The climb up the cliff to the village was steep. At the top stood a shack shop where we bought coffee and batteries for Joy's torch.

Some days ago we'd all come over for the meagre market with its stalls of chillies, onions, poor bananas and cloth. There had been plenty of tobacco, *kallu* and *arrack*. Kondamodhalu had more than its share of tobacco-curing barns and illicit stills. Distilling by Hindu incomers had long weaned tribals from toddy onto spirits, creating dependency on alcohol and cash: need and indebtedness only satisfied finally by loss of land.

Arrack was just one of the tools by which non-tribals had taken control of tribal territory. A beggar did a pathetic dance for me in the hope of buying some more booze. A drunk with a heavily scarred belly, who turned out to be the village headman, repeatedly offered to be my faithful guide, his few words of English not enhanced by his addiction. It was very like market day at home in Devon. Yuniah had an animated exchange with some wild-looking men and women.

'This people, bear village,' he explained.

They talked amongst themselves in Koya, a dialect of Gondi. Yuniah said I could understand about as much as he. It seemed, he assured me, that they would be happy to see us.

Now we were on our way. But first – always there was a 'but first' to put my impatient soul on the rack – we had to scour Kondamodhalu for the supplies Yuniah felt Joy and I needed. We could tick coffee and batteries off our list, but problem items were bananas and tomatoes, papaya and prawns. The anonymous Post Office had firm bananas which would keep for us, but its paw-paws were soft. We tried at several houses. Unripe or too ripe. Yuniah left me with village women while he sniffed around.

I stared into a baby's pale face, his kohl-black eyes. They gave the boy to me, laughing, and urged me to take him home. More sign language warned me about going with Yuniah: wide-eyed, they clawed at their legs. Bears or tigers, I didn't know which. I said farewell gratefully and accompanied him anyway, pleased to be on the road to whatever it was we were going to see.

The road was being renewed. Between chilli fields, women were sifting soil and gravel under the eye of a foreman in white shirt and *lungi*. Apart from the lorry with a puncture downriver at Takuru, I hadn't seen a wheeled vehicle since I boarded the launch at Polavaram. Not even an ox-cart. There was no current on this east bank either. But was this dirt road preparing to usher Kondamodhalu a little faster into the twentieth century? Beside it, on a white launch-pad decorated with Telugu script, towered a red rocket out of Thunderbirds with, mounted at the nose-cone, a spherical sputnik flying a silver hammer and sickle.

It was thirty feet of art-deco cement work: an incongruous memorial to Naxalite martyrs erected amongst red chillies and jungly hills between the river and the Papikondalu. Only a month ago thirteen Naxalites of the Maoist People's War Group had been shot dead in neighbouring Khammam district; as part of a campaign to ban *arrack* sales they'd set fire to a liquor store and set a land-mine booby-trap in the road for a police jeep. Seven hours of rifle fire followed.

'If there was a bit of moonlight the toll would have been higher,' a police officer said.

'They set their mothers' wombs on fire,' said Manchiraju Venkata Rao, quoting the Telugu proverb. 'That God has failed. Why offer these Telugu young men as the last of the sacrificial goats? Year after year, the people's war, the glorious thousand – head-chopping ritual – must it go on? Must Andhra bleed?'

'What are we doing?' asked an ex-Naxalite. 'We harass the villagers at night, the police do it in the day. Nothing else is happening there.'

The Naxalites organized Koyas, Konda Reddis and Kammaras,

the blacksmith 'caste' of the Godavari region, to resist the alienation of land and exploitation of labour by landlords and merchants. At their instigation, the people of Kondamodhalu and its satellite hamlets harvested paddy fields occupied by non-tribals. In 1969, for instance, they'd won six hundred and eighty sacks of rice and were rewarded with multiple arrests. Some *girijans* had been held in jail, waiting for their cases to come up, for six or seven years. Since then the authorities have filed suits against non-tribals for occupying Koya and Reddi land in contravention of a Land Transfer Act dating back to British legislation of 1917.

Do *girijans* have written deeds and registered property? Can they afford to hire lawyers? Have the authorities got the will?

'The government claims to have allocated funds for *girijan* areas,' the Telugu Desam party's spokesman complained soon after I left the hills, 'but nothing has reached them. Whatever funds were allocated appear to have been misused.'

Beyond the Naxalite monument and the new dirt road, the landscape between small hills was a lush idyll: palms, paddies, cattle, and egrets rising, lifting the eye to the mountains. Skirting the hill folk climbed in time of flood, we entered the spacious village of Kokiragudem. A boy collected feathers for arrows. Ploughs leant at a tree. Goats huddled and nudged and masticated unstoppably. The sunlight was warm, the place dusty yellow, dun, brown, parchment. Pennants of meat hung from bamboo prongs above woven fences. Yuniah roused some residents and bought a big parcel of flesh wrapped in banana leaves for six rupees. The hunter's left eye was deeply inflamed. Yuniah gave him five rupees to buy eye medicine and bore the meat off in triumph.

'For Missamma,' he said, 'she like very much.'

'What is it?' I asked.

'Men hunt,' he said, miming bow and arrow, 'for eat.'

'Yes,' I said, 'but what animal?'

'Jungle mutton.'

Well, that's how it translated. It turned out to be meat of a sambar, the largest Indian deer, that hunters of Kokiragudem had brought down with bows and arrows.

That evening, Joy was delighted with it, and with the other

supplies Yuniah had arranged to pick up on our way home: eggs packed in paper and string, coffee, tomatoes, bananas, papaya, sweets and batteries. We called at fishermen's shacks on the silent beach under a sickle moon to check up on the prawns. All was well. They'd been ferried across to Sivagiri and were already in Suguna's pot. The night's prawn curry was very good.

Meanwhile, Yuniah and I walked on round the hill and met a little procession of Koya men and cockerels on their way to the east bank's regular Thursday cockfight. Then a toddy-tapper in a red shirt and white *lungi*. Then another, whom Yuniah knew well, naked but for a towelling turban and a *langoti* or small loincloth tucked into a string of twisted creeper tied round his waist. Over his shoulder he carried a length of bamboo with his climbing tackle looped over one end and a gourd for *kallu* hanging from the other. His moustache was white and his veins stood proud, but his body was firm and lithe.

'His name, Madimsingaya,' said Yuniah.

Madimsingaya grinned and turned to display wounds in buttock and thigh, old furrows ploughed by the claws of a bear. Yuniah pointed to his calves, scarred by the tusks of a wild boar. The old man looked happy to be still on his feet, or perhaps just mightily relieved never to have met with enraged tiger or panther or gaur, the wild bison which gave a name to these hills.

Between the small hill and the big ones we came upon the village of Pedagudem. Yuniah sent a child to fetch a thin, mournful man with enormously in-turned big toes. After a little palaver the man retreated into his compound and returned, doing awkward dance steps through his gate, with a big black bear in his arms. He stood it up on the dust and stepped aside. He looked slight beside it. It was a mangy, boneless, gutless shell of a beast, but it was seven feet tall. It had splayed yellow claws as distorted as its dancing-master's toes.

A tiny girl with kohl-black eyes studied me as I studied the hollow bear skin. A young lad made an entrance with a bamboo bow and arrows in his hands. His deep dark eyes regarded me frankly. His curly hair was luxuriant. His cheek bones were broad but finely sculpted. Reluctantly he played the part of the

great huntsman, the stalker, the bear-killer. He drew the bow
and let a bamboo arrow fly. Its iron head sank without a quiver
into the belly of a mud and bamboo-weave granary.

The Koys have the character of possessing great magical
powers, so much so as to charm the tiger, and bind him to
their plough. Such are, or rather were, the commonly
received notions regarding them. They have, however, of
late become better known; still they are objects of terror to
those who would oppress them, which is especially the case
with those landed proprietors who hold the hill districts.

I rather wished that William Bowden's description of 1860 still
applied. A little terror might keep downriver farmers and
foresters at bay. The *sarpanch* or president of Pedagudem stared
at me hard, but he was mild-mannered enough. He was
expecting us and, yes, he'd organize his people to perform the
horn dance.

He spoke Koya to them, and Telugu to Yuniah. I didn't know
that Yuniah had requested this honour. I hadn't thought they'd
perform a dance usually reserved for marriage rites in front of
strangers. Was it cultural prostitution? Should it be allowed?
They had to decide. I hadn't dared imagine that I'd see it.

The women, who gathered in the space between leaf-roofed
houses and bamboo fences in the centre of the village, looked
unlikely to do anything against their will; the men, by contrast,
seemed pliable. Gond women are said to be independent in spirit
and self-reliant despite the fact that the clan, or joint family, is
patrilineal. Mature women marry boys by parental arrangement
or, more frequently now, by mutual choice. In the past a young
man and his peers might kidnap a bride without agreement, but
now *pisi watana*, marriage by capture, has become a piece of
theatre staged to avoid the cost of full-blown nuptials.

A little to the north, on the border with Orissa state, the
Koyas merge with another Gond people called the Dandami, or
Bisonhorn Marias. Like them, these Koyas possess headdresses
on which horns of gaur, the world's biggest wild ox, are
mounted. One basketwork helmet and horns was fitted on the
head of a teenage boy, another on a girl. While Dandami

headdresses sport 'veils' of cowrie shells, here sari lengths were stretched and wound tightly around the base of the bison horns. At the rear of each helmet a spike impaled a raffia quiverful of peacock feathers. The glittering plumes stood tall. The saris' loose ends hung blue and green to the ground behind.

Before I saw what was happening the boy and girl faded away. The curved, viciously pointed horns were on the heads of two men wearing long skirts of pink and saffron, adorned with printed peacocks above the hem. The *sarpanch* wore one too, and all three carried long double-ended drums suspended around their necks and struck with hand and stick. Their noise was stunning.

The women, two dozen of them, coalesced into a ring around these three, grasped each other above the elbow and stepped sideways, forward, back, stamping the earth, raising the dust, slowly round and round to a rhythm the drums' staccato barely but powerfully suggested, gaining momentum, their chant gathering force, eyes glinting, skins glistening. The circle swelled and tightened. The drumming grew more frantic. The dance spun faster. The *sarpanch* and his men grew wild, the women wilder.

The angry bison taunted, charged and seemed to pass through one another, horns untangled. An archer appeared in the ring, stalking with bow and arrow, women urging him on as a bride urges her lover to his utmost, hunter tracking spoor, bisons' horns lowered like spears, peacocks' eyes like temptation, music like intoxication, the air thick with sweat and toddy.

My excitement grew and grew. The hunter mimed a fatal shot. The climax. The kill. The little death. One horned man lay still in the dust. The dance slowed, the dancers watchful. The men disputed whose was the prize, whose the horned beast, whose the desired flesh they bent to grasp, their tall drums suddenly dumb in the arena.

Before I saw what was happening, the dance was over. The archer triumphant. Dust settling. The sun setting. Drums stood upright, horns resting on them, saris trailing. Gladly I gave the *sarpanch* money. Then women came for their share loud and strong, ritually abusing Yuniah, glaring at me, surrounding us both. Their scent was raw. Yuniah smiled, sweating, gave what little he had. I quailed. They could not be denied.

39

KEEPING MY HEAD

Geddapalli

WOMEN STOPPED early morning pounding and emerged from their compounds, standing in ones, twos and small groups on the village street as Yuniah and I set out from Sivagiri. They gazed at me and cried out excitedly with drawn faces and flailing hands.

'Namaskaram,' I said. 'Namaskaram, namaskaram.'

I'd slept well after the horn dance and the prawn curry, but clambered out between the narrow twisting walls of night and woke up early. I washed and shaved at 5.30 a.m. and pump-filtered water in the dark. I repacked my rucksack with bare essentials, even barer than usual, and fitted my feet into comfortable baseball boots ready for the hill climb to come. The night before, I'd tripped on the house step and ripped my right sandal apart. It was months since I'd worn shoes. My feet had spread. Suguna roused herself, though she was suffering sweats and pains, to make a breakfast of tea, *chapatis* and scrambled eggs. I said grateful goodbyes to her and to Joy. Joy seemed to think we'd all meet again some day.

'Namaskaram,' I kept saying, and a few more choice Telugu phrases of which I was proud, to the village women we passed.

I couldn't understand what they were stirred up about and Yuniah didn't translate. Ahead of us, Santi Babu, a lad hired as a porter, sprang along the path. I'd expected to carry my own rucksack but now it swung – with Yuniah's few things, food, water and bedding – from Santi Babu's bamboo yoke. Beneath shirt and *dhoti* his thighs and calves were taut, his feet bare.

A tide of mist rode up the river. We walked between the hills and Shiva's hill. Chillies glowed, embers in first light. We strode between the burning bushes, between plants gravid with aubergines of beryl, between marigolds of topaz and gamboge; we skirted fields of emerald paddy and tobacco on a path flanked by coconut and palmyra palms of malachite and henna. We headed for the hills, at the point where they fell steeply to the Godavari.

There, like a minor interruption in their descent, on a small shelf, stood the village of Koruturu. To me it seemed a major interruption before we'd even begun our ascent. Compulsory stops at houses. Drinks. Snacks. Obligatory politeness. My anxiety about the climb. I wanted to get as high as possible in the cool of morning. But as soon as we left one house we were offered an irresistible invitation to the next.

'Not to say no,' said Yuniah. I shook my head.

William Bowden was a gracious guest here in 1856, I know, almost certainly not his first visit. By the end of the century the government was auctioning bamboo and timber concessions in the surrounding hills. Since then Koruturu became accustomed to outsiders, though, until 1936, its inhabitants were all *girijans*, three-quarters Konda Reddis, a quarter Koyas. In 1937 Satyam, a timber merchant's clerk, moved in. Now, of Koruturu's population of three hundred or so, more than a quarter are non-tribals.

'You like see forest bungalow?' asked Yuniah.

'No,' I said. 'Let's go.' I pointed up into the forested depths of unrealizable hills. It was already heating up.

At the edge of the village the warden conducted me round the Forest Rest House's living room, bedroom and bathroom. He went to unlock the dining room. I stood on the terrace outside and wouldn't move. The view was glorious but I couldn't see it. The forest guard came out of his house and wagged his finger at us. Yuniah led me back into the village. Back! A girl of twelve was waiting, all dressed up in tangerine with shocking-pink ribbons in her hair. A cloth bag was slung from her shoulder. She'd got her mother's permission to accompany us. I called her the Pink Panther, because of her ribbons and her soft watchful eyes.

Ninety minutes after we arrived at Koruturu we climbed out of it, up behind its mud and leaf houses, on tree roots, slithery gravel and rough stones up to the old road, an abandoned truck route where, Joy had told me, a man called Yacob had died when his Public Carrier overturned. Great plinths of rock overlooked the shining Godavari and the shimmering forest canopy, the thickening upholstery of the hills. We climbed the track for a while, then stopped. The pause was welcome. I was hot and wet.

'Monkey,' whispered Yuniah.

A troop of langurs gazed from the jungle before scuttling into its darkness. Where the track made a hairpin bend Santi Babu took off upwards on a barely perceptible rocky path through mixed forest. Santi Babu and the Panther bounded up on bare feet without a care. Yuniah breathed a little. I was wet from head to foot. I thought of the fears Sivagiri's children expressed about herding goats or cattle in the jungle. A man had been taken by a tiger a month before. At Koruturu they'd killed three panthers ten days earlier. It was good that I, who consider myself goat-footed, had to concentrate so hard on standing up.

'Always here, I sit,' said Yuniah, laying his hand on a rock like a butcher's slab. 'You sit also.'

I sat on Yuniah's Rock. He told me how he'd met a sloth bear on this track. I thought of the toddy-tapper Madimsingaya's old wounds. But Yuniah had had his tambourine with him.

'I bang, like this, and I sing. The bear, it goes.'

We went, hit another stretch of track with a sign, 'Dawson Road 1935', scrambled up another narrow path and, after two and a half hours' climbing, entered teak plantations labelled with enamelled tin notices, '1938 Teak Plantation 6.07 Hec', '1942 T.P. 8.3 Hec', and later slabs the size of headstones, 'T.P. 1970'. Huge mottled leaves hung like tattered flags. Occasional chocolate-coloured termite mounds dwarfed the Panther. Clumps of bamboo soared, gothic pillars springing arches. Here and there a pipal tree, rosewood, satinwood. Lianas lassoed trunks, played cat's cradle, twisted and frayed. An unseen bird chimed like a dinner gong. Something far away in the forest's vaults whooped.

About noon there were lilac umbelliferous flowers, sky-blue forget-me-nots, deep pink thyme and the track dropped into a small river and climbed out again. We did too. I took off my baseball boots. My feet were parboiled and blistered, especially the big and little toes. The water was chill and blissful. I waded upstream to a waterfall. A pair of bird-size butterflies, light and dark blue, black and white, danced across the water.

We sat down to eat jungle mutton, bean curry, rice, tomatoes and bananas out of our tall stack of tiffin tins. Sambar venison tasted great. Suvarthamma had got up two hours before I did to cook it. There was plenty for the Panther too. I listened to the stream chirrup and throb. I imagined big cats padding down here to drink. I longed to see them and recalled the tiger emerging from scrub and coming to water at Hyderabad Zoo; it had plucked a piece of chicken out with its mighty paw. The size of it, the luxuriance of its expensive suspension and shock absorber system, its casual ferocity and grave placidity had brought tears to my eyes. I longed to see one here and prayed I wouldn't.

'You won't at noon, idiot,' I told myself. 'And I'll be out of this jungle by dusk.'

In the shade by the stream I and my imagination cooled down. I dried out. Sweat stopped pumping from my pores. From now on it was still more up than down, but stiff climbs were finished for we'd reached the plateau. Up here there was the plushness of mosses and ferns, and Yuniah's memory of hearing and seeing, just beneath where we walked, a herd of 'bisons' running. The gaur had caught his scent, and Suvarthamma's, but ignored them. Black hairless bulls weighing well over a ton, younger beasts like toasted gold, horns in their proper place, fearsome momentum. I longed to feel their thunder but prayed I wouldn't.

'Bear take man here,' Yuniah said, pointing to the exact spot as if he'd been an eye-witness.

Just before two o'clock we passed a grass roof off to the left. Then cattle and a crushed-mint smell underfoot. Mud houses and ragged bamboo fences: the old village of Geddapalli. A decayed concrete hostel/school put up, soon after Koruturu's, in the 'sixties. A villainous watchman with one half-closed eye under a rough turban. A schoolteacher who seriously introduced himself as M. John Victorbob. Was this farce or light opera?

M. John Victorbob spoke fair English. Clever old Yuniah, bringing me ten miles and more up into the jungle fastnesses to a man who could answer my questions. M. John Victorbob released his pupils and conducted us to a house with a peaked roof: grey thatch where its ribs weren't bare, where it wasn't patched with new straw and a vine heavy with gourds wasn't scaling its summit. In its shade, on a deep mud verandah, Yuniah and I sat down with coffee and chilli-and-onion fries to meet M. John Victorbob's mother, wife, sister-in-law, father, brother, children and all the hangers-on. They were warm. M. John Victorbob was diffident, slow to converse with an English writer. Perhaps he was shy.

'Where next?' I asked Yuniah quietly.

'Here, here!' he grinned conspiratorially.

We'd reached our destination. I hadn't known what to expect so I wasn't expecting anything. And this was it. I was prepared for anything of course. Tiger. Gaur. Human skulls. But this was it. Santi Babu and the Panther were already bustling about with the family, doing domestic chores, getting on with life.

A bamboo kitchen filled the verandah at one end. Beside it a wooden door opened into a narrow room: the threshold decorated with *muggu*, a mud floor, mud walls, the roof's ribs and a door on to the back verandah. Inside a charpoy bed and some boxes and chests which M. John Victorbob's wife insisted on rearranging and tidying *ad infinitum*. Such solicitude drove my impatient soul to distraction. At last she left me in darkness with my throbbing feet. It was hot and airless but I was alone.

I must have slept. On the verandah, Pink Panther pounds ginger in a mortar. A bitch suckles puppies, two of whom play tug-of-war with one of my shoes. On the ground before the high verandah sister-in-law blows up a fire between big stones with a bamboo pipe. She weeps as she blows. Her daughter died of TB two months ago. Yuniah stands on the washing stone with a *bindi* of water and rubs himself down. Beyond weeds, at the compound gate, Santi Babu slits a chicken's throat, bleeds it, beheads it. He and the villainous watchman build a pile of white feathers and a pile of twigs. They light the twigs and singe the pink bird. I feel pink too, and singed. Must remember to keep my head.

'You will come to see villages here also?' asks M. John Victorbob. He smiles. 'I am your guide.'

'Not too far?' My feet, freshly crammed into my shoes, are burning. But I'm keen to see what's around the next corner.

'Near,' says Yuniah. 'Near only.'

Up the mud track we go in a bunch, then single file through grass, M. John Victorbob, Yuniah, Santi Babu, the watchman, the Panther and I. This plateau is like heathy parkland with a backdrop of forested hills. We walk and walk until we enter a village of low houses and bamboo fences. Goats tinkle. Cattle graze. In an enclosure a woman grasps a calf's head between her hands and butts it up against its mother's udder. Only when it grasps a teat does she stand straight and stare at us.

'This is Cheymaluru,' says M. John Victorbob. 'Here are ten families, all Konda Reddis, like Geddapalli.'

He wanders off. Seats are brought. I rest my feet, watched by three women standing shoulder to shoulder, ear-rings, ear-bells and nose-studs glinting in low sun. One wears a gilded pendant that pierces her nasal septum and hangs before her lips. Another carries a baby girl with jasmine blossom in her hair and a thread round her waist strung with beads and hung with coins. The bass beat of invisible pounding never stops. Sorghum. Sorghum.

Where forest has not been stolen by timber merchants and paper mills, Konda Reddis are still slash-and-burn cultivators. While Koyas use ploughs and hoes, Reddis use the axe to create rough *podu* fields. They broadcast small millets without even scratching the soil. To prepare ground for dibbling sorghum millet and pulses they prod holes in it with a digging stick. In the days before wage slavery and imported paddy that only money can buy, they subsisted, and some like these still subsist in lean times, on roots, pith of the caryota palm and mango kernels.

M. John Victorbob reappears with the *pedda kappu* or headman, a personage with tousled hair and hypnotic eyes whose hereditary role is more spiritual than temporal. He it is who knows when *konda devata* pronounce the season favourable for sowing. He it is who presides over sacrifices that must propitiate the hungry sisters. He gives me a long look and signals to the dancers.

In their hot pinks and pale blues the women of Cheymaluru

grasp hands and rattles of dried pods full of seeds. As the sun sets, their steps are like the horn dancers', but languid. Their chant ebbs and flows like the Koyas', but mournfully. Rattles drop with their hands on each backward step. Taken up with their own pulse, they drift away into low scrub. They cast long shadows. Their sound is the sound of desiccated souls in parched husks.

But these people, said Swami Balananda of Perantapalli, are the fresh people of the world. *Girijans, adivasis*, scheduled tribes, whatever you want to call them, they are those who, in Adam's words, 'have just completed their progress as non-humans and who have joined the human race for the first time'. More experienced and intellectually advanced folk 'have already taken birth in human bodies one or more times previously'. They are the re-embodied people. Selfishness, instinct, survival of the fittest, equips beasts to embody as fresh people. Unselfishness is humanness by which the spirit can escape *samsara*, the cycle of reincarnation. Fresh people, naive and spiritual, can achieve *moksha*, release, in one lifetime. But if they persist in their selfishness they, like the rest of us, may gain success, profit, knowledge. Then, like us, they may exploit the fresh people and earn yet another life sentence. One life is quite enough.

M. John Victorbob said he'd lead us home by a short-cut. It was dusk. Soon it would be dark. M. John Victorbob's short-cut was through the jungle and his breath was laden with toddy. He and the *pedda kappu* had been hitting the gourd. We climbed single file through thick vegetation and almost collided with a hunter and a toddy-tapper. While M. John Victorbob conversed earnestly with the latter, the former surreptitiously 'lost' his bow and arrows near the path. Yuniah didn't know the way. The Pink Panther looked nervous. Her mother had trusted us to look after her. I was angry with our tipsy guide on her behalf. I didn't want re-embodying either, though my feet could have done with it.

'Don't worry, we will be back before night,' said M. John Victorbob unconvincingly. 'We are among friends, no problem. The animals, they go their way and we go ours.'

His English became both more fluent and more repetitive.
'No problem, they go their way and we . . .'
We emerged into a golden village. No one appeared.
'There are many people here, if we call.'

M. John Victorbob found the headman and his hooch while
the villainous watchman led us onwards through darkening
forest. The next village was quite deserted. We dragged our so-
called guide away before he could so much as sniff his poison.
I could have done with some myself, but no one so much as
offered.

'Your short-cut is a very long-cut,' I shouted at him, 'and
you're more than half cut.'

He put his arm round me and smiled. Soon he was left behind
and I was thinking uncharitable thoughts about tigers taking
tail-enders. Pink Panther started. We all froze. Movement in the
darkness. Men carrying long beams on their shoulders. Then
one saw us. He cried out and they all ran off panic-stricken in
different directions, but without dropping their burdens.

'We're not forest guards!' Yuniah yelled after them, and in
English, 'Teak. Smugglers.' We all laughed very loudly.

Soon afterwards I saw, up ahead, horns and straight backs of
massive beasts. Even Yuniah looked twice, but they were cattle
magnified by night, not 'bisons'. After a four-hour short walk
we reached old Geddapalli and the fire-light of home.

The men there were pissed too. The women had prepared
a fine meal. We ate gratefully. The watchman was my hero.
M. John Victorbob stumbled in and stood on the verandah
clutching his youngest daughter. Yuniah touched my feet. I
embraced him.

I bathed under the stars and the gaze of women squatting at
the fire. My toes were red hot bladders. My oil lamp smoked. I
blew it out. My charpoy was highly strung and cut off the blood
supply to my arms. I considered laying my sheet on the floor,
but a snuffling, scuttling rat put me off. I thought I'd never sleep.
At 4.30 I crept out of the compound to crap. I listened as hard
as I could. Nothing else stirred.

I woke with stiff arms and a rigid neck to the sound of hymns
and prayers in the house. Santi Babu had lit a fire by the gap
in the fence. I stood with him and warmed myself. Things had

calmed. The Panther was smiling. Yuniah took me down to the stream. The men had asked him to pray for them. They would never drink again. Yuniah smiled tenderly at the very idea.

'Women all baptized,' he explained, 'men not baptized.'

He led me to *jiliga chettu* palms near the new village of Gedda-palli. *Jiliga kallu*, M. John Victorbob's father told us, was as strong as whisky. Much stronger, Yuniah said, than *thatti kallu*, palmyra wine. The heroic watchman materialized and, grasping a bamboo pole lashed to the trunk, strode straight up on the old leaf bases for demonstration purposes only. This morning everyone was keen to be kind. M. John Victorbob was contrite.

They took me to the *sarpanch*'s, or village president's, house. It would not be polite not to call. He could not be roused. The compound behind his fine mud house was stacked with plastic cans. He was the registered vendor of *sava*, or cane spirit. It was a customary arrangement, but what did the Naxalites have to say about it? From a nearby flagpole the hammer and sickle flew.

'All people here, communists,' said Yuniah.

After bowls of *oopma* and fried eggs we undertook a round of heartfelt farewells notable for their intoxicating sobriety. We'd planned to leave at eight. At 9.15 Santi Babu set off with our baggage, the Panther followed him and M. John Victorbob's brother, a malaria control officer, accompanied us for the first mile. On the outskirts of old Geddapalli he pointed to a house.

'This man attacked by bear,' he enthused, 'one week since.'

He said goodbye and turned back without a second look. It was mostly downhill. My toes crammed into the front of my baseball boots like meat into a mincer. I'd bound them with sticking plasters, but it was going to be a very long walk. I concentrated on the beauties of the forest, on flowers, trees, the cries of birds, the yelps of monkeys. The Panther cut her big toe open on a stone. I staunched the blood and put a plaster on it too. Soon we were paddling in the stream.

Yuniah smiled to himself and giggled.

'Women, Sivagiri,' he said. 'Forest guard, Koruturu, yes?'

Yes, I remembered their looks, their urgent chatter, their impenetrable gestures.

'Yes?' I said.

'Not go. Not now. They look for man . . .'

Yuniah drew his fingers across his throat. Now he told me. They'd been warning me against going into the hills at the very season when the people were looking for a stranger to sacrifice.

40

THRILLER

Sivagiri

FROM THE chirruping stream it was a long way, and a very steep descent through the jungle towards Koruturu. I couldn't believe we'd climbed it. It was like paddling in molten metal. We tacked across gullies, tiptoed down rocky, rooty ladders. Upon Yuniah's Rock I rested for a token few moments. When I stood, my dark sweat prints on the stone shrank to nothing almost at once.

Already it was as though I had never been here. And that was good. A memory in a handful of heads, that's all. A memory in my echoing head. A pain in the foot. Was travelling any more than that? It was vanity, the notion that I should see the world or that it should see me. Vanity to sit on my butt for months writing a travel book. Perhaps I should stay put for the rest of my life. For a moment I dreamt of comfortable slippers. But comfortable slippers were not part of my nature, not part of the luggage I travel with, even from room to room, at home. Curiosity was. One of the few appetites worth satisfying.

It was not idle curiosity that brought William Bowden down this slope in April 1856, twenty years to the month since he set sail for India on the *Peace*, and twenty years before his death downriver at Rajahmundry. At the midpoint of his Indian life he set out to tour the hill villages, to find out their population, whether the tribespeople were Koyas or others, and in what circumstances they lived. William had two companions on the expedition, old Gadhamchetti Simeon and young Alisahib.

Gadhamchetti Simeon was a farmer of the Balji caste, a grey-haired guru and a devotee of Shiva. When he broke caste and was baptized, his people mounted a bitter campaign against him. But he stuck to his home – Panigi, near Kovvur, where William had first preached in 1841 – though his wife treated him like a dog until he died, putting his food outside the house. Alisahib was a clever young Muslim who practised medicine near Palakol, the Bowdens' first convert from Islam.

The three of them approached the hills from the south-west. A Konda Reddi headman warned them that the path ahead was rugged. William sent Gadhamchetti Simeon around the hills with his horse, to rendezvous with them upriver. He and Alisahib took a guide to lead them up through dense jungle, 'the track getting more and more difficult, the forest hamlets tinier and further apart'.

I stood on a rock plinth that protruded from the forest's flank. I looked back to the upholstered heights and listened to unearthly sounds pooled in the amphitheatre of hills. Then, as I gazed down on the glorious Godavari below, on beaches and patches of peppers like spilled blood, I felt what Alisahib and William must have felt. Gratitude. Recognition. Wonder.

Down, down, we came until Yuniah suggested a short-cut. Yuniah's short-cuts were better than M. John Victorbob's but this one looked more or less perilous in my condition. It was a long last slither down to the palm-leaf roofs of Koruturu. I was walking on my own hot tin one. I paid Santi Babu his wages and thanked him as heartily as I could. Within the darkness of one mud house I found Joy and Suguna waiting for me.

Well, not for me. They were eating a meal before going to an afternoon meeting in the village that Joy was due to address. Yuniah's short-cut ensured that he was in time for it. We drank coffee together. Then I sat on the mat Joy vacated and ate fish and bean curries followed by squelchy papaya. The Pink Panther's smiling mother took me down the burning road to her house and gave me the run of it. I sat there in splendour and took stock.

In his centenary record of the Godavari Delta Mission, E. B. Bromley describes William and Alisahib's arrival here:

A very steep and rough descent brought them down to Koruturu, on the Godavari, and here they were disappointed to find no trace of the boat that had been arranged to meet them at this point. Instead of embarking

here for Bhadrachalam as planned, Mr Bowden had to set
off back along the bank, in shoes almost to pieces after the
previous rough walking.

I dared not yet remove my shoes. I hadn't intended to follow
so exactly in great-great-grandfather's footsteps.

The house of the Pink Panther was a delightful haven. Above
the mud verandah a ceiling of bamboos rested on thick poles
lashed together with fibres, overlapped by a palmyra-leaf roof
supported by pillars like crutches. The ochre mud walls were
decorated at top, middle and foot with horizontal bands of dots.
White points, as on a graph or oscilloscope, precisely painted in
thick lime-wash, a quasi-random scatter of uniform spots hinting
at sophisticated wave-forms. They pleased me enormously.
    A coconut painted with a grotesque face hung in a net from
the verandah ceiling. It was to keep demons at bay and might
once have been a human skull. On the verandah itself were
hints of *muggulu*. There were many patterns in the village, and
in pattern-books which notated the living tradition, including
one which struck me. It was the maze I'd found carved in the
cave temple at Ondavalli beside the Krishna river, the labyrinth
whose pattern was repeated at Knossos, Pompeii and Pylos, in
Peru, Iceland, Scandinavia, Britain and Sumatra.
    It is Troy, Jerusalem, Amaravati. It is the *omphalos*, the navel
of Lord Vishnu. It is carved on rocks in the Nilgiri hills, tattooed
on southern skin, cut into stone in Mysore, drawn and painted
on Tantric manuscripts. It is outlined in ochre on bronze plates,
rinsed off with Ganges water and given to women to speed birth.
It is the place of initiation where the pure hero takes on occult
forces. In the *Mahabharata*, Abhimanyu tells his uncle the
Pandava king that he can get to the heart of the wheel of
battle, the labyrinth, but not out again. His father Arjuna has
not yet told him how, and he is killed with arrows there.
    Trickled in chalk dust before a threshold here, the maze is
called *kolam*, the fort, and it defends the house. Up in the jungle
the gaur I never met was the minotaur, and mother-mother
with her garland of human skulls, Kali on her tiger, was mistress

of the labyrinth. Up there the fresh people confronted re-embodied greed; up there the child confronted the man's fear; up in the inaccessible place I met something of myself. But briefly. If the path out is the path of initiation and rebirth, I had taken a short-cut.

Here, in the Panther's simple beautiful home, I was safe. My feet were on fire but my head was on my shoulders. It knew that the journey was, as always, only just beginning. Between the tightly woven split bamboos of the compound fence many eyes, splinters of darkness, peered at me unremittingly. But I refused to let my face fall into the grimace of impatient tolerance I'd grown to recognize. I smiled at them, and smiled, and two by two they dropped away and vanished as silently as they'd appeared.

People in Sivagiri welcomed me back with relief. Unless they were putting on a good act, their anxiety had been real enough. On the painful walk from Koruturu we'd seen a whitebreasted kingfisher which cackled as it flew; Joy pointed out the exact spot where a man had lain drunk on toddy all night; the massy rocks of Shiva's hill looked darker and more bruised, and its vegetation brighter and airier, than before I set out.

I sat on the step of the government house and eased off my baseball boots. They'd once been so comfortable. Three of my smallest toe-nails had been uprooted and rode quivering on bags of fluid. My other toes were glued together with sweat and blood. I washed them gingerly and anointed them with Indian Balm before bandaging them as best I could. I bound my broken sandal up with sticking plaster too. I walked up Jesus's Hill with Yuniah to inspect the completed church foundations.

That night Sai Baba came to inspect me. The girls came to dance and sing and giggle at my door. A man came to Joy's house, reeking of toddy and brandishing a bow. He said he wanted to sell it, and three arrows. I wanted it badly and prepared to barter. He asked thirty-five rupees. Ridiculous, how could he ask that price? I offered seventy. Done, he said, pleased with his night's work.

The bow was sturdy bamboo. The bowstring was bamboo strip

notched at each end and attached with coir cord. The arrows were straight young bamboo, flight feathers fixed with fine bamboo lashing. One arrow head, like a cork, was for knocking birds out of trees. The others were slender steel, forged by Kammara 'caste' blacksmiths, wed to shafts by wound and plaited bamboo.

Joy wanted some too. While I was climbing to Geddapalli she'd seen a big hunting party take off from Kondamodhalu, fully equipped with bows and arrows and gourds of *arrack* and *kallu*. They had not taken her interest kindly. But now Sheik Baji, the Muslim boat-owner, did the business. He obtained another set for her, cheap at half the price and who knows what commission. He regretted that we were leaving, that we had not eaten with him, that we could do no further business, but rejoiced to show us the smart wardrobe, the double bed and the bright fluorescent tube newly installed in his government house.

That night, my last in Sivagiri, he had yet another surprise in store. I revelled in my last bath under Sivagiri's stars. I exchanged gifts and hugs and kisses with Yuniah and Suvarthamma. They gave me a bamboo walking-stick with a fine notched handle. We all went early to bed. I woke out of a nightmare in a sweat, but the nightmare was being awake. My ears were full of pop music and dubbed Telugu. It was worse than Narsapur's pre-dawn temple music. Sheik Baji's compound was packed with people who'd paid two rupees to see Sivagiri's first ever video.

Michael Jackson's *Thriller* had dropped by just days after the current came to town. It was my privilege to witness this historic moment. I wished I'd stayed in Geddapalli with the rat. So many ironies. Did they know that this little rich boy had once been dark as any *girijan* before fading to a pale shade of Brahmin? For the first time in their lives, most of these people were seeing what passed for a vision of the outside world. There was no doubting their love of novelty; I just hoped, foolishly, for their undiminished hatred of change.

Thriller finished at 1.30 a.m. I started packing at 4.30 and had breakfast by hurricane lamp. Suguna gave us a species of hot porridge and cold hard-boiled eggs. She was sweating again and aching, not looking forward to the launch trip, but longing to be home in Narsapur. I trudged up and down the beach in my sandals, past the red hot peppers and the scales, trying to keep my bandaged toes out of the sand. Then my bandaged sandal broke again. I kicked them off. Doesn't the Telugu proverb say, 'To a man who wears sandals the whole world is covered with leather.' I wanted to wear this sand, this dirt for a bit longer.

Two boys waded down from the shelf of beach. The older one held an electric plug; at the end of the lead the younger one carried the TV on his shoulder, his cheek pressed at the screen, down to the river that would bear it, for the time being, away.

At the shore an old man, whom I'd seen when Joy laid the church foundation stone, waited to see us off and guarded our accumulating baggage. He wore *banian* and *pajama* and his face was that of a little boy, which was what his name, Chinnabhai, meant. The oldest Christian in these parts, he'd come from Cheeduru to help us. Two little girls in their best dresses stood near him and watched for the launch. One was solemn, the other fizzed like a firework. They were new recruits for Joy's hostel. They half knew how lucky they were.

The launch puttered across from Kondamodhalu, its bow waves rocking the Bison Hills in Godavari's misty depths. Everybody was tearful. Yuniah came aboard and helped stow everything. We went astern before going full ahead. Yuniah wouldn't let us go.

'Get off, Yuniah,' I said. 'Get off!'

He jumped into the water. I waved at him standing there waist-deep, at Suvarthamma, Sai Baba and old Chinnabhai, at the whole colourful crowd that wouldn't stop waving. I watched until the Welcome sign was out of sight. I turned and grinned sheepishly at the two girls. They were ready for anything. I started to bandage my sandal again, but it could wait. The throb of the diesel engine gently massaged my feet. If I couldn't wear Sivagiri any longer, I'd wear these bilge boards for a bit. And bandages. And W. Bowden's Indian Balm.

SELECT BIBLIOGRAPHY

Adam, *Mankind in General Against Itself*, Nidadavole 1987.

M. J. Akbar, *Riot After Riot*, New Delhi 1988.

Salim Ali, *The Book of Indian Birds*, Bombay 1979.

Swami Balananda, *The World, India, The Emergency*, Kakinada 1976.

C. A. Bayly (ed), *The Raj: India and the British 1600–1947*, London 1990.

E. B. Bromley, *They Were Men Sent from God*, Bangalore 1937.

Joseph Campbell, *The Masks of God: Oriental Mythology*, New York 1962.

K. N. Chaudhuri, *The English East India Company: The Study of an Early Joint-stock Company 1600–40*, London 1965.

N. C. Chaudhuri, *Thy Hand, Great Anarch!*, London 1987.

Alfred Deakin, *Irrigated India*, London 1893.

C. Fawcett (ed), *The English Factories in India, 1670–1677*, London 1936.

W. Foster (ed), *The English Factories in India, 1618–1669*, London 1906–27.

Christoph von Fürer-Haimendorf, *Tribes of India*, Delhi 1989.

Brian Gardner, *The East India Company*, London 1971.

W. S. Hadaway, *Cotton Painting and Printing in the Madras Presidency*, Madras 1917.

Lady Hope, *General Sir Arthur Cotton: His Life and Work*, London 1900.

An Indian Romance, Blackwood's Magazine, Edinburgh and London, June 1897.

John Keay, *The Honourable Company*, London 1991.

Hermann Kern, *Labyrinthe*, München 1982.

John Layard, 'Labyrinth Ritual in South India', *Folklore XLVIII*, London 1937.

Letters from Madras during the years 1836–39 by a Lady, London 1843.

Henry Morris, *A Descriptive and Historical Account of the Godavari District in the Presidency of Madras*, London 1878.

R. S. Nathan (ed), *Symbolism in Hinduism*, Bombay 1983.

Olive Rogers, *The Origins of the Godavari Delta Mission and its Distinctive Tenets (Thesis)*, Secunderabad 1980.

Mrinalini Sarabhai, *The Sacred Dance of India*, Bombay 1979.

Percival Spear, *A History of India*, vol. 2, London 1965.

I. Stone, *Canal Irrigation in British India*, Cambridge 1984.

Romila Thapar, *A History of India*, vol. 1, London 1966.

George T. Walch, *The Engineering Works of the Godavari Delta*, Madras 1896.

INDEX

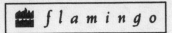

flamingo

Flamingo is a quality imprint publishing both fiction and non-fiction. Below are some recent titles.

Fiction

- ☐ No Other Life *Brian Moore* £5.99
- ☐ The Kitchen God's Wife *Amy Tan* £4.99
- ☐ A Thousand Acres *Jane Smiley* £5.99
- ☐ A Yellow Raft in Blue Water *Michael Dorris* £5.99
- ☐ Tess *Emma Tennant* £5.99
- ☐ Pepper *Tristan Hawkins* £5.99
- ☐ Dreaming in Cuban *Cristina Garcia* £5.99
- ☐ Happenstance *Carol Shields* £5.99
- ☐ Blood Sugar *Suzannah Dunn* £5.99
- ☐ Postcards *E. Annie Proulx* £5.99

Non-fiction

- ☐ The Gates of Paradise *Alberto Manguel* £9.99
- ☐ Sentimental Journeys *Joan Didion* £5.99
- ☐ Epstein *Stephen Gardiner* £8.99
- ☐ Love, Love and Love *Sandra Bernhard* £5.99
- ☐ City of Djinns *William Dalrymple* £5.99
- ☐ Dame Edna Everage *John Lahr* £5.99
- ☐ Tolstoy's Diaries *R. F. Christian* £7.99
- ☐ Wild Swans *Jung Chang* £7.99

You can buy Flamingo paperbacks at your local bookshop or newsagent. Or you can order them from HarperCollins Mail Order, Dept. 8, HarperCollins*Publishers*, Westerhill Road, Bishopbriggs, Glasgow G64 2QT. Please enclose a cheque or postal order, to the order of the cover price plus add £1.00 for the first and 25p for additional books ordered within the UK.

NAME (Block letters)_____

ADDRESS_____

_____

_____